FROMMER'S

COMPREHENSIVE TRAVEL GUIDE

ST. LOUIS & KANSAS CITY '91-'92

by Beth Reiber

PRENTICE
HALL
PRESS

NEW YORK • LONDON • TORONTO • SYDNEY • TOKYO • SINGAPORE

FROMMER BOOKS

Published by Prentice Hall Press
A division of Simon & Schuster Inc.
15 Columbus Circle
New York, NY 10023

ISBN 0-13-337841-1
ISSN 1051-6840

Design by Robert Bull Design
Maps by Geografix Inc.

**PRENTICE
HALL
PRESS**

Manufactured in the United States of America

FROMMER'S ST. LOUIS & KANSAS CITY '91-'92
Editor-in-Chief: Marilyn Wood
Senior Editors: Judith de Rubini, Pamela Marshall, Amit Shah
Editors: Alice Fellows, Paige Hughes
Assistant Editors: Suzanne Arkin, Ellen Zucker

CONTENTS

PART TWO—KANSAS CITY

LIST OF MAPS

ABOUT THIS FROMMER GUIDE

What is a Frommer City Guide? It's a comprehensive, easy-to-use guide to the best travel values in all price ranges—from very expensive to budget. The one guidebook to take along with you on any trip.

WHAT THE SYMBOLS MEAN

 FROMMER'S FAVORITES—hotels, restaurants, attractions, and entertainments you should not miss

 SUPER-SPECIAL VALUES—really exceptional values

 FROMMER'S SMART TRAVELER TIPS—hints on how to secure the best value for your money

IN HOTEL AND OTHER LISTINGS

The following symbols refer to the standard amenities available in all rooms:

A/C air conditioning   TEL telephone   TV television
MINIBAR refrigerator stocked with beverages and snacks

The following abbreviations are used for credit cards:

AE American Express	DISC Discover	EU Eurocard
CB Carte Blanche	ER enRoute	MC MasterCard
DC Diners Club		V VISA

TRIP PLANNING WITH THIS GUIDE

Use the following features:

What Things Cost in . . . to help you plan your daily budget
Calendar of Events . . . to plan for or to avoid
Suggested Itineraries . . . for seeing the city and environs
What's Special About . . . Checklist a summary of the city's highlights—which lets you check off those that appeal most to you
Easy-to-Read Maps . . . showing walking tours; city sights; hotel and restaurant locations—all referring to or keyed to the text
Fast Facts . . . all the essentials at a glance: climate, currency, embassies, emergencies, information, safety, taxes, tipping, and more

OTHER SPECIAL FROMMER FEATURES

Cool for Kids—hotels, restaurants, and attractions
Did You Know?—offbeat, fun facts
Famous People—the city's greats
Impressions—what others have said

INVITATION TO THE READERS

In researching this book I have come across many wonderful establishments, the best of which are included here. However, I'm sure that many of you will come across other wonderful hotels, inns, restaurants, guest houses, shops, and attractions. Please don't keep them to yourself. Share your experiences, especially if you want to comment on places that I have covered in this edition that have changed for the worse. You can address your letters to:

Beth Reiber, c/o Prentice Hall Press, Travel Books
15 Columbus Circle, New York, NY 10023

A DISCLAIMER

Readers are advised that prices fluctuate in the course of time and travel information changes under the impact of the varied and volatile factors that affect the travel industry. The author and publisher cannot be held responsible for the experiences of the reader while traveling. Readers are invited to write the publisher with ideas, comments, and suggestions for future editions.

INTRODUCING ST. LOUIS & KANSAS CITY

In 1803, Thomas Jefferson made one of the best real estate deals in history: the Louisiana Purchase, for which the United States paid France $15 million (about 3¢ an acre), doubling the nation's size. This heralded the start of the great westward expansion, and throughout the 1800s Americans and newly arrived immigrants streamed through the middle of the continent in search of a better life.

Some settlers recognized Missouri as that better life and settled in places with names such as St. Louis and the Town of Kansas—later changed to Kansas City. Most, however, used St. Louis and the Town of Kansas as springboards for their journeys to someplace else, traveling westward on the California and Oregon trails and later on the railroads.

Kansas City and St. Louis have had a complex about this situation ever since. The automobile has replaced the Conestoga wagon, but travelers still race through the Midwest on their way to someplace else, giving Kansas City and St. Louis nothing more than a passing glance from their cars on Interstate 70. Although the natives have always been convinced that their hometowns were especially nice, tourist meccas the two cities have not been. But that situation is slowly changing.

1. CULTURAL LIFE & ATTRACTIONS

In the past decade, both St. Louis and Kansas City have undergone a renaissance. They have shaken off the dust of their frontier and backwater image, renovated their downtowns, capitalized on their rich historic legacies, assumed once again their roles as leaders in blues and jazz, and regained the pride that they once had when both cities served as bustling gateways to the West. Vacationers may still go racing by, but they also stop over in numbers greater than ever before and are astonished at all the things to do. If it's been ten years since you've seen either Kansas City or St. Louis, you're in for a huge surprise.

Tourism now rates as one of Missouri's top-three revenue-producing industries and is one of the fastest-growing factors in the state's economy. St. Louis, after all, is within a day's drive of almost

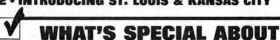

☑ WHAT'S SPECIAL ABOUT ST. LOUIS

Monuments
☐ Gateway Arch, America's tallest monument honors the westward expansion in the 1800s

Parks and Gardens
☐ Forest Park, now home of the St. Louis Zoo, Science Center, St. Louis Art Museum, St. Louis History Museum, and recreational facilities

☐ Missouri Botanical Garden, the oldest botanical garden in the country

☐ Laumeier Sculpture Park, a 96-acre park with sculpture from more than 30 artists

Shopping
☐ Union Station, the world's largest rail terminal when built in 1894, now a shopping center with more than 80 specialty shops

☐ St. Louis Centre, one of the largest downtown enclosed malls in the country

☐ Antique Row, with more than 50 antique shops on one street

☐ Soulard Market, St. Louis' city market

Food
☐ Great Italian restaurants, particularly on the Hill

☐ New American cuisine, innovative dishes combining regional specialties with international spices and ingredients

Free Attractions and Clubs
☐ Free admission to many top attractions, including the St. Louis Art Museum, St. Louis Zoo, Anheuser-Busch Brewery, and Grant's Farm

☐ Many nightclubs with free entertainment, in Laclede's Landing and Soulard

A Paradise for the Kids
☐ Six Flags Over Mid-America, a theme park loaded with rides, amusements, and entertainment

☐ St. Louis Zoo

☐ Grant's Farm, a 281-acre estate with a zoo, a game preserve, and the Ulysses S. Grant cabin

☐ St. Louis Science Center and the Magic House, where children learn through hands-on displays

---

one-third of the nation's population, and Kansas City is less than a four-hour drive farther west. According to a survey conducted by the St. Louis Convention and Visitors Commission, 85% of the visitors polled said that St. Louis was their destination, and almost 50% said that it was their summer vacation spot.

It's easy to see why. For one thing, both Kansas City and St. Louis offer a staggering variety of things to see and do. Both towns have first-rate professional baseball teams; a score of unusual museums, including renowned art museums; historic homes and buildings; theme parks that do a roaring business; nearby horseracing tracks; and riverboat rides.

In St. Louis alone there are the 630-foot Gateway Arch, symbolizing the nation's westward expansion; the renovated Union Station with its shops and restaurants; the St. Louis Zoo; the Missouri Botanical Garden; the Anheuser-Busch Brewery; and museums as diverse as the National Bowling Hall of Fame and the Dog Museum. Laclede's Landing, a riverfront warehouse district where the city's history began, is now the most popular nightlife district. St. Louis is one of the best places to hear rhythm and blues, much of it absolutely free, and the city dishes out some of the best Italian food in the country.

Kansas City adds to the list of attractions with its Country Club Plaza (the nation's oldest shopping center, modeled after Seville, Spain); the Truman Museum and boyhood home in adjacent Independence; the nation's only museum devoted to World War I; the NCAA Visitors Center; and the Kansas City Stockyards, once the nation's largest and still the scene of weekly cattle auctions. History lives on in three restored forts near Kansas City—Fort Osage, Fort Scott, and Fort Leavenworth. But most surprising to visitors is the architectural wealth of Kansas City, where more than 1,000 structures have been entered into the National Register of Historic Places. Whereas the old buildings in many cities were torn down in the zeal for urban renewal, Kansas City's buildings have survived, thanks in large part to decades of abandonment and neglect. In fact, some of the nation's best examples of art deco can be seen in the heart of Kansas City. And, of course, Kansas City is famous the world over for its barbecue, steaks, and jazz.

Not only are Kansas City and St. Louis good destinations for what they have to offer, but also they are very affordable. Prices for accommodations, meals, and entertainment run as much as 30% less than those on either coast, making these cities great places for family vacations. Many of St. Louis' attractions are absolutely free, and both cities have scores of things for youngsters to do, ranging from educational yet also fun learning centers to theme parks.

2. THE PEOPLE

The most compelling reason to visit the Midwest is the Midwesterners themselves. They're friendly, open, honest, neighborly, and down-to-earth with few pretensions. It's little wonder that the region has produced three of the nation's presidents: Harry S. Truman from Independence, Missouri; Dwight D. Eisenhower from Abilene, Kansas; and Abraham Lincoln from Springfield, Illinois. The people of the Midwest are hard workers, products of the people who came before them—waves of immigrants from first France and then Germany, Italy, Sweden, and other European countries, lured to these rich lands to hunt, trap, farm, set up shop, and make better lives for themselves. Their rich ethnic heritage lives on to this day and is most visible in small towns such as the French settlement of Ste. Genevieve, the German Rhine–like town of Hermann, and the Swedish community of Lindsborg, all of which make good overnight excursions from Kansas City or St. Louis.

However, Kansas City and St. Louis are markedly different from each other, despite the fact that they're both Midwestern towns and have intertwined histories. Although St. Louis has always looked

✓ WHAT'S SPECIAL ABOUT KANSAS CITY

Food
- ☐ Some of the best barbecue in the country, with more varieties of barbecue sauce than anywhere else in the world
- ☐ Kansas City steaks, including huge cuts at inexpensive prices
- ☐ Ethnic foods, including Mexican, Italian, and Greek

Jazz
- ☐ Many jazz clubs, including piano bars, classic jazz clubs, and the Mutual Musicians Foundation's after-midnight jam sessions
- ☐ A Jazz Hotline, with tips on what's going on in Kansas City's jazz scene

Buildings
- ☐ The Garment District downtown, with buildings dating from the 1800s
- ☐ Some of the best examples of art deco architecture in the country

Shopping
- ☐ Country Club Plaza, the nation's oldest shopping center (modeled after Seville, Spain), with more than $1 million worth of art
- ☐ Crown Center, financed by Hallmark Cards, Inc., with more than 50 boutiques, shops, and restaurants
- ☐ City Market, especially on Saturday

Historic Forts
- ☐ Fort Leavenworth, established in 1827 to protect travelers on the Santa Fe Trail, now a U.S. Army education center
- ☐ Fort Osage, a reconstruction of the first U.S. outpost following the Louisiana Purchase
- ☐ Fort Scott, established in 1842 and now restored

eastward, identifying itself with Chicago and even New York, Kansas City has always been distinctly western, perhaps because it was here that the trails for Santa Fe, Oregon, and California began.

With all the diversity the Midwest has to offer, vacationers are stopping by these days to take in the sights, delight in the food, and revel in the music and people of the heartland of America.

3. GEOGRAPHY

Both Kansas City and St. Louis owe their existence to rivers—St. Louis to the Mississippi and Kansas City to the Missouri. Also, both are located on the Missouri state borders—St. Louis on the eastern border next to Illinois and Kansas City on the western end straddling both sides of the Kansas-Missouri border. They are separated by approximately 250 miles of rolling Missouri countryside, with Interstate 70 serving as the main highway between the two. In the central and southern part of the state are the Missouri Ozarks, which serve as a recreational getaway for those in both metropolitan areas.

Metropolitan St. Louis, with a total population of 2.4 million, is 295 miles from Chicago, 346 miles from Cincinnati, 546 miles from Cleveland, and 543 miles from Detroit. Metropolitan Kansas City has a population of approximately 1.5 million and is 604 miles from Denver, 500 miles from Dallas, and 457 miles from Minneapolis.

4. HISTORY

Before white people came, the Mississippian, Osage, Kansa, and other Native American tribes lived and hunted the hills and plains that are now known as Kansas, Missouri, and Illinois. The first white people to venture into this vast interior were Spanish, seeking gold and fortune, and they were followed by French explorers, trappers, and traders. In the mid-1730s the French established the region's first permanent white settlement, Ste. Genevieve. For the next 30 years this tiny outpost on the west bank of the Mississippi River survived alone in this vast Upper Louisiana Territory. But then in 1764 French fur traders Auguste Chouteau and Pierre Laclede founded St. Louis as a trading post 65 miles farther north. Naming their post after King Louis IX of France, they soon had a lucrative business trading with the Osage, Missouri, Sauk, and Fox tribes. Because game was plentiful and the post's excellent location near the confluence of the Mississippi and Missouri rivers gave it quick and easy transport on to New Orleans, St. Louis was destined to become the largest settlement in the state and one of the nation's larger cities. By the 1770s St. Louis was a town of 339 white settlers, 33 free blacks, and 274 Native American and black slaves. By 1800 the number of inhabitants had grown to 2,447. Ste. Genevieve, on the other hand, remained a small settlement, and it is still in existence today, boasting 50 buildings from its French colonial times.

In 1803 Napoleon Bonaparte, anxious to rid himself of the vast and troublesome frontier so that he could wage more effective war against England, sold the Louisiana Territory to the United States for a mere $15 million. To find out what he had acquired, President Thomas Jefferson sent two trusted explorers, Lewis and Clark, to explore the

DATELINE

- **700–1500** Mississippian tribes settle along the Mississippi River
- **1735** Ste. Genevieve founded, first permanent white settlement west of the Mississippi
- **1764** St. Louis founded as a fur trading post
- **1803** Louisiana Purchase.
- **1804** Lewis and Clark depart St. Louis for their 7,689-mile expedition.
- **1817** The first steamboat arrives in St. Louis
- **1820** Missouri Compromise allows slavery in Missouri but forbids it in all future western and northern states.
- **1821** Missouri admitted to the Union as a slave state. A fur-trading post established on the Missouri River later becomes Kansas City.
- **1827** Wagon trains depart Independence on the Santa Fe Trail. Fort Leavenworth established.
- **1833** John C. McCoy establishes outfitters' post in

(continues)

DATELINE

Westport on the Santa Fe Trail, rivaling Independence.

1841 First organized wagon train leaves Westport for Oregon. St. Louis ranks second in the nation in river traffic, behind New Orleans.

1849 Cholera epidemic in St. Louis, kills 7,000; fire also destroys 400 buildings.

1854 The Kansas-Nebraska Act allows the people of Kansas and Nebraska to decide whether they want slavery.

1857 Dred Scott decision

1860 St. Louis, (pop. 160,000) eighth largest city in the nation.

1861 Civil War. Missouri, a slave state stays in the Union

1863 The anti-slavery town of Lawrence is ransacked, and 150 men are killed by a posse led by William Quantrill.

1864 Battle of Westport, the last major Civil War battle west of the Mississippi River.

1865 Missouri-Pacific Railroad reaches Kansas City.

1869 Hannibal Bridge, the first to span the Missouri River, allows Kansas City to establish rail-

(continues)

region. They left St. Louis in 1804 and covered 7,689 miles during the next two years.

The Louisiana Purchase opened the west to a flood of eager newcomers. Anglo-Americans flocked to St. Louis. Although it wasn't long before the English language became dominant, St. Louis' early French influence is still reflected in such street and district names as Laclede's Landing, Chouteau, LaSalle, and Soulard.

In 1820 the Missouri Compromise was struck, allowing slavery to continue in Missouri but forbidding it in all future states north of an imaginary line extending west and north. As a result, when Missouri was admitted to the Union in 1821, it entered as a slave state. During that same year, a fur-trading post was established on the western end of the state, on land that is now Kansas City. For years, however, it remained nothing more than a trading post for a few French families, while nearby Independence grew as the starting point for wagon trains departing on the Santa Fe Trail as early as 1827.

Then in 1833 an entrepreneur named John C. McCoy saw that there was money to be made from the Santa Fe Trail, so he set up an outfitters store in a place called Westport. His scheme worked, and it wasn't long before Westport rivaled Independence as an equipment center. Its dusty streets—if you could call them that—were filled with Native Americans, Mexicans, mountain men, buffalo hunters, and mule skinners, all hoping to cash in on the riches of the trade. Westport, an outpost of whisky and guns, was crude, rowdy, and undisciplined. To protect the interests of the Santa Fe Trail, which was primarily a commercial trail for merchants traveling the 900 miles back and forth between Santa Fe and Westport, forts such as Fort Leavenworth and Fort Scott were established in Kansas. In 1838 McCoy founded the Town of Kansas four miles north of Westport on the banks of the Missouri River, on land that is now downtown Kansas City.

While the western edge of Missouri remained a rough frontier, St. Louis became gentrified. After it was proved in 1815 that sternwheelers could travel upriver on the Mississippi, St. Louis found new prosperity as a port town, as steamboats brought new products from Europe via New Orleans. By 1841 St. Louis was outranked only by New Orleans in terms of the nation's river traffic, with 186 steamboats landing in St. Louis that year.

But goods weren't the only things the steamboats transported. They also brought people by the thousands, many of whom stayed in St. Louis but most of whom traveled onward via the Missouri River to Independence and Westport, where they then joined others on the Oregon Trail. By 1860, as many as 100,000 emigrants had dared the five-month, 2,000-mile journey to Oregon. As for St. Louis, between 1830 and 1860 it grew from a town of only 5,825 to a city of 160,000, making it the eighth-largest city in the nation. As many as 50% of the newcomers were European immigrants, most of them Germans fleeing religious persecution back home and Irish escaping the Potato Famine.

THE CIVIL WAR

St. Louis seemed destined for greatness, but then in 1861 came an event that thwarted its ambitions—the Civil War. As a slave state, Missouri had already attracted national attention with the Dred Scott case, which had opened in 1846 in the new St. Louis Courthouse. Dred Scott, a slave, had sued for freedom after his owner had taken him to free territory, but after years of court battles the U.S. Supreme Court finally ruled that Scott was not a citizen and therefore couldn't sue.

The Supreme Court also ruled that Congress couldn't exclude slavery in the territories. With the passage of the Kansas-Nebraska Act, the people in Kansas and Nebraska were given the option of deciding whether to permit slavery. To help swing the vote, the New England Emigrant Aid Company sent both men and weapons to keep Kansas a free state, while armed "border ruffians" rode over from Missouri to fight for slavery. Civil war broke out with the first shots fired in "bleeding Kansas." In 1863 the anti-slavery town of Lawrence was attacked by a posse of pro-slavery men led by William Quantrill, killing 150 Lawrence men and setting fire to the town.

The Civil War tore Missouri in half.

DATELINE

road links east and west.

- **1874** Eads Bridge completed over the Mississippi River, linking St. Louis with the east.
- **1880** St. Louis becomes the nation's fourth-largest city.
- **1894** St. Louis Union Station built, the largest rail terminal in the world.
- **1900** Kansas City hosts the Democratic National Convention, which elects William Jennings Bryant.
- **1904** The St. Louis World's Fair attracts 19 million visitors.
- **1926** Charles Lindbergh makes the first nonstop flight from New York to Paris in the "Spirit of St. Louis," backed by St. Louis businessmen. The St. Louis Cardinals win the World Series against the New York Yankees led by Babe Ruth.
- **1928** Republican National Convention held in Kansas City.
- **1945** Harry S Truman of Independence becomes president of the United States.
- **1965** Gateway Arch, the nation's tallest monument, completed in St. Louis.

(continues)

DATELINE

• **1976** Kansas City hosts the Republican National Convention.

• **1985** St. Louis Union Station re-opens as a luxury hotel and a shopping and dining complex.

Although Missouri was a slave state, its governor was driven from office after trying to align the state with the Confederacy. And even while Missouri remained with the Union throughout the Civil War, it sent men to both sides in the conflict. But the biggest blow to Missouri occurred when the Confederates blocked the Mississippi River and the Union placed trade restrictions on the state, depriving St. Louis of its livelihood. By default, Chicago emerged as the Midwestern giant in trade, attracting the railroads and the support of New York merchants. It would be years before St. Louis would recover.

The Civil War also crippled Kansas City because warfare cut off trade along the Santa Fe Trail. In 1860 Kansas City had boasted 9 boarding houses, 16 hotels, and 26 saloons, with as many as 700 steamboats landing each year. As the Civil War raged, half the city's population simply packed their bags and left, while Confederate sympathizers were ordered to leave by official decree. Throughout the state, as many as 20,000 Missourians sympathetic to the South were driven from their homes. Kansas City, once a booming, bawdy, and raucous frontier city, was transformed into a virtual ghost town. In 1864 the last major Civil War battle west of the Mississippi took place in Westport.

BOOMTOWNS

Once the war was over, Kansas City jumped to its feet in its bid to attract the railroad. Competition was fierce because every town around knew that the railroads were the key to success in any city's future. But Kansas City ultimately won, beating out Leavenworth and Lawrence, and in 1865 the Missouri-Pacific reached the town. That was followed in 1869 with the completion of the Hannibal Bridge over the Missouri River, which meant that Kansas City could now ship goods both east and west. Kansas City turned its back on the river and before long emerged as one of the largest rail centers in the country and the marketing hub of the Great Plains.

Between 1865 and 1870 Kansas City's population surged from a mere 6,000 to 32,000. It was also the beginning of Kansas City's cowtown era and the cattle boom, as Texas longhorns were driven north along the Chisholm Trail to Abilene and then shipped to the stockyards of Kansas City. Wild Bill Hickok, Wyatt Earp, Jesse James, Bat Masterson, and Doc Holliday all strolled the streets of Kansas City, rubbing elbows with cowboys, merchants, more immigrants, and a newly emerging wealthy class. Before long, the bustling cowtown boasted a public library, an opera house, a board of trade, a stock exchange, a medical college, and uniformed police and firemen. By 1900 Kansas City had come so far that it was chosen as the site for the Democratic National Convention, which nominated William Jennings Bryan. Later, in 1928 and again in 1976, it would serve as headquarters for Republican conventions.

St. Louis, too, slowly recovered from setbacks suffered from the Civil War, growing as a commercial and manufacturing center for meat-packing, brewing, refining, and mining. By 1870 the city boasted 31 flour mills, 85 brickyards, and 40 breweries. In 1874 the

Eads Bridge was completed, spanning the Mississippi River and finally linking the city with the east. Like Kansas City, St. Louis turned its back on the river and concentrated its energies on the growth of the city, installing city parks and public facilities.

By 1880 St. Louis was the nation's fourth-largest city, a position that it would retain for the next four decades. To accommodate the waves of people pouring in off the railroads, the city constructed St. Louis Union Station. Completed in 1894, it was the world's largest rail terminal, twice as big as its nearest competitor in Boston. In 1894 St. Louis also established a convention bureau, the purpose of which was to advertise St. Louis to the rest of the world.

THE 20TH CENTURY

The convention bureau's efforts bore fruit in 1904 with the St. Louis World's Fair. A celebration of the 100-year anniversary of the Louisiana Purchase, the fair was held in Forest Park in the western end of the city and began with an address by William Howard Taft and music conducted by John Philip Sousa. Approximately 50 nations participated, erecting a total of 1,576 buildings and drawing more than 19 million visitors. Among the many exhibits was Thomas Edison's display of his newfangled phonograph and the light bulb. The seven-month fair is also credited with serving the first hot dog, iced tea, and ice-cream cone.

Throughout the 20th century, both Kansas City and St. Louis have continued to enjoy steady growth and prosperity. St. Louis led the way with the revitalization of its riverfront when its Gateway Arch was erected in 1965, followed through the next decades with the renovations of Laclede's Landing and Union Station. Today Kansas City and St. Louis are Missouri's two largest cities, with a combined population of almost 4 million.

FAMOUS ST. LOUISANS

General William Clark (1770–1838) An explorer, military officer, and public official, Clark is best known for the expedition he led with Meriwether Lewis to explore the Louisiana Purchase, departing St. Louis in 1804 and returning two years later. Clark remained in St. Louis, becoming the Indian Agent for Missouri Territory.

Thomas Hart Benton (1782–1858) Missouri's first senator, serving in that capacity for 30 years, Benton was a noted Congressional orator and historian. He was responsible for the eastern portion of the Missouri Pacific Railroad starting at St. Louis, thus making the city a 19th-century railroad center.

Mark Twain (1835–1910) Born in Hannibal, a small river town north of St. Louis, Mark Twain lived for several years in St. Louis, where he wrote and set type on the *St. Louis Evening News and Intelligencer* and began his career as a river pilot.

Adolphus Busch (1838–1913) A German-born American brewer, businessman and philanthropist, Busch (with his father-in-law) founded the Anheuser-Busch Brewery, today the world's largest brewery.

Eugene Field (1850–1895) A writer and journalist, Field is best known as the "children's poet" for such works as *Wynken, Blynken* *and Nod* and *Little Boy Blue.* His boyhood home in St. Louis is now a museum containing a large collection of antique toys and dolls.

Kate Chopin   (1851–1904) Kate Chopin grew up in St. Louis, moved to Louisiana when she married, and returned to St. Louis with her children after she was widowed. In St. Louis she wrote her most well known book, *The Awakening,* about a woman who seeks love outside a stuffy, middle-class marriage.

T. S. Eliot   (1888–1965) Critic, author, and winner of the Nobel Prize for Literature in 1948, Eliot is considered St. Louis' most famous poet, even though he left St. Louis for Harvard as a student and eventually moved to London, where he lived most of his adult life.

Tennessee Williams   (1911–1983) Playwright Thomas Lanier "Tennessee" Williams grew up in St. Louis, living in several locations with his family before he headed for the East Coast. The view from the apartment described in *The Glass Menagerie* fits the view from an apartment that he lived in during his youth.

Scott Joplin   (1868–1917) The legendary "King of Ragtime," Joplin spent some of his most formulative and productive years in St. Louis, where he composed "The Cascades" and "The Entertainer."

Chuck Berry   (b. 1926) This rock-'n'-roll legend grew up in St. Louis listening to recordings of Charlie Christian, T. Bone Walker, and Carl Hogan, first imitating then expanding on their guitar techniques. By 1954 he was packing them in at the Cosmo Club in East St. Louis, performing his own compositions and covering the blues, country, and pop demanded by his audiences. Blueberry Hill, a bar in University City in St. Louis, claims to have more Chuck Berry memorabilia than anywhere else in the country, including the guitar on which he composed "Roll over Beethoven."

William S. Burroughs   (b. 1914) A beat generation novelist, Burroughs was born in St. Louis and lived here until he was ten. He now resides in Lawrence, near Kansas City.

FAMOUS KANSAS CITIANS

Thomas Hart Benton   (1889–1975) One of Kansas City's best-known artists, Benton has many works in the Nelson-Atkins Museum of Art as well as a mural at the Harry S Truman Library in Independence. The Kansas City home where Benton lived and painted from 1937 until his death is now a state historic site.

Harry S Truman   (1884–1972) Thirty-third president of the United States, Truman is one of Missouri's most famous native sons. He served as a Jackson County judge, U.S. senator, and vice president before taking office as president in 1945 upon Franklin D. Roosevelt's death. He was elected to a second term in 1948. The home where he lived with his wife, Bess, and the Truman Library and Museum where the Trumans are buried are open to the public in Independence.

Walt Disney   (1901–1966) Although he was born in Chicago, Disney came to Kansas City as a young man in 1919 and found employment first as a commercial artist and then as an animator for Kansas City *Film Advertising.* He then formed his first—and soon bankrupt—production company. After this, he moved to Hollywood in 1923, where he went on to produce *Pinocchio, Fantasia,* and other Disney greats.

Count Basie   (1904–1984) A composer and band leader, Basie was largely responsible for bringing Kansas City to the fore of jazz. He performed with the Benny Moten Band in local clubs from 1929 to 1936 before moving on to greener pastures on the East Coast.

5. RECOMMENDED BOOKS

ST. LOUIS

Primm, James N., *Lion in the Valley* (Pruett, 1990). This is the most exhaustive history of St. Louis and the area.

Kirschten, Ernest, *Catfish and Crystal* (Patrice Press, 1989). Less scholarly in tone than the book above, this is an older history book that has just been re-released.

Fifield, Barringer, *Seeing St. Louis* (WA University Campus). This is a guide book divided into specific tours and written from an architect's point of view. It is not pedantic, however, and can be enjoyed by a wide audience.

Ebenhoh, Tom, *Arch Celebration* (Spiritgraphics, 1990). This new book celebrates the 25th anniversary of the Gateway Arch with color photographs, interviews, and reflections on the meaning of St. Louis' role as the gateway to the West.

KANSAS CITY

Grant, William D., *The Romantic Past of the Kansas City Region* (Lowell Press, 1987). This is a portrait of Kansas City from 1540 to 1880.

Reddig, William, *Tom's Town: Kansas City and the Pendergast Legend* (University of Missouri Press, 1986). Tom Pendergast was the undisputed "Boss" of Kansas City politics in the 1920s and through the Depression; although the years of his regime were undoubtedly corrupt, it was also under him that many of the city's art deco buildings were constructed. Interesting reading.

CHAPTER 2

PLANNING YOUR TRIP

This chapter will help you prepare for your trip to St. Louis and Kansas City. Also, reading through the other chapters before leaving home will help you plan your travels and itinerary.

1. INFORMATION

One of the best and easiest ways to prepare for your trip is to send away for the wealth of brochures and pamphlets just waiting for you. For general information on Missouri, send for the 140-page free annual booklet called *Missouri Travel Guide,* which has information on everything from attractions and campgrounds to wineries and caves. Contact the **Missouri Division of Tourism,** Truman State Office Building, Department MT-90, P.O. Box 1055, Jefferson City, MO 65102 (tel. 314/751-4133).

A similar booklet on Kansas, called *A Guide to Kansas,* which lists attractions city by city, is available from the **Kansas Department of Commerce,** Travel & Tourism Division, 400 West 8th St., 5th Floor, Topeka, KS 66603-3957 (tel. 913/296-7091, or toll free in Kansas 800/2-KANSAS). Maps and a calendar of events also are available.

For information specifically on St. Louis, including a map of the city and brochures, contact the **St. Louis Convention and Visitors Commission,** 10 S. Broadway, Suite 300, Dept. MT-90, St. Louis, MO 63102 (tel. 314/421-1023, or toll free 800/247-9791).

Similarly, for information and a map on Kansas City, contact the **Convention & Visitors Bureau of Greater Kansas City,** City Center Square, 100 Main St., Suite 2550, Dept. MT-90, Kansas City, MO 64105 (tel. 816/221-5242, or toll free 800/767-7700).

If you plan to visit Abilene, Hannibal, Hermann, Springfield, or any of the other recommended excursions in this book, you may also wish to contact that city's local tourist office before you depart. Refer to Chapter 11 for the addresses and telephone numbers of the local tourist offices for each town.

Both Kansas and Missouri maintain a number of state information centers to assist travelers arriving by car. For a list of these centers and their locations, refer to the "Getting There" section later in this chapter.

2. WHEN TO GO

WHAT THINGS COST IN ST. LOUIS	U.S. $
Taxi from airport to downtown St. Louis	$18.00
Bus from downtown to Clayton	.85
Local telephone call	.25
Double (at Adam's Mark Hotel—expensive)	165.00
Double (at Drury Inn Union Station—moderate)	88.00
Double (at Coral Court Motel—inexpensive)	40.00
Lunch (for one at Cardwell's—moderate)	12.00
Lunch (for one at Miss Hullings—budget)	5.00
Dinner for one, without wine (at Tony's—expensive)	44.00
Dinner for one, without wine (at Gian-Peppe's—moderate)	27.00
Dinner for one, without wine (at Blueberry Hill—budget)	5.00
Pint of beer	2.00
Coca-Cola	1.00
Cup of coffee	.75
Roll of ASA 100 Kodacolor film, 36 exposures	5.50
Admission to Gateway Arch and Tram	3.50
Movie ticket	5.00
Ticket to The Muny	5.00 to 30.00

The most pleasant time to visit the Midwest as far as weather is concerned is in late spring or early autumn, except then you miss out on all those festivals and events that make the rest of the year so much fun. If you're willing to brave the elements, Kansas City and St. Louis make good destinations at any time of the year.

THE CLIMATE

There's a saying around these parts that the weather is so fickle, it can change in the amount of time it takes you to visit the outhouse. About the only thing you can rely on is that the weather is reliably unpredictable—which means that it can be cold and chilly or warm and sunny in both July and November and sometimes even both of those extremes in the same day. But one of the great things about the weather is that the sky is often a deep blue, with more than 200 sunny days per year.

One can say with certainty, however, that Missouri has four distinct seasons. Winters are usually brisk and stimulating but seldom severe, with snowfalls up to a depth of 10 inches or more very rare. More likely are snowfalls of only an inch or two, with the average yearly snowfall ranging from about 17 to 20 inches per year. Winter temperatures usually remain around 30°F, although December 1989 brought the coldest reading of the century, when an Arctic cold front sent the mercury to a freezing 23 degrees below zero in Kansas City. Usually, however, temperatures of zero or below occur only two or three days a year, usually in January.

Early spring brings a period of frequent and rapid fluctuations in weather, including those great thunderstorms that roll in from the west off the prairies. Of course, each thunderstorm can bring the thing that got Dorothy out of Kansas—a tornado. Tornado season is April through June, but even though I've lived in Kansas most of my life, I've never seen one. In St. Louis in the past 116 years there have been only four tornadoes that have produced extensive damage and/or loss of life. Both television and radio stations carry weather alerts, and almost every town around has warning sirens.

Summer can be very hot and humid, with temperatures of 90° or more occurring 35 days a year and a humidity of 70 to 80 percent. Autumn is glorious as the leaves change color and the sky turns that incredibly deep shade of blue. Indian summers are frequent, and the first frost usually occurs in late October.

For a tape-recorded message of the temperature and forecast, call St. Louis at 314/321-2222 or Kansas City at 816/471-4840.

Missouri's Average Daytime Temperature and Rainfall

	Jan	Feb	Mar	Apr	May	June	July	Aug	Sept	Oct	Nov	Dec
Temp. °F	29	33	43	55	65	75	80	79	71	59	44	34
Rainy days	8	8	11	11	11	9	8.6	7.6	8	8.3	9	9.5

ST. LOUIS & KANSAS CITY CALENDAR OF EVENTS

If you're lucky, your trip may coincide with one of the area's many annual festivities, most of which are linked to the Midwest's rich ethnic heritage or historical events. All those listed here are easily accessible, with either free admission or tickets sold at the gates as you enter.

MARCH

✪ **ST. PATRICK'S DAY PARADE, KANSAS CITY** More than 300,000 people flock to downtown

Kansas City to take part in this annual event, the country's third-largest St. Patrick's Day parade.
  Where: *From Crown Center via Grand Avenue to 6th Street.* ***When:*** *March 17.* ***How:*** *Simply show up—and wear green. For more information, call 816/931-7373.*

✪ **ST. PATRICK'S DAY PARADE, ST. LOUIS** *This parade has been an annual event for more than 20 years.*
  Where: *Downtown, starting at 14th and Washington.* ***When:*** *Saturday before St. Patrick's Day.* ***How:*** *Show up.*

MAY

✪ **STORYTELLING FESTIVAL, ST. LOUIS** *This annual festival features both nationally recognized and local storytellers, with a special performance for the hearing impaired.*
  Where: *Gateway Arch.* ***When:*** *Early May (dates vary).* ***How:*** *For more information, call 314/553-5911 or 425-4465.*

✪ **MAIFEST, HERMANN, MO** *This is a German celebration featuring a parade, tours of historic homes and wineries, crafts, German food, and dance.*
  Where: *Stone Hill and Hermannhof wineries and downtown.* ***When:*** *Third full weekend in May.* ***How:*** *Admission free, winery tours $1.50. For more information, call 314/486-2410.*

JUNE

✪ **GOOD OLD DAYS, FORT SCOTT, KS** *Free entertainment, a parade, eight blocks of arts and crafts, and an antique show are just some of the events of this re-creation of an 1890 street fair.*
  Where: *Downtown Fort Scott.* ***When:*** *First weekend after Memorial Day.* ***How:*** *For more information, call 316/223-2334.*

✪ **KANSAS STATE BARBECUE CHAMPIONSHIP, LENEXA, KS** *Lenexa, a suburb of Kansas City, is host to a statewide competition with free admission and free samples.*
  Where: *Sar-Ko-Par Park, 87th and Lackman.* ***When:*** *Fourth Saturday in June.* ***How:*** *Free admission. For more information, call 913/541-8592 or 888-6570.*

JULY

✪ **VEILED PROPHET FAIR, ST. LOUIS** *This is one of the nation's largest July 4 celebrations, featuring five days of events including air shows, water shows, craft booths, live entertainment, a parade, and a fireworks display.*
  Where: *Gateway Arch, Mississippi riverfront, Laclede's Landing.* ***When:*** *Four or five days around July 4.* ***How:*** *For more information, call 314/535-FAIR.*

✪ *LINCOLNFEST, SPRINGFIELD, IL* This street festival offers food, drink, entertainment, music, crafts, and fireworks.
  Where: Downtown Springfield. **When:** Closest weekend prior to July 4. **How:** Free admission. For more information, call 217/789-2360, or toll free 800/545-7300.

✪ *INDEPENDENCE DAYS, LAWRENCE, KS* Canoe races, crafts booths, live entertainment, and fireworks are the draws of this annual Independence Day celebration.
  Where: Burcham Park, on the riverfront. **When:** July 4 and nearest weekend. **How:** Tickets available at the gate. For more information, call 913/865-4476.

✪ *KANSAS CITY INDIAN CLUB POW WOW, KANSAS CITY* Midwestern tribes compete in dance and skill during a three-day event.
  Where: Wyandotte County Fairgrounds, 98th and State. **When:** Mid-July. **How:** For more information, call 913/421-0039 or 421-7609.

✪ *STRASSENFEST, ST. LOUIS* Entertainment includes music by local and German oompah bands, a juried arts-and-crafts show and sale, rides, and children's stage. Proceeds go to charity and scholarship funds.
  Where: Westport Plaza, off I-270 at Page Avenue. **When:** Late July or early August (dates vary). **How:** For more information, call 314/721-7454.

AUGUST

✪ *ILLINOIS STATE FAIR, SPRINGFIELD, IL* Illinois' biggest, this fair features livestock shows, tractor pulls, milking contests, horse racing, music, and more.
  Where: Illinois State Fair Grounds. **When:** Eleven days, beginning with the second Thursday in August. **How:** Tickets available at the gate. For more information, call 217/789-2360, or toll free 800/545-7300.

✪ *JOUR DE FETE, STE. GENEVIEVE, MO* Missouri's oldest permanent settlement celebrates its French and German heritage with old-style French clogging, German bands, tours of historic homes, and arts and crafts.
  Where: Throughout Ste. Genevieve. **When:** Second full weekend in August. **How:** For more information, call 314/883-7097.

✪ *KANSAS CITY JAZZ FESTIVAL, KANSAS CITY* This is the largest annual free festival in Kansas City and is one of the top jazz concert productions in the country, with performances by local, regional, and national artists.
  Where: Volker Park, 47th and Oak. **When:** Usually last weekend in August. **How:** Free admission. For more information, call 816/722-4258.

✪ *JAPANESE FESTIVAL, ST. LOUIS* This annual celebration features taiko (drummer) groups, martial arts exhibitions, Kabuki dance groups, Suzuki violinists, and flower arranging.

Where: Missouri Botanical Gardens. **When:** Last weekend of August. **How:** For more information, call 314/577-5125.

SEPTEMBER

✪ **RENAISSANCE FESTIVAL, BONNER SPRINGS, KS** This is a great medieval getaway, complete with bards, musicians, beggars, damsels, knights, royalty, jousts, and sorcerers. A benefit of the Kansas City Art Institute, this re-creation of a 16th-century village features crafts, food booths, and old-fashioned games as well as continual entertainment on a number of stages. Plan to spend the entire day.

Where: Agricultural Hall of Fame, off I-70. **When:** Weekends only, from Labor Day weekend to mid-October. **How:** Tickets available at the gate or in advance by writing 207 Westport Road, Kansas City, MO 64111. For more information, call 816/561-8005.

✪ **SPIRIT FESTIVAL, KANSAS CITY** Entertainment from gospel to jazz and blues, cultural activities, food booths, and fireworks are featured in this annual festival celebrating things unique to Kansas City.

Where: Barney Allis Plaza, downtown Kansas City. **When:** Labor Day weekend. **How:** Tickets available at the gate. For more information, call 816/221-4444.

✪ **SANTA-CALI-GON DAYS, INDEPENDENCE, MO** A celebration of the city's pioneer heritage—when the Santa Fe, California, and Oregon trails led westward from Independence—this festival features an arts-and-crafts fair, entertainment, an interpretive area with demonstrations and food and crafts booths.

Where: Independence Square, downtown. **When:** Labor Day weekend, Friday to Monday. **How:** For more information, call 816/252-4745 or 836-8300.

✪ **POLISH FESTIVAL, ST. LOUIS** This is an annual feast of homemade food and pastry, including cabbage rolls, polish sausage, cheese dumplings, and bow-tie cookies, and features live polka bands and folk dancing.

Where: 2013 St. Louis Avenue. **When:** Dates vary. **How:** For more information, call 314/921-1192.

✪ **PLAZA FINE ARTS FAIR, KANSAS CITY** This arts fair on Country Club Plaza has been a tradition for more than 60 years. Artists from around the country display and sell their artwork, including oils, watercolors, drawings, prints, photography, and sculpture.

Where: Country Club Plaza. **When:** Dates vary. **How:** Free admission. For more information, call 816/753-0100.

OCTOBER

✪ **OCTOBERFEST, HERMANN, MO**   The area wineries
host a variety of activities and entertainment, including
tours, tastings, German bands, and dancing.
  Where: Stone Hill, Hermannhof, and Bias vineyards.
When: Every weekend in October. **How:** Free admission,
wine tours $1.50.

✪ **SVENSK HYLLNINGSFEST, LINDSBORG,
  KS**   Held every other year on odd years, this festival in the
town of Lindsborg is a celebration of the early Swedish
pioneers who founded the town. It features a smorgasbord,
Swedish folk dancing, a parade, and music.
  Where: Events held throughout Lindsborg, including
Bethany College. **When:** October 18–20, 1991. **How:** For
more information, call 913/227-3706.

✪ **HISTORIC FOLKLIFE FESTIVAL, HANNIBAL,
  MO**   Street musicians, artisans demonstrating crafts of the
mid-1800s, storytellers, and abundant food make Mark
Twain's river town come alive.
  Where: Downtown Hannibal. **When:** Third weekend in
October. **How:** For more information, call 314/221-6545.

NOVEMBER

✪ **AMERICAN ROYAL LIVESTOCK, HORSE SHOW
  AND RODEO**   Since 1899 the American Royal has
attracted competitors from across the nation to take part in
one of Kansas City's most famous traditions, a 15-day
event that includes a livestock show, a rodeo, livestock
auctions, and a barbecue contest.
  Where: 1701 American Royal Court and Kemper Arena.
When: First Saturday in November to mid-November.
How: For more information, call 816/221-9800.

✪ **PLAZA CHRISTMAS LIGHTING CEREMONY,
  KANSAS CITY**   Every Thanksgiving evening, Kansas
Citians crowd the streets of Country Club Plaza to witness
the turning on of more than 155,000 colored bulbs that
outline the 14-block district. The lights remain on
throughout the Christmas season.
  Where: Country Club Plaza. **When:** Thanksgiving
evening. **How:** Simply show up—and dress warmly. For
more information, call 816/221-5242 or 753-0100.

3. TIPS FOR THE DISABLED

For a list of hotels, restaurants, and tourist attractions in St. Louis that
provide handicapped parking and wheelchair accessibility, contact

the **Office on the Disabled,** City Hall, Room 30, St. Louis, MO 63103 (tel. 314/622-3686 for voice, 622-3692 for TTY). This office's brochure listing these facilities is called *Access St. Louis.* As for public transportation, many buses in St. Louis are equipped with lifts for wheelchairs. For more information on these buses, call the **Bi-State Transit** system at 314/231-2345 (outside Missouri, toll free 800/2233-BUS).

For information in Kansas City about access to city buildings, programs and activities, and other information, contact the **Mayor's Office on the Disabled,** City Hall, 29th Floor, 414 E. 12th St. (tel. 816/274-1235).

4. GETTING THERE

St. Louis and Kansas City are located in the heart of America, making them easy to reach by plane, train, car, and bus. St. Louis, for example, is within a four-hour flight of every major city in the country and within a day's drive of almost one-third of the nation's population.

BY AIR

PLANE ECONOMICS

Ever since Congress passed the Airline Deregulation Act of 1978, the airfare market has been a free-for-all, allowing such special fares as APEX (advanced purchase fare), discount travel agents, and other confusing options.

Your best strategy for securing the best airfare, therefore, is to shop around. Use the toll-free lines to call all the airlines that go to your destination and then call several travel agents to see whether they can find a better deal. Always ask for the lowest priced fare available. Sometimes you can purchase a low priced ticket at the very last minute, because airlines will discount tickets if the flight is not fully booked. Another good strategy is to consult the travel sections of major newspapers, since they often carry advertisements for cheap fares and special promotions.

Most airlines offer an assortment of fares, ranging from first class, the most expensive, to business class to economy. First and business class offer large seats with more leg room, more personal service, and better meals. Economy is the lowest-priced regular fare, of which there are usually two types: one that carries no special restrictions or requirements and one that is cheaper and carries some restrictions, such as tickets that are only 50% refundable. Of course, you can also assume that seats in economy class will be small and cramped and that you'll be served typical airline food. All these classes can be booked at the last minute, if there's space on the flight.

If you're trying to save money, the cheapest way to travel is by a promotional fare, the most common of which is usually called APEX but can also be referred to as Excursion, Super Saver, and other

FROMMER'S SMART TRAVELER —AIRFARES

1. Shop all the airlines that fly to Kansas City or St. Louis.
2. Keep calling the airlines, since the availability of cheap seats changes daily. As the departure date nears, you might be able to obtain a seat at a great discount, since an airline would rather sell a discounted seat than fly with it empty.
3. Read the advertisements in newspaper travel sections, since they often offer special deals and packages.
4. You can save money by buying your ticket as early as possible, since the cheapest fares, such as APEX (Advance Purchase Excursion), require that you purchase your ticket in advance, usually 21 days in advance.

names. Offering savings as much as 35% off the regular fare, they carry stringent restrictions, which do vary, but usually include a 21-day advance purchase requirement, usually allow no changes and are nonrefundable and nontransferable.

Airlines that serve both Kansas City and St. Louis include **Air Midwest** (tel. toll free 800/272-6433), **American** (tel. toll free 800/433-7300), **Continental** (tel. toll free 800/525-0280), **Delta** (tel. toll free 800/221-1212), **Northwest** (tel. toll free 800/225-2525), **Southwest** (tel. 816/474-1221 in Kansas City, 314/421-1221 in St. Louis), **TWA** (tel. toll free 800/892-4141; 816/842-4000 in Kansas City, 314/291-7500 in St. Louis), **United** (tel. toll free 800/241-6522; 816/471-6060 in Kansas City, 314/454-0088 in St. Louis), and **U.S. Air** (tel. toll free 800/428-4322).

Fares

Fares vary widely among the airlines, so the fares listed here should be used only as a guideline. From New York, round-trip fares on TWA to St. Louis at the time this book is going to press are $1,236 for first class, $832 for business class, $792 for economy class with no restrictions, $376 for economy class with some restrictions, and $307 for APEX fare. To Kansas City, round-trip fares on United from New York are $946 for first class (there is no business class), $808 for economy class with no restrictions, $421 for economy with some restrictions, and $330 for APEX fare.

From Los Angeles, TWA round-trip flights to St. Louis cost $1,668 for first class, $1,102 for business class, $1,060 for economy class with no restrictions, $491 for economy class with some restrictions, and $399 for APEX fare. Round-trip fares from Los Angeles to Kansas City on United are $1,614 for first class (there is no business class), $712 for economy class with no restrictions, $305 for economy class with some restrictions, and $240 for APEX fare.

If you wish to fly between Kansas City and St. Louis, the round-trip fare on U.S. Air is $750 for first class, $568 for business class, $438 for economy class with no restrictions, $216 for economy class with some restrictions, and $148 for APEX fare.

Remember, fares are subject to change without notice. Be sure to contact your travel agent or the airlines for current information.

Other Options

Besides contacting airlines and travel agencies and consulting newspapers, you may also contact a discount travel agent. Each agent has his or her own set of rules and usually charges small fees for such services as delivering tickets and changing reservations. Discount travel agencies that serve customers nationwide are **Travel Avenue** in Chicago (tel. 312/876-1116, or toll free 800/333-3335), **Travelbrokers** in New York City (tel. toll free 800/999-8748), and **Smart Traveller** in Miami (tel. 305/448-3338, or toll free 800/226-3338).

BY CAR

According to a survey conducted by the St. Louis Convention and Visitors Commission, almost 95% of that city's visitors arrive by car. St. Louis is easily reached by Interstate 70, as well as from Interstate 55 from Chicago and New Orleans, Interstate 44 from Oklahoma City, and Interstate 64 from Norfolk, Virginia. Driving time to St. Louis is approximately 10 hours from Atlanta, 5 hours from Chicago, 12 hours from Dallas, 16 hours from Denver, 34 hours from Los Angeles, 13 hours from New Orleans, and 18 hours from New York.

Kansas City is served by two major highways: Interstate 70 from Denver and St. Louis and Interstate 35 from Minneapolis and Dallas. Kansas City is about a four-hour drive west of St. Louis on Interstate 70.

Missouri law requires that all front-seat passengers wear a seat belt. In addition, children under four must be in a child safety seat in the front or wear a seat belt in the back seat. If you need emergency assistance on a Missouri highway or wish to report an accident, intoxicated drivers, or vehicle problems, call toll free 800/525-5555.

If you arrive in Missouri by car, you'll find state information centers on Interstate 44, near the Oklahoma border; on Interstate 270 in north St. Louis, just west of the Missouri-Illinois state line at the Riverview exit; in southeast Missouri on the north-bound lane of Interstate 55, near Marston; on Interstate 29 in northwest Missouri; in Hannibal on Highway 61; and in east Kansas City, near the Truman Sports Complex on Interstate 70.

Kansas Visitor Information Centers are located west of Kansas City on I-70 (for westbound traffic only), on I-70 in Abilene, on I-70 in Goodland in western Kansas, and on U.S. 55 near Fort Scott.

BY TRAIN

One of the most interesting ways to travel between Kansas City and St. Louis and enjoy the Missouri countryside is by Amtrak. Two trains depart daily from each direction, and the trip takes slightly more than five hours. Tickets cost $40 one way and $47 round trip.

You can also reach both Kansas City and St. Louis by Amtrak from Los Angeles, Chicago, New Orleans, and points in between. The round-trip fare from Chicago is $45 to St. Louis and $81 to Kansas City. From Los Angeles, the round-trip fare is $203 to both Kansas City and St. Louis.

For information on **Amtrak,** call toll free 800/872-7245 or 800/USA-RAIL.

BY BUS

The cheapest way to get to St. Louis or Kansas City via public transportation is probably by bus, with **Greyhound/Trailways.** The cost of a round-trip bus ticket with no restrictions from New York to Kansas City, for example, is $179. Promotional and seven-day advance-purchase tickets also are available. For more information, contact your nearest bus carrier.

CHAPTER 3

FOR THE FOREIGN VISITOR

1. PREPARING FOR YOUR TRIP

2. GETTING TO THE UNITED STATES

• FAST FACTS: THE FOREIGN TRAVELER

f you're traveling to St. Louis or Kansas City, you'll have most likely visited the United States at least once before—it is rare to find a visitor in the Midwest who has not already seen New York and California. However, should you have questions about your stay, this chapter will hopefully answer them. Be sure, too, to read Chapters 1, 2, 4, and 12.

---

1. PREPARING FOR YOUR TRIP

ENTRY REQUIREMENTS

Except for Canadian nationals (who need only proof of residence) and British and Japanese nationals (who no longer need visas but only passports), each foreigner entering the United States must have two documents: (1) a valid passport, with an expiration date at least six months longer than the scheduled end of the visit to the United States, and (2) a tourist visa, available without charge from the nearest U.S. Consulate (you must fill out a special form and provide a passport photograph).

In most instances, you will be given your visa immediately or at least within 24 hours. Try to avoid the summer rush in June, July, and August, when Consulates may be packed. If applying by mail, enclose a large, stamped, self-addressed envelope and expect to wait at least two weeks for the visa. You can obtain visa application forms from U.S. Consulates as well as from airline offices and leading travel agents. The U.S. tourist visa (visa B) is theoretically valid for a year and good for any number of entries, but in reality the U.S. Consulate issuing your visa will determine the length of stay for a multiple- or single-entry visa. Keep in mind that there is some latitude here, so dress neatly and responsibly if applying in person; it helps if you can give the address of a relative, friend, or business connection living in the United States.

MEDICAL REQUIREMENTS

No inoculations are required for entry into the United States unless you come from, or have stopped over in, an area known to be infectious, especially for cholera or yellow fever. Only applicants for immigration visas are required to undergo a screening test for AIDS.

If you have an ailment requiring treatment with syringes or medications containing narcotics or drugs, be certain to carry a valid, signed prescription from your physician to avoid any suspicions from customs officials that you are carrying illegal drugs.

TRAVEL INSURANCE (BAGGAGE, HEALTH, AND LOSS)

Insurance—even health insurance—is voluntary in the United States. However, because of the very high cost of medical care, you'd be wise to arrange for appropriate coverage before setting out. There are specialized insurance companies that will, for a relatively low premium, cover the following: loss or theft of your baggage; trip-cancellation costs; guarantee of bail in case you are jailed; sickness or injury costs (medical, surgical, and hospital); and costs of an accident, repatriation, or death.

Such packages may be sold by insurance companies, travel agencies, banks, some airports, and even automobile clubs. If you carry a lot of camera equipment, it's worth getting the equipment insured as well. I can't stress enough the importance of having medical insurance.

2. GETTING TO THE UNITED STATES

Travelers from overseas can take advantage of APEX (Advance Purchase Excursion) fares, which are offered by all major U.S. and European airlines. In addition, Icelandair from Luxembourg offers inexpensive fares to New York or Orlando, and Virgin Atlantic is an inexpensive way to get from London to New York via Newark airport or Miami.

Some airlines (such as TWA, Northwest, United, and Delta) offer discount tickets on their transatlantic or transpacific flights under the name Visit USA, allowing travel between a set number of U.S. destinations at minimum rates. Such tickets are not for sale in the United States and must therefore be purchased before you leave your foreign point of departure. This system is the best way to cover much of the country at a low cost.

 THE FOREIGN TRAVELER

Accommodations Hotel and motel chains are big business in the United States, accounting for the majority of accommodations nationwide. Chain hotels offer uniformity in the quality of their rooms, as well as prices, but lack the charm of privately owned, smaller hotels. Generally speaking, motels, which are one- or two-story accommodations often located near highways, are cheaper than hotels, particularly those on the outskirts of town. Another choice in inexpensive accommodations are bed and breakfasts, which are similar to pensions in Europe. Bed and breakfasts are often historic homes offering a half-dozen or so guest rooms with or without private bathrooms.

Refer to the accommodations chapters for St. Louis and Kansas City for more information on the various types of hotels, motels, and bed and breakfasts.

Auto Organizations If you plan to travel by automobile, you may wish to join an auto club, which entitles you to maps, recommendations on routes, guide books, accident insurance, and emergency road service. One of the largest automobile clubs is the American Automobile Association (AAA), which maintains an office in St. Louis at 3917 Lindell Blvd. (tel. 314/531-0700) and in Kansas City at 3245 Broadway (tel. 816/931-5252). A one-year membership for both Americans and foreigners is $45.

Business Hours   Most government offices and businesses are open Monday through Friday from 9am to 5pm. Banks usually are open Monday through Friday from about 9am to 3 or 4pm, with slightly longer hours sometimes offered on Friday and morning hours offered on Saturday. Post offices generally are open Monday through Friday from 8am to 5:30 or 6pm and Saturday from 8am to noon.

Stores in downtown areas usually are open only during regular business hours—that is, Monday through Saturday from 9 or 10am to about 5:30 or 6pm. Shopping malls have longer hours, usually Monday through Saturday until 9pm and Sunday until 5 or 7pm. Drugstores and supermarkets are open even later—and in some cities they never close. Some Americans, to avoid crowds, do all their grocery shopping in the middle of the night.

Museum hours vary widely. The average hours for large museums are Tuesday through Saturday from 10am to 5pm, opening perhaps at noon on Sunday and closed on Monday. Some of the major museums are open on national holidays, with the exception of Thanksgiving, Christmas, and New Year's Day.

Climate   Refer to Chapter 2 under the "When to Go" section for a discussion of the Midwestern climate.

Currency and Exchange   The U.S. monetary system has a decimal base: one dollar ($1) = 100 cents (100¢). The most common denominations come in the form of $1 (a "buck"), $5, $10, $20, $50, and $100 notes—all green in color. There's also a $2 bill, but it's rarely used. Most store clerks do not like taking a $50 or $100 bill for a small purchase.

There are six denominations of coins: 1¢ (one cent, or penny); 5¢ (five cents, or nickel); 10¢ (ten cents, or dime); 25¢ (twenty-five cents, or quarter); 50¢ (fifty cents, or half dollar); and—prized by collectors—the rare $1 piece (both the older, large silver dollar and the newer, small Susan B. Anthony coin).

The foreign-exchange bureaus so common in Europe are rare even at airports in the United States and nonexistent outside major cities. Try to avoid having to change foreign money or traveler's checks denominated in foreign currency—it may prove to be more of a nuisance than it's worth. The best policy is to put the bulk of your money into U.S. dollar traveler's checks and then bring a credit card. If you must change money, there are major banks in Kansas City and St. Louis that will do so for you. In St. Louis, try the **Mercantile Bank,** 8th and Locust (tel. 314/425-2525), open weekdays from 8:30am to 4:30pm; or the **Commerce Bank of St. Louis County,** 8000 Forsyth on the corner of Merimac (tel. 314/854-7463), open Monday to Thursday from 9am to 4pm and Friday from 9am to 6pm.

In Kansas City, a convenient place to exchange foreign currency is downtown at the **United Missouri Bank,** 1010 Grand (tel. 816/556-7000), open Monday to Thursday from 8am to 4:30pm and Friday from 8am to 5pm.

Customs and Immigration   Every adult visitor to the United States may bring in the following, free of duty: one liter of wine or hard liquor (which isn't much, regrettably); 1,000 cigarettes or 100 cigars (but *no* cigars from Cuba) or three pounds of smoking tobacco; and $400 worth of gifts. These exemptions are offered to travelers who spend at least 72 hours in the United States and who have not claimed the exemptions in the preceding 6 months. It is absolutely forbidden to bring into the country foodstuffs (particularly cheese, fruit, cooked meats, and canned goods) and plants (vegetables, seeds, tropical plants, and so on). Foreign tourists may bring in or take out up to $5,000 in U.S. or foreign currency with no formalities. Larger sums must be declared to Customs on entering or leaving.

No matter what your point of entry into the United States, you should anticipate a long wait. U.S. Customs and Immigration officials are among the slowest and most suspicious on earth. At some of the busiest international airports, such as New York's John F. Kennedy Airport, you may have to wait two hours just to get your passport stamped. When you add to that the time it takes to clear Customs and get your luggage, it'll become clear that you should allow at least three hours if you're changing planes.

It's a different story altogether if you're arriving by car or rail from Canada because border-crossing formalities between the two neighbors are little more than that. And for some flights by air from Canada, Bermuda, and some points in the Caribbean, Customs and Immigration are handled at the point of *departure,* which is much quicker and less painful.

Drinking Laws Although Americans can vote and die at war for their country at 18, they can't drink until they reach 21 years of age in Missouri and Kansas. That applies to visitors as well. For hours of operation of liquor stores and bars, check the individual city listings.

Electricity Although in Europe the current is 220 volts and 50 cycles, in the United States it's 110 to 115 volts and 60 cycles. Try to avoid traveling with foreign appliances unless you wish to buy a volt converter and a plug adapter with two flat, parallel pins.

Embassies and Consulates All embassies are located in Washington, D.C.; consulates in the Midwest are usually located in Chicago. There are no English-speaking consulates in either Kansas City or St. Louis. For the telephone number of your nation's embassy in Washington, D.C., call information at 202/555-1212.

Emergencies Throughout the United States, dial 911 to get the police or an ambulance or to report a fire. U.S. hospitals usually have emergency rooms, with a special entrance for quick attention. See the Fast Facts section for each city for more information under "Dentists and Doctors," "Drugstores," and "Hospitals."

Gasoline (Petrol) One U.S. gallon equals 3.75 litres, while 1.2 U.S. gallons equals one imperial gallon. Although leaded gas (short for gasoline) costs less, recent makes of cars, including those from rental agencies, take unleaded gas only.

Holidays Banks, government offices, and post offices are closed on the following national holidays: New Year's Day (January 1), Martin Luther King Jr. Day (third Monday in January), Presidents Day/Washington's Birthday (third Monday in February), Memorial Day (last Monday in May), Independence Day (July 4), Labor Day (first Monday in September), Columbus Day (second Monday in

October), Veteran's Day/Armistice Day (November 11), Thanksgiving (last Thursday in November), and Christmas (December 25).

If Christmas or New Year's Day falls on a Sunday, the following Monday is a holiday. Finally, the Tuesday following the first Monday in November is Election Day and is a legal holiday every four years during the presidential election.

Information For local tourist information, refer to the "Getting to Know St. Louis" and "Getting to Know Kansas City" chapters. If you wish to obtain information before your trip, see chapter 2, "Before You Leave," for telephone numbers and addresses of local and state tourist offices.

Legal Aid The foreign tourist will probably never come up against the U.S. legal system. The most that's likely to happen is that you'll be pulled over for speeding (65 miles per hour is achingly slow if you're used to German autobahns), in which case you should never attempt to pay the fine directly to the police officer. It could be interpreted as a bribe and land you in serious trouble. Pay fines by mail or directly into the hands of the clerk of the court. If you're accused of a more serious offense, it is wise to say and do nothing before consulting a lawyer. Under U.S. law, an arrested person is allowed one telephone call to a party of his or her choice. Call your embassy or consulate.

Mail Mailboxes in the United States are painted blue with a red-and-white stripe and carry the inscription "U.S. Mail." Don't forget to add the five-figure postal code (Zip code) to all letters addressed to a U.S. destination. If you're unsure of the postal code, telephone or inquire at any post office.

You can receive your mail on your vacation, even if you aren't sure of your address, by having your mail sent to you in care of General Delivery at the main post office of the city where you expect to be. You must pick it up in person and produce proof of identity (driver's license, credit card, or passport will do). If you want your mail forwarded, you need only to fill out a change-of-address card at any post office. The post office will also hold your mail for you up to one month.

Medical Emergencies See "Emergencies," above. Also refer to the "Getting to Know St. Louis" and "Getting to Know Kansas City" chapters for information on local hospitals and doctors.

Newspapers and Magazines Most newspapers in the United States are local, not national. In St. Louis it's the *St. Louis Post-Dispatch;* in Kansas City it's the *Kansas City Star.* Other newspapers available in both cities are *USA Today, The New York Times, The Wall Street Journal,* and the *Christian Science Monitor.* As for magazines, weekly news magazines include *Newsweek, Time,* and *U.S. News & World Report.* It is difficult to get the airmail editions of foreign newspapers and magazines in the Midwest—and they're often out of date by the time they get here.

Post See "Mail," above.

Radio and Television Most hotels have televisions in their rooms, so you'll have a chance to see that most American of institutions—commercials. There are three coast-to-coast networks—ABC, CBS, and NBC—as well as the Public Broadcasting System (PBS) and the cable network CNN. Many hotels subscribe to cable, allowing viewers the choice of about a dozen channels, including channels devoted entirely to sports, news, music, and movies. There are also local radio stations that each broadcast a particular kind of music—classical, country, jazz, or pop—punctuated by news broadcasts and frequent commercials. If you're hungry for international news, tune into the local National Public Radio station, which broadcasts news programs in the morning and again in the late afternoon.

Safety   Whenever you're traveling in an unfamiliar city or country, stay alert. Be aware of your immediate surroundings. Wear a money belt and keep a close eye on your possessions. Never carry large amounts of cash and leave your expensive jewelry at home. Be particularly careful with cameras, purses, and wallets—all favorite targets of thieves and pickpockets.

Generally speaking, the Midwest is safe, particularly in rural areas, but there are parts of Kansas City and St. Louis where you should exercise extreme caution. Use common sense when walking at night—keep to areas where there are lots of people and the streets are well lit. Avoid such isolated areas as gardens, alleys, and parking lots after dark. If you find yourself driving through an area that looks like it's been through a war (and there are ghettolike areas in both Kansas City and St. Louis), keep your doors locked and your windows up and don't stop. East St. Louis is considered the most depressed part of St. Louis; in Kansas City this area lies east of downtown along the Paseo and side streets.

Before you start worrying that you're about to enter a crime-ridden country, be assured that I have never been mugged, nor have I ever had anything stolen from me in this country. As with many things, being the victim of a crime is largely being in the wrong place at the wrong time.

Taxes   There is no VAT (Value-Added Tax) in the United States, nor is there any other indirect national tax. Every state, however, can set its own sales tax: in Missouri it's 4.425%; in Kansas it's 4.25%. In addition, each city can add its own General Revenue tax. In St. Louis, for example, it's 1.5%. These taxes are added to everything you purchase, from clothing to a meal in a restaurant. Liquor taxes are even higher. Thus, if you're making a major purchase, taxes can really add up. Just a $100 purchase, for example, will cost you more than $5 extra in tax.

Telephone, Telegraph, Telex   Public telephones can be found virtually everywhere—on the street and in restaurants, bars, public buildings, stores, and gas stations. Outside metropolitan areas, gas stations and stores are your best bet.

Local calls cost a quarter (25¢). For long-distance or international calls, stock up on a supply of quarters; the pay phone will instruct you when and in what quantity you should put them into the slot. For direct overseas calls, first dial 011, followed by the country code (Australia, 61; Republic of Ireland, 353; New Zealand, 64; United Kingdom, 44; and so on), and then by the city code and the number of the person you wish to call. For calls to Canada and long-distance calls in the United States, dial 1 followed by the area code and number you want. Generally speaking, it's much cheaper calling from the United States to other countries rather than the reverse. It's also cheaper if you call between 10pm and 8am or on Saturday and Sunday.

Before calling from a hotel room, always ask the hotel phone operator if there are any telephone surcharges, since these can be shockingly high. It's best to use a public phone. Phone cards such as those sold in England, Japan, and many other countries are not used here.

For reversed-charge or collect calls and for person-to-person calls dial 0 (zero, not the letter O) followed by the area code and the number you want. The operator will then come on the line, and you should specify that you are calling collect, or person-to-person (the most expensive way to call), or both. If your operator-assisted call is international, ask for the overseas operator.

If you need local directory assistance, dial 411. If you need a long-distance number, dial 1, followed by the appropriate area code and 555-1212. Thus, if you're in Kansas City and need a number in St. Louis, dial 1-314-555-1212.

Telegraph and telex services are provided by private corporations (as is the telephone system), such as ITT, RCA, and above all, Western Union. You can bring your telegram in to the nearest Western Union office or even dictate it over the phone (tel. toll free 800/552-5959). You can also telegraph money or have it telegraphed to you very quickly over the Western Union system. Some hotels also provide these services.

Telephone Directories   There are two kinds of telephone directories available, both of which should be in your hotel room. The general directory is the so-called *White Pages,* which contains private residential numbers and business subscribers, listed in alphabetical order. The inside front cover contains the emergency number for police and other vital numbers, such as a poison control center and a crime hotline. It also contains a guide to long-distance and international calling, complete with country codes and area codes.

The second directory is printed on yellow paper—and therefore called the *Yellow Pages*—and lists all local services, businesses, and industries by type of activity, with an index in the back. The listings cover everything from restaurants to specialized shops and services. The book also includes a city map. In small cities, the *Yellow Pages* and *White Pages* often are combined into one directory.

Time   The United States is divided into four time zones (with the exception of Alaska and Hawaii), and both St. Louis and Kansas City follow Central Standard Time (CST). When it's noon in Kansas City, it's 1pm in New York and 10am in Los Angeles. Kansas City is seven hours behind Central European Time, which means that when it's noon in Kansas City, it's already 7pm in much of Europe. Daylight Savings Time is in effect from the last Sunday in April (when clocks are set one hour ahead) through the last Saturday in October (when clocks are set one hour back).

Tipping   Tipping is very much a part of the American way of life. Indeed, waiters and waitresses depend on it for the majority of their income. Here are some rules of thumb:

Bartenders: 10%–15%
Bellhops: at least 50¢ per piece; $2–$3 for a lot of baggage
Cab drivers: 15% of the fare
Cafeterias, fast-food restaurants: no tip
Chambermaids: $1 a day; more in upper-class hotels
Cinemas, movies: no tip
Checkroom attendants: 50¢ per garment
Doormen (hotels or restaurants): not obligatory, but $1 at top hotels
Hairdressers: 10%–15%

Parking-lot attendants: $1 or $2

Porters (airport and railroad stations): at least 50¢ per piece; $2–$3 for a lot of baggage

Restaurants, nightclubs: 15%–20% of the check to your service person

Toilets The United States does not have as many public toilets as you'll find in many other countries. Rather, Americans use those in bars, fast-food restaurants, hotels, museums, department stores, or gasoline stations. Often the toilets are clean—sometimes they are not, with those at gas stations clearly the worst offenders. I usually carry some pocket tissues with me in case toilet paper is nonexistent.

Some gas stations and restaurants have a sign saying that its restrooms (as public toilets are often called) are for the use of its patrons only. Buy a cup of coffee if you must. And although it is now rare, some public toilets require you to insert one dime (10¢) into a slot on the door before the door will open.

Traveler's Checks and Credit Cards The United States is basically a cashless society. Going about with only cash, it seems, is just too risky, since there may not be enough to pay for unforseen accidents or expenses. In fact, many hotels and most car-rental agencies will not deal with customers who cannot produce a credit card. In addition, many Americans avoid carrying large amounts of cash on them, since loss, theft, and muggings are always possibilities.

Paying with credit cards (and personal checks), therefore, is the most widely used method in the United States. Most common are Visa (BarclayCard in Britain), MasterCard (EuroCard in Europe, Access in Britain, Diamond in Japan, and so on), American Express, Diners Club, Carte Blanche, and Discover. Of these, Visa and MasterCard seem to be preferred by the greatest number of establishments. Credit cards can be used in almost all hotels and motels and in most restaurants and shops (except for liquor stores). A credit card can serve as a deposit when you rent a car or allow you to draw cash from banks that accept them. It is also accepted as proof of identity, often carrying more weight than a passport.

As for traveler's checks, buy them in U.S. dollars. They're accepted as cash almost everywhere, so be sure to have both $20 and $100 denominations. There's no fee charged for cashing them.

Yellow Pages See "Telephone Directories," above.

PART ONE

ST. LOUIS

CHAPTER 4

GETTING TO KNOW ST. LOUIS

1. ORIENTATION
2. GETTING AROUND
- **FAST FACTS: ST. LOUIS**

This chapter will answer any questions that you might have upon your arrival in St. Louis and during your stay—from how to get to your hotel from the airport and around the city to numbers to call during an emergency.

1. ORIENTATION

Located on the western shore of the Mississippi River, which divides the state of Missouri from the state of Illinois, St. Louis prides itself on having been the gateway to the West.

ARRIVING

BY PLANE

The **St. Louis–Lambert International Airport** (tel. 314/426-8000) is conveniently located 10 miles northwest of the city, just north of Interstate 70. Facilities include the usual restaurants, car-rental companies, lockers for storage of luggage, shoe-shine stands, and a hair salon, but of most interest to arriving visitors is the **St. Louis Visitor Information** booth located on the lower level by the luggage carousels. Be sure to pick up a copy of the *St. Louis Visitor Guide,* with information on the city's top attractions, as well as brochures and a map of the city.

GETTING INTO TOWN   The easiest way to get to your hotel is by **taxi,** which costs about $18 for the ride downtown and takes approximately 40 to 60 minutes, depending on traffic. Fares from Lambert Airport to Clayton or Mid-County run about $14. Up to five passengers can ride and share the meter fare, making a taxi ride very reasonable if there are several of you.

An alternative is to take the **Airport Limousine** (tel. 314/429-4940), which is actually a six- or eight-passenger van depositing passengers directly at hotels. The fare is $6 one way or $9 round trip. The hours of operation from the airport are daily from 6:30am to 10:30pm. Among the many hotels served by Airport Limousine in the downtown area are the Adam's Mark Hotel, the Clarion Hotel, the Holiday Inn Downtown Riverfront, the Hotel Majestic, the Marriott Pavilion Hotel, the Embassy Suites Hotel, the Hyatt Regency at Union Station, the Mayfair, and the Drury Inns at both the Convention Center and the Union Station locations. Other hotels served by the Airport Limousine include the Cheshire Lodge and Forest Park Hotel and the Radisson and Ritz-Carlton hotels in Clayton. Even if you aren't staying at one of these hotels, you may find it cheaper to take the limousine to the hotel nearest your destination and then continue your trip by taxi.

The cheapest way to get from the airport to downtown is via **public bus no. 4,** known as the Natural Bridge bus and operated by the **Bi-State Transit System** (tel. 314/231-2345). The fare is 85¢, and the final destination is Broadway and Olive streets in the heart of downtown.

BY TRAIN

If you're arriving in St. Louis via train, you'll most likely arrive at the main **Amtrak** terminal at 550 South 16th St. (tel. 241-8806) in downtown St. Louis. From there taxis are easily available to your final destination.

BY CAR

If you're driving to St. Louis, the main thing to keep in mind is to time your arrival so that you miss rush hour. Particularly bad is the bottleneck that develops on the Poplar St. Bridge crossing the Mississippi from Illinois, which is also the route served by highways 70, 55, and 64. As in most big cities, traffic here is worst heading into St. Louis in the morning and again after 5pm as commuters head back for the suburbs.

Since parking can be expensive in St. Louis, you'll save considerably if you stay in a hotel that offers free parking. (Check Chapter 5 for parking information for individual hotels.) Generally speaking, hotels on the outskirts are more apt to provide free parking than those in the downtown area. As for public parking facilities, St. Louis has parking garages everywhere to accommodate the crowds who flock to Busch Stadium, Union Station, the Arch, and other top attractions.

BY BUS

The **St. Louis Bus Terminal** (tel. 314/231-7800), served by Greyhound, is at 801 N. Broadway in downtown St. Louis, conveniently located near many of the city's hotels. However, keep in mind that the future expansion of a new convention facility will call for the eventual relocation of the bus terminal. Although no new location

IMPRESSIONS

The first time I saw St. Louis I would have bought it for $6 million. It is bitter now to look abroad over this domed and steepled metropolis, this solid expanse of brick and mortar, and remember that I allowed this opportunity to go by. . . .
—MARK TWAIN, 1874

has been announced at press time, it might be wise to check beforehand whether the new terminal is in operation by the time of your trip.

TOURIST INFORMATION

The main information office is the downtown **St. Louis Convention and Visitors Commission,** 10 S. Broadway (third floor of the Equitable Building) Suite 300, St. Louis, MO 63102 (tel. 314/ 421-1023)—open daily from 8:30am to 5pm. Stop here to arm yourself with brochures, guides, and maps of St. Louis and vicinity.

There's another visitor center located in the **Mansion House Center,** 445 N. Memorial Drive (tel. 314/241-1764)—open daily from 9:30am to 4:30pm—and also one on the airport's lower level which is open daily from 10am to 8pm.

For a quick rundown of what's happening in St. Louis, call 421-2100 for a recorded message outlining special exhibits and music and theater events and even giving a schedule of Cardinal home baseball games.

CITY LAYOUT

St. Louis was founded on the western banks of the wide Mississippi, and it's here that its heart remains. Downtown St. Louis, guarded over by the shining Arch, includes Busch Stadium; Union Station; and a restored warehouse district now housing restaurants and bars, called Laclede's Landing. Less than a 10-minute drive due west from downtown is Forest Park, home of the St. Louis Zoo, a fantastic art museum, and a number of other fine attractions. Spreading like a fan toward the north, west, and south is the rest of St. Louis, which is completely contained in one county, St. Louis County. Natives often refer to a certain part of St. Louis according to where it is in the county, such as South County along the southern perimeter, North County, and West County. Mid-County refers to such neighborhoods as Brentwood, Clayton, University City, and Kirkwood. Incidentally, the Mississippi River serves as the dividing line between Missouri and Illinois. East St. Louis, therefore, is in Illinois and is a separate city altogether, although many residents who live in East St. Louis commute across the river to work.

MAIN ARTERIES AND STREETS

For orientation downtown, let the Arch be your guide. Located on an expanse of green called the Jefferson National Expansion Memorial Park beside the Mississippi River, the Arch serves as the gateway to the West both in symbol and in fact. From about the middle of the Arch stretching west is Market Street, which passes the Old Courthouse and continues on to Union Station. It's one of the most important streets in the city, serving as a dividing line for the north and south street addresses. The streets running westward and parallel to Market Street were named in the 1800s after trees. Walnut, Chestnut, Pine, Olive, and Locust are all downtown streets lined with office buildings, restaurants, and shops.

Bisecting Market Street are the numbered streets (that is, streets that run north and south). At 18th and Market Street, for example, stands Union Station, which is 18 blocks west of the Mississippi River. As Market Street is the dividing line between north and south addresses, North 4th Street is north of Market Street, while South 4th Street is its continuation south of Market.

Downtown St. Louis is connected to the rest of the county via a number of major thoroughfares and highways. Most important for east-west traffic are I-70 (which leads past Lambert Airport and continues through Missouri to Kansas City); U.S. Highway 40/I-64 (also called the Daniel Boone Expressway), which skirts Forest Park; and I-44, which continues on to Six Flags and Meramec Caverns. Also passing through downtown is I-55 in its run from Chicago on to the Ozarks. If you picture St. Louis as a fan spreading out from its downtown hub on the Mississippi, its outer perimeter is marked by I-270, a circumferential expressway that surrounds the city in a half-circle. Another important thoroughfare that loops around the city is Lindbergh Boulevard.

FINDING AN ADDRESS

As previously mentioned, downtown St. Louis is composed of a grid, with numbered streets paralleling the Mississippi River and running north and south and streets named after trees and Market Street running east to west. Remember that Market Street divides the north and south street designations. Thus, the Holiday Inn at 200 N. 4th Street is located two blocks north of Market; and the Campbell House Museum, at 1508 Locust, is located near the intersection of Locust and 15th Street.

NEIGHBORHOODS IN BRIEF

Laclede's Landing   A neighborhood of restored 19th-century warehouses just north of the Arch and beside the river, Laclede's Landing is where the city of St. Louis was born. It was here that Pierre Laclede, a French fur trapper, set up a trading post on the banks of the Mississippi in 1764, and it was from here that the city grew and prospered. Today Laclede's Landing is a nine-block area of brick buildings and cobblestone streets, filled with restaurants, clubs, shops, and offices. This is one of St. Louis' most famous nightlife districts, noted for its many establishments offering live music from jazz to rock-'n'-roll.

Central West End   In the late 1880s, with the increase in smog and noise, many well-to-do St. Louisans moved farther west to greener pastures, and this is where many of them settled. By the time the World's Fair opened in nearby Forest Park in 1904, the Central West End was a booming residential area of imposing mansions and neighborhood stores. Stretching along Euclid Avenue and branching off onto side streets such as Maryland Avenue and McPherson, today the Central West End is one of the city's most interesting neighborhoods, a lively mix of trendy clothing boutiques, sidewalk cafés, antiques shops, and restaurants.

The Hill   No trip to St. Louis would be complete without a visit to the Hill to chow down on Italian cuisine. This is the city's Italian district, where even the fire hydrants are painted red, white, and green, the colors of the Italian flag. Practically every block has its own Italian eatery, some of which are very expensive and hushed within, others of which are a riot of families and noise. There are also Italian bakeries, mom-and-pop groceries, and neatly maintained small brick homes. The heart of the Hill is the St. Ambrose Church, located at the corner of Wilson and Marconi streets, where there's a bronze statue memorializing the Italian immigrants who came to America to begin new lives. The Hill, which is not much of a hill at all, is located south of Forest Park and west of the Botanical Gardens.

Soulard   Located south of downtown on and around Russell Boulevard, Soulard (pronounced "sue-lard") is another neighborhood of brick homes, these built primarily by 19th-century German immigrants, many of whom worked in the city's breweries. In fact, Soulard is where you'll find Anheuser-Busch, the area's only surviving brewery, where tours are offered most days of the week. Soulard Market, the city's main produce market, at Seventh and Lafayette, has been selling fruit, vegetables, meats, and spices since 1845. Near Soulard is Cherokee Street, lined with dozens of antiques shops. But the main draws of Soulard are its small music clubs and restaurants, where jazz, blues, and Irish music reign supreme.

The Loop   Named after an old streetcar turnaround, the Loop is a five-block area between 6200 and 6700 Delmar Boulevard in University City, and it is the closest thing St. Louis has to a SoHo. The Loop is home to a number of art galleries, ethnic restaurants serving everything from Mexican to Jamaican food, bookstores, and bars. Blueberry Hill, a bar that pays tribute to rock-'n'-roll, is said to have the world's best jukebox, and out on the sidewalk is St. Louis' own Walk of Fame, with markers highlighting the lives of such famous St. Louisans as Tennessee Williams, Chuck Berry, and baseball great Stan Musial.

Clayton   Located in Mid-County west of Forest Park, Clayton is the city's corporate and financial center. The home of many of St. Louis' most notable hotels and restaurants, it has the subdued and relaxed pace of suburbia but also the flair of metropolitan smartness. Because Clayton is in the middle of town, it's a convenient spot from which to explore the city.

MAPS

The St. Louis Visitor Information Center offers a free map that includes both an outline of the city and its vicinity and a detailed map of the downtown area. It's adequate for most purposes, but if you wish to explore the backroads of St. Louis, you might wish to purchase one of many city maps available. The Automobile Association of America, for example, has a map of St. Louis with a street index.

2. GETTING AROUND

St. Louis cannot compete with European cities or East Coast cities when it comes to public transportation—in the Midwest, most people get around in their own cars. Even most visitors to the city arrive by car.

BY PUBLIC TRANSPORTATION

BY BUS

In 1993, **Metro Link** will open a light rail service linking Lambert Airport with downtown. Until then, the only mode of public transportation in St. Louis is the bus, operated by the Bi-State Transit System. Most bus routes start downtown and then fan out to outlying districts, which means that buses are convenient if you're traveling to or from the downtown area. However, bus stops do not identify the destination or route of buses that stop there, so plan beforehand which bus you want to take. Bus no. 93, for example, begins at 3rd and Washington downtown and passes through St. Louis University and the Central West End on its way past Forest Park to Clayton. Bus no. 40 is convenient for travel from Washington Avenue downtown to Anheuser-Busch and Soulard Market. For more information on specific bus routes, call the **Bi-State Transit System** at 231-2345 (outside Missouri, you can call Bi-State by dialing toll free 800/2233-BUS). Simply say where you are and where you want to go, and you'll be told which bus to board.

Most buses are equipped with lifts for wheelchairs and operate from approximately 5am to 11pm or midnight, with slightly shorter hours on Sunday and holidays. Fares for local buses are 85¢ for adults and 40¢ for children 5 through 12. Express buses (identified with an X added to their number, as in 140X) cost $1.15 for adults and 55¢ for children. Transfers between buses cost 15¢ to 30¢, depending on the bus.

For visitors, the great news is that you can ride throughout the downtown area for free. Downtown is known as the Free Ride Zone, in which passengers can ride from one point downtown to any other point downtown without paying, all year round. In addition, during the summer months there's also the **Levee Line**, special buses that transport passengers between Union Station and the Arch, with stops along the way such as at Laclede's Landing and the St. Louis Centre. The Levee Line is also free, and the buses are easily identifiable because they are painted like paddlewheel steamboats. Hours of operation for the Levee Line are daily from about 10:50am to 9:40pm (to 5:55pm on Sunday).

BY TAXI

There are approximately 20 taxicab companies listed in the St. Louis *Yellow Pages*, each with its own system for fares. **County Cab Co.** (tel. 991-5300), in business since 1937, serves the entire St. Louis County and charges $2.35 for the first mile and 90¢ for each additional mile. **Allen Cab** (tel. 241-7722) charges 85¢ when you get into the cab, then $1 per mile. It also has vans for the handicapped. **ABC** (tel. 427-8888) charges 75¢ for the first eighth of a mile, then 10¢ for each additional eighth of a mile. Most companies also charge an extra 50¢ for an additional passenger, and some also add a 50¢ gas surcharge. It costs approximately $18 to take a taxi from Lambert Airport to the downtown area.

BY CAR

That St. Louis is a driving town is evident especially during rush hour. A plus is that drivers in the Midwest tend to be courteous, civil, and forgiving, qualities to be grateful for if you're navigating unfamiliar territory.

Arm yourself with a good map, and keep in mind that during rush hours the freeways tend to be congested. In the downtown area, it seems that every street is a one-way, so you'll probably want to park and then walk around. Have plenty of quarters handy if you plan on parking at the meters on the street. Otherwise there's public parking downtown, at the Arch, Laclede's Landing, and Union Station. Unless otherwise posted, you can turn right at red stoplights.

If you need to rent a car, **Avis** has an office both downtown (tel. 241-5780) and at the airport (tel. 426-7766), as does **Hertz** (tel. 421-3131 downtown; 426-7555 airport) and **National** (tel. 621-0060 downtown; 426-6272 airport). The base price for rentals begins at about $30 per day, which includes 150 free miles but excludes gas.

ON FOOT

There are many areas of St. Louis that you'll want to explore on foot, including the downtown area, the Hill, Forest Park and its many museums, the Loop in University City, and the Central West End. It's approximately 16 blocks from the Arch to Union Station (about a mile), which you can walk in less than a half hour.

FAST FACTS: ST. LOUIS

This section is designed to make your stay in St. Louis as problem-free as possible. Keep in mind, too, that the concierge at your hotel is an invaluable source of information, as is the **St. Louis Convention and Visitors Commission** (tel. 314/421-1023).

American Express American Express Travel Services is located at 1 Mercantile Center (tel. 314/241-6400).

Area Code The telephone area code for St. Louis is 314. On the Illinois side, in East St. Louis, it's 618.

Airport The St. Louis–Lambert International Airport (tel. 314/426-8000) is conveniently located 10 miles northwest of the city. Refer to the "Orientation" section at the beginning of this chapter for more information.

Auto Rentals See the preceding section, "Getting Around," for information on car-rental agencies and prices.

Babysitters Most of St. Louis' major hotels provide babysitting service or can contact a babysitter should the need arise.

Buses Many bus routes start in the downtown area and then fan out to the outskirts, but of most interest to visitors is the fact that passengers can travel within the downtown area absolutely free. Refer to the preceding section, "Getting Around," for more information.

Business Hours Office hours are generally weekdays from 9am to 5pm, and most banks are open weekdays from about 8:30 or 9am to about 4pm. Shops are open longer, especially those at such shopping centers as Union Station and the city's many enclosed shopping malls. Although hours vary, most shopping centers are open Monday through Saturday from about 10am to 9 or 10pm, until 5pm on Sunday.

Car Rentals See "Auto Rentals," above.

Climate See "When to Go" section in Chapter 2.

Currency For a discussion of U.S. currency, see Fast Facts in Chapter 3.

Currency Exchange See Fast Facts in Chapter 3 for banks in St. Louis that will exchange foreign currency into dollars.

Dentists and Doctors Some of the expensive hotels offer the services of an in-house doctor or a doctor on call. Otherwise, check the *Yellow Pages* for a list of area doctors. An alternative is to call the **Doctor Referral Service of the St. Louis Metropolitan Medical Society** (tel. 314/371-5225) or the **Dentist Refer-**

ral Service of the Dental Society of Greater St. Louis (tel. 314/965-5960).

Drugstores   Many drugstores have normal business hours. If you need a prescription in the middle of the night, **Walgreens, 4** Hampton Village Plaza (tel. 314/351-2100), fills prescriptions 24 hours. For more information on 24-hour pharmacy service, telephone 314/721-2033.

Emergencies   As throughout the United States, the number to call in an emergency is 911 for police, fire, and ambulance. Also see "Dentists and Doctors" and "Hospitals" in this section.

Eyeglasses   If you need to replace eyeglasses in a hurry, two convenient locations are Lenscrafter, 176 Crestwood Plaza in Southwest County (tel. 314/968-9090), and Sterling, 7901 Forsyth Blvd. in Clayton (tel. 314/862-0255). Both can supply you with a new pair within a few hours.

Gay Hotline   The local gay and lesbian hotline is 314/367-0084.

Hairdressers and Barbers   If your hotel does not have a barber shop or beauty salon, the concierge may be able to direct you to one to suit your style. Otherwise, refer to the *Yellow Pages.*

Holidays   For a list of U.S. national holidays, see Fast Facts in Chapter 3. For information on St. Louis' special annual events, see the "When to Go" section in Chapter 2.

Hospitals   There are approximately 30 hospitals in the St. Louis area. Some of the most centrally located include **Barnes Hospital,** Barnes Hospital Plaza (tel. 362-5000), which specializes in surgery and transplants; **Deaconess Hospital,** 6150 Oakland (tel. 768-3000); **St. Mary's Health Center,** 6420 Clayton Rd. (tel. 768-8000), which also has a doctor-referral service; **St. John's Mercy Medical Center,** 615 S. New Ballas Rd. (tel. 569-6000); **St. Louis Children's Hospital,** 400 S. Kingshighway (tel. 454-6000); **St. Louis Regional Medical Center,** 5535 Delmar Blvd. (tel. 361-1212); and **St. Louis University Hospital,** 3635 Vista at Grand Blvd. (tel. 577-8777).

Information   Locations of the St. Louis visitor centers are given in the "Orientation" section at the beginning of this chapter.

Laundry/Dry Cleaning   All of the expensive and most of the medium-priced hotels offer laundry and/or dry-cleaning service. Some of the budget-priced ones offer coin-operated laundry machines. If yours does not, ask the staff where the most convenient laundry facility is.

Liquor Laws   The minimum drinking age is 21. Otherwise, liquor laws vary somewhat according to municipality. Bars close by 1:30am throughout much of the city, except in selected nightlife areas, such as Laclede's Landing, where they often stay open until 3am. Liquor stores stay open until 1:30am, but nowhere can you buy liquor at a store on Sunday, even though it is served in restaurants and bars.

Lost Property   There is no central lost-property office. If you lose something, call the nearest police station to report the loss.

Luggage Storage   Lambert Airport has lockers for storing luggage in all its concourses.

Mail   The main post office of St. Louis is located at 1720 Market St. (tel. 436-4458), next to Union Station. It's open Monday through Friday from 7am to 8pm and Saturday from 8am to 3pm. Vending machines selling stamps are accessible 24 hours. In addition, a full 24-hour retail postal center is located at the **Lambert Airport Mail Facility,** 9855 Air Cargo Rd., just east of Lambert Airport's East Terminal.

Maps   The St. Louis Visitor Centers distribute a free map of the downtown area and city vicinity. In addition, hotels often carry maps of their surrounding region.

Newspapers/Magazines   The local newspaper is the *St. Louis Post-Dispatch.* Other newspapers readily available include *USA Today* and *The New York Times.* It's difficult to find international newspapers in St. Louis. Foreign magazines are a bit easier to locate, and your best bet for doing so is at **World News,** which has three locations: 314 N. Broadway in downtown (tel. 621-8686)—open Monday through Friday from 7am to 6pm; 4 S. Central Ave. in Clayton (tel. 726-6010)—open Monday through Friday from 7am to 11pm, Saturday from 7am to midnight, and Sunday from 7am to 10pm; and 308 West Port Plaza in West Port (tel. 434-9449)—open Monday through Friday from 9am to 10pm, Saturday from 10am to 11pm, and Sunday from 10am to 6pm. **The Daily Planet,** 243 N. Euclid in the Central West End (tel. 367-1333), is also a good source for newspapers and magazines. Open Mon–Sat 8am–8:30pm, Sun 8am–7:30pm.

Photographic Needs   Both Union Station and the St. Louis Centre downtown have photo shops that specialize in quick film processing and also sell film. Otherwise, ask the concierge at your hotel for the nearest photo shop.

Police   The emergency number for police throughout the United States is 911.

Post Office   See "Mail."

Radio and Television   You'll find CBS on channel 4, NBC on channel 5, and ABC on channel 2. The local PBS station is on channel 9. Among the many radio stations in St. Louis, KMOX (AM 1120) is your best bet for international news, with newscasts, talk shows, and sports broadcast throughout the day.

Religious Services   The Saturday edition of the *St. Louis Post* carries a religious section with a list of area churches and times of their services.

Restrooms   If you need to use a public restroom, your best bet is a hotel or fast-food chain. Refer to the accommodations chapter for the nearest hotel.

Safety   Whenever you're traveling in an unfamiliar city or country, stay alert. Be aware of your immediate surroundings. Wear a money belt and keep a close eye on your possessions. Never carry large amounts of cash and leave your expensive jewelry at home. Be particularly careful with cameras, purses, and wallets—all favorite targets of thieves and pickpockets.

St. Louis' crime rate is as high as that in any major U.S. city, so exercise caution, especially at night. Keep your car locked at all times, and do not wander from nightlife districts at night. You are perfectly safe walking around Laclede's Landing, Soulard, or the Central West End at night, especially if there are two or more of you. The downtown area, however, tends to empty out after the shops and businesses close, so keep to lighted areas if you're walking from Laclede's Landing to a downtown hotel.

Shoe Repair   You can have your shoes repaired while you wait at the **Centre Shoe Care,** located in the second level of the St. Louis Centre, 6th and Washington streets (tel. 231-4014). It's open

Monday through Saturday from 10am to 6pm and Sunday from noon to 5pm. Another shop downtown is **Broadway Shoe Repair,** 308 N. Broadway (tel. 342-9983), open Mon–Fri 8am–5:30pm, closed Sat. and Sun.

Taxes A 5.925% tax is added to all goods, food, and services in St. Louis; it's composed of a 4.425% Missouri sales tax and a 1.5% General Revenue tax. If you're staying in a downtown hotel, both the 5.925% tax and a 3.75% hotel tax will be added to your bill (for a total of 9.675%), as well as a $2 occupancy fee per room per night; if you're staying in a hotel outside the downtown area, the total tax added to your bill will be 13.175%, but there is no occupancy fee.

Taxis Refer to the preceding section, "Getting Around," for information on taxis and their fares.

Telephone A local telephone call costs 25¢. Be sure to ask at your hotel whether a surcharge is added to calls made from your hotel room, since sometimes these surcharges can be pretty stiff, even if you're making a credit-card call. If you need directory assistance, dial 1-411. For local numbers when calling from a pay phone, dial 411.

Time Zone St. Louis follows Central Standard Time. If it's noon in St. Louis, it's 1pm in New York and 10am in Los Angeles.

Tipping As elsewhere in the United States, serving people should be tipped 15% to 20%, and bartenders should get at least 10%. Bellhops should receive 50¢ for each piece of luggage, cab drivers expect a tip of 15% of the fare, and chambermaids should be left $1 per night of stay. Valet parking is in vogue in a big way at St. Louis' hotels and better restaurants, where attendants expect $1 or $2 in tips, even if they just drive your car across the parking lot.

Transit Information For information on St. Louis's Bi-State Transit System, call 314/231-2345. Outside Missouri, you can call Bi-State toll-free by dialing 800/2233-BUS.

Weather For the time and temperature, call 321-2522. Weather information and the forecast can be obtained by dialing 421-5555. In addition, the National Weather Service in St. Louis may be able to answer other questions at 928-1197.

CHAPTER 5

ST. LOUIS ACCOMMODATIONS

As in any city, your biggest expense in St. Louis will be for a place to sleep at night. Luckily, there's a wide choice in accommodations, from deluxe hotels near the Arch to inexpensive motels on the outskirts of town and even quaint bed-and-breakfasts and a youth hostel. No matter where you stay, you won't be very far from the city's main attractions.

The rates given below are the standard rack rates, but remember there are often discounts available but only if you ask. In fact, some hotels offer so many discounts and packages that virtually no one ever ends up paying the full rack rate. Many hotels, for example, offer weekend discounts that amount to 50% off the rack rate and corporate rates for business travelers; others offer cheaper rates in winter. In any case, keep in mind that in addition to the rates given, a hotel tax will be added to your bill. If you're staying at a downtown hotel, a 9.675% tax will be added to your bill, as well as a $2 occupancy fee per room per night. If you opt for a hotel outside the downtown area, a tax of 13.175% will be added to your bill, but there is no occupancy fee.

Keep in mind, too, that although every effort was made to be accurate, rates may go up during the lifetime of this book. It's always a good idea to reserve a room in advance to avoid disappointment or waste time searching for a room. In addition, rooms downtown become scarce if there's a big convention taking place at the downtown convention center or if the Cardinals are having a good season.

Many hotels now include in their rates a continental breakfast that consists of rolls, coffee, and perhaps juice and fruit. Some even offer complimentary cocktails during afternoon happy hours. Some offer free parking as well, while others may charge as much as $8 a night for a space. Some offer free local phone calls from your room, while others add a stiff surcharge. It pays to shop around, asking for the absolutely best rate and keeping in mind what services are included in the price. Wherever possible, toll-free numbers have been included below.

The hotels are divided according to their location and are further subdivided according to their price. (Unless otherwise noted, all provide private baths.) The expensive hotels charge more than $100

IMPRESSIONS

The inhabitants of St. Louis believed in enjoying life. There was a
fiddle in every house, and dance somewhere every night. They
were honest, hospitable, inviting and generous. . . .
—JOHN DARBY, 1818

---

per night for two persons but provide first-rate accommodations and
a wide range of services, which may include a health club and
swimming pool guests can use for free, a concierge to help you with
any problems you may have, cocktail lounges with live music, and fine
restaurants. Hotels in the moderate category charge $50 to $100 for
two persons and offer comfortable rooms with all the usual
amenities—TV, with cable programs or in-house movies at an extra
charge; radio; and telephone. Some have swimming pools as well.
Inexpensive lodgings, offering rooms for less than $50, are simple but
adequate, with all the basics. If you're on a rock-bottom budget,
consider staying in the youth hostel in Soulard or at one of the
outlying campgrounds.

The circled dollar symbol beside certain listings below represents
especially good value for the money, and the circled star designates
one of my particular favorites, usually given for a combination of
outstanding service, ambience, and comfort.

1. DOWNTOWN

All these hotels are within easy walking distance of the Arch,
Laclede's Landing, and other downtown attractions. Downtown is an
especially convenient place to stay if you do not have a car, because
buses depart from downtown for the rest of the county.

EXPENSIVE

**ADAM'S MARK HOTEL, Fourth and Chestnut, St. Louis,
MO 63102. Tel. 314/241-7400,** or toll free 800/444-ADAM.
816 rms, 94 suites. A/C TEL TV

$ Rates: $140 single; $165 double; $185 Concorde Executive
Level. Extra person $15. Children under 18 stay free in parents'
room. Weekend, family, senior citizen, and corporate discounts
available. AE, CB, DC, DISC, MC, V. Parking: $9.

Located in the shadow of the Arch, the Adam's Mark Hotel is
one of St. Louis' premier hotels, the flagship of the Adam's
Mark group of hotels. Its lobby is a three-story atrium,
impressive with such features as a half-dozen Regency chandeliers in
the foyer and a pair of nine-feet-tall cast-bronze horses galloping
across the marble floor. Many visitors to St. Louis include a stroll
through the hotel, stopping off for a meal at one of its fine restaurants,
an afternoon tea at Tiffany Rose, or a beer at AJ's, one of downtown's

ST. LOUIS
Downtown

Adam's Mark Hotel 8
Clarion Hotel 9
Days Inn 4
Drury Inn
  Convention Center 3
Drury Inn Union Station 12
Embassy Suites 1
Holiday Inn
  Downtown/Riverfront 7
Hotel Majestic 6
Hyatt Regency St. Louis 11
Marriott Pavilion
  Downtown 10
Mayfair 5
Thrifty Inn 2

most popular night spots. The Adam's Mark indoor and outdoor pools are on the roof, offering breathtaking views of the city.

Each room provides all the comforts you'd expect from a first-class hotel, including cable TV with in-house movies, an extra phone in the bathroom, and full-length mirrors. There's a no-smoking floor. As in many downtown hotels, rooms facing the Arch and the mighty Mississippi are more expensive, but if you really want to splurge, consider staying on the hotel's Concorde Executive Level,

DOWNTOWN ST. LOUIS ACCOMMODATIONS

which includes its own concierge services, a lounge, and a full-service complimentary breakfast in its rates.

Dining/Entertainment: Faust's is the place to go for fine dining in an atmosphere of old-world charm, where continental and American cuisine are complemented by an extensive wine list. Chestnut's is the hotel's more casual restaurant, where an international buffet is offered every Friday and Saturday evening. Tiffany Rose features afternoon tea and live piano or jazz music Monday through

Saturday, while Players caters to sports fans with screens depicting the latest in ESPN sports. AJ's draws in a nightly crowd with its live music, dance floor, and special events.

Services: 24-hour room service, babysitting referral service, airport shuttle, laundry/shoe-shine service, concierge desk.

Facilities: Indoor and outdoor swimming pools, racquetball courts, whirlpool, sauna, exercise room, aerobic classes, gift shop, florist, barber/beauty shop, airline/car-rental services, business center.

CLARION HOTEL, 200 South 4th St., St. Louis, MO 63102. Tel. 314/241-9500, or toll free 800/762-2333. 826 rms, 27 suites. A/C TEL TV

$ Rates: $120 single or double; from $275 suite. Extra person free. AE, DC, DISC, MC, V. Parking: $8.50.

Popular as a convention hotel, the Clarion can be crowded and noisy at times, but maybe that's the excitement you're looking for. The hotel features two towers of rooms; the North Tower is taller, with 27 floors topped by a revolving restaurant. Each room features a TV with pay video, an alarm clock, and a sink and counter space separate from the bathroom. Rooms with refrigerators also are available. Unfortunately, rooms are not sound-proofed against traffic noise.

Dining/Entertainment: Top of the Riverfront, the city's only revolving restaurant, offers a bird's-eye view of the Arch and the city. The Lobby Bar also has a view of St. Louis' famous landmark. The Dugout Bar is a popular pre-game watering hole, while Zelda's Deli offers snacks and sandwiches. The Coffee Grove serves three meals a day in a casual setting.

Services: Room service to 11pm, laundry service, concierge service.

Facilities: Indoor and outdoor pools, health club, game room, barber shop, beauty salon.

EMBASSY SUITES, 901 N. 1st St., St. Louis, MO 63102. Tel. 314/241-4200, or toll free 800/362-2779. 298 suites. A/C TEL TV

$ Rates (including American breakfast): $120 single; $135–$200 double. Extra person $10. Children under 17 stay free in parents' room. Weekend rates and senior-citizen discounts available. AE, CB, DC, DISC, MC, V. Parking: $5.75.

Located in the historic district of Laclede's Landing, just north of the Arch, Embassy Suites is part of a nationwide chain of hotels that does its best to provide guests with extra touches and services that make staying here a pleasure. Its eight-story inner atrium is a comfortable oasis complete with a courtyard, a bubbling fountain, and well-tended plants. Breakfast, which is cooked to order and includes eggs and pancakes, is served beside the fountain; in the early evening, from 5:30 to 7:30pm, there also are complimentary cocktails.

Every room at the Embassy Suites as its name implies, is a two-room suite, all of which ring the atrium and have windows on the outside overlooking the city. Rooms on the lowest floor have balconies, but those higher up facing the Arch have a better view, all at the same price. The living room of each two-room suite contains a sofa-bed, a refrigerator, and a coffee machine and coffee, and in each suite are two TVs with remote control and pay movies, two telephones, and two sinks. Handicapped-equipped and no-smoking suites are available.

Dining/Entertainment: The hotel's bar is the Landing's Lounge. Joe B's Restaurant offers everything from chili dogs to prime rib, including a bargain lunch buffet Monday through Friday.

Services: Room service to 11pm, valet service, 24-hour fax service.

Facilities: Indoor pool, exercise room, sauna, whirlpool, pool tables, video games, coin-operated laundry, gift shop.

THE HOTEL MAJESTIC, 1019 Pine St., St. Louis, MO 63101. Tel. 314/436-2355, or toll free 800/451-2355. Fax 314/436-2355. 91 rms. A/C MINIBAR TEL TV

$ Rates (including continental breakfast): $125–$155 single; $140–$170 double. Extra person $15. Children under 12 stay free in parents' room. Weekend, corporate, and other packages available. AE, CB, DC, DISC, MC, V. Parking: $8.

 If your idea of a fine hotel is a smaller, older establishment with old-world European charm, this hotel is for you. First opened in 1913 and built in the Renaissance revival style, the Hotel

---

ⓕ FROMMER'S SMART TRAVELER —HOTELS

VALUE-CONSCIOUS TRAVELERS SHOULD TAKE ADVANTAGE OF THE FOLLOWING:

1. Weekend discounts of up to 50% available at most expensive and moderate hotels in St. Louis.
2. Corporate rates available to business travelers—even if you're on vacation, it doesn't hurt showing a business card and asking for corporate rates.
3. Winter discounts offered at some inexpensive hotels.
4. Hotels on the outskirts of the city, which are often cheaper than those downtown.
5. Accommodations that include breakfast in the price.
6. A youth hostel and campgrounds at rock-bottom prices.
7. In St. Louis, rooms without a view of the Arch, which are usually cheaper than rooms with a view.

QUESTIONS TO ASK IF YOU'RE ON A BUDGET

1. Is breakfast included in the price? Is it buffet-style, allowing you to eat as much as you want?
2. Is there a parking charge? (In many downtown St. Louis hotels, as much as $8 may be charged for each overnight stay. Parking is free at hotels outside the downtown area.)
3. Is there a surcharge on local and long-distance calls? (Some hotels offer free local phone calls.)
4. Are there any discounts available? (Weekend rates are sometimes half of the rack weekday rate.)

Majestic is a National Historic Landmark, a member of the Small Luxury Hotels Association, and it has long been a guarded St. Louis secret. Both business people and visiting stars stay here for the privacy it affords (Billy Joel was checking in during my last visit) as well as for all the extra amenities and facilities, including one of the city's premier restaurants. There is no front desk—check in is at a concierge desk that provides the individualized treatment repeat customers appreciate.

Each guest room is slightly different, but each is outfitted with either a king-size or two double beds, a hairdryer, two-line phones, a TV with remote control and pay movies, terrycloth robes, a minibar, and a coffee machine. There's maid service twice a day, including turndown service with chocolates. Although the hotel itself does not have a health club, guests can use free of charge a nearby YMCA, which includes a pool, racquetball courts, and a gym.

Dining/Entertainment: Under the direction of Richard Perry, the Richard Perry Restaurant is renowned for its service and innovative cuisine, which relies upon the American Midwestern heritage. See "Hotel Dining."

Services: Complimentary fruit plate upon arrival, complimentary shoe shine, free morning newspaper, free shuttle downtown, 24-hour room service, babysitting, 24-hour concierge.

MARRIOTT PAVILION DOWNTOWN, 1 Broadway, St. Louis, MO 63102. Tel. 314/421-1776, or toll free 800/228-9290. Fax 314/331-9029. 670 rms, 11 suites. A/C TEL TV
$ Rates: $130 single; $145 double; Concierge Floor $15 extra. Extra person $10. Children under 18 stay free in parents' room. Weekend and other packages available. AE, DC, DISC, MC, V. Parking: $8.

Located beside Busch Stadium and just two blocks from the Arch, this is a large hotel with a lot of facilities, attracting both baseball fans and convention groups. It consists of an east tower and a newer, taller west tower, and some rooms even provide a view of the stadium or Arch at no extra charge. All rooms are comfortable, each containing two phones and remote-control cable TV with pay movies; some rooms also have a small refrigerator. There are also no-smoking rooms and rooms for the handicapped. If you really feel like being pampered, stay on the 23rd or 24th Concierge floors of the west tower, where you'll have a king-size bed, an automatic shoe polisher, and a communal lounge in which you'll receive a complimentary continental breakfast and afternoon hors d'oeuvres.

Dining/Entertainment: The Pavilion Restaurant offers everything from a buffet breakfast or light snack to a quick lunch and hearty dinner. J. W. Carver's is more elegant and formal. One Broadway, a sports bar, is the place to meet for pre-game cocktails.

Services: Room service to 11pm, laundry service, concierge desk.

Facilities: Indoor swimming pool, whirlpool, sauna, health club with weight room, gift shop, barber shop, travel agency, game room.

MAYFAIR, 806 St. Charles St., St. Louis, MO 63101. Tel. 314/421-2500, or toll free 800/444-3313. Fax 314/421-6254. 165 rms, 19 suites. A/C MINIBAR TEL TV

$ Rates: $125–$155 single; $140–$170 double; suites from $180 single, $205 double. Extra person $15. Children under 12 stay free in parents' room. Weekend packages available. AE, DC, DISC, MC, V. Parking (in public lot across street): $3.

Originally built in 1925 and completely renovated in 1990, the Mayfair is located in the heart of downtown and is on the National Historic Register. Its lobby is small and comfortable. Although the guest rooms have been modernized, they still retain such features as old-fashioned double-paned windows and spaciousness. Each room is decorated with floral-print bedspreads and curtains and features a TV with videocassette player and a bathroom with a phone, a magnifying mirror, a hairdryer, and even a small TV. The Mayfair's most expensive suite, on the 18th floor, boasts a fireplace and a Jacuzzi.

Dining/Entertainment: The Mayfair Room, wood-paneled and restored to its original elegance, serves lunch and dinner. The Hofbrau serves three meals a day in a clublike bar and grill.

Services: 24-hour room service, complimentary morning shuttle downtown, free morning newspaper.

Facilities: Rooftop outdoor pool and sundeck, fitness and exercise room.

MODERATE

DAYS INN, 333 Washington Ave., St. Louis, MO 63102. Tel. 314/621-7900, or toll free 800/325-2525. 179 rms, 3 suites. A/C TEL TV

Ⓕ FROMMER'S COOL FOR KIDS
HOTELS

Cheshire Inn and Lodge *(see p. 59)* The child in everyone will be enchanted by the nine Fantasy Suites here, which include the Tree House and the Safari Country suites.

Henry VIII Hotel *(see p. 61)* Kids will love the game room, pool, and tennis courts here, plus the space outside to run around in.

Holiday Inn Airport West *(see p. 62)* Kids love the facilities of the Holidome, including its indoor pool, whirlpool, video-game room, indoor putting green, billiard table, and Ping-Pong tables.

Hyatt Regency St. Louis *(see p. 53)* Camp Hyatt is a program offering special room rates, children's menus in restaurants and room service, and a welcome check-in packet for kids, making the Hyatt Regency a great place for families to stay. What's more, it's located in Union Station. The hotel also offers a supply of games available to borrow, and there's even a supervised room for children on Friday and Saturday night.

$ Rates: $85 single; $99 double. Extra person $10. Children under 18 stay free in parents' room. AE, CB, DC, DISC, MC, V. Winter discounts available. Parking: $4.50.

With a great location just a stone's throw from Laclede's Landing and the Arch, this 25-year-old property has recently been renovated. Simple but comfortable, each of its rooms features double-paned windows to shut out traffic noise, full-length mirrors, an alarm clock with radio, and a large bathroom with counter space. Rooms facing the Arch have the best view, and there are also no-smoking rooms.

Services: Fax services.

Facilities: One restaurant, one lounge, indoor swimming pool, sauna, coin-operated laundry.

DRURY INN CONVENTION CENTER, 711 N. Broadway, St. Louis, MO 63101. Tel. 314/231-8100, or toll free 800/325-8300. 142 rms, 36 suites. A/C TEL TV

$ Rates (including continental breakfast): $68–$74 single; $78–$84 double; suites from $79 single, $88 double. Extra person $8. Children under 18 stay free in parents' room. Free cribs available. Corporate rates available. AE, DC, MC, V. Parking: Free.

This new hotel near the Convention Center and Laclede's Landing makes it easy to understand why the Drury Inn chain of hotels is taking the Midwest by storm. Offering a variety of services but without a correspondingly high price tag, it's a great choice for both the business traveler and families. Guests start their day with a complimentary QUIKSTART breakfast consisting of cereals, fruit, doughnuts, muffins, coffee, and juice, served buffet-style in the airy atrium near the indoor pool. The building itself, built in 1925, once served as the city market; the hotel's cool and spacious lobby is on the ground floor, and the two top floors contain the guest rooms. In between is a parking garage, where guests can park for free. Rooms face either the inner atrium or toward the outside, with sound-proof windows to cut down on noise. Particularly good deals are the suites, each of which comes with a microwave, a refrigerator, and two satellite TVs with remote control. A couple of suites even feature lofts. There are also no-smoking and handicapped rooms. Although there are no restaurants in the hotel, there are many in the immediate area. All in all, you can't go wrong staying here.

Services: Free local phone calls.

Facilities: Indoor swimming pool, whirlpool.

HOLIDAY INN DOWNTOWN/RIVERFRONT, 200 N. 4th St., St. Louis, MO 63102. Tel. 314/621-8200, or toll free 800/325-1395. Fax 314/621-8073. 371 rms, 87 suites. A/C TEL TV

$ Rates: $89 single; $99 double; suites $135–$250. Extra person $5. Children under 12 stay free in parents' room. Free cribs available. AE, DC, DISC, MC, V. Parking: Free.

This downtown property was built in 1974 as an apartment complex, reflected in the enormity of most of the hotel's rooms. Some even have balconies, while others have kitchenettes complete with stoves and refrigerators (but without pots and pans). Close to the Arch and all downtown sights, the Holiday Inn boasts a rooftop pool with an observation deck offering a great view of the city. Although there's no health club in the hotel, guests can use a nearby YMCA for free.

Services: Concierge desk, room service until 10pm.

Facilities: One restaurant, one deli, coin-operated laundry, pharmacy, gift shop, beauty shop.

INEXPENSIVE

THRIFTY INN, 1100 N. 3rd St., St. Louis, MO 63102. Tel. 314/421-6556. 48 rms. A/C TEL TV

$ Rates: $42.88 single; $49.88 double. Winter discounts available. AE, CB, DC, DISC, MC, V. Parking: Free.

Located off I-70 near the 6th Street exit, this older hotel doesn't look like much from the outside, but it's under the management of the Drury Inn hotel group and offers inexpensive lodging in the heart of the city. Rooms were recently refurbished, each with a king-size bed, a desk, a TV with pay movies, and a sink and counter space separate from the bathroom. Complimentary coffee is served mornings in the lobby, where there are vending machines selling sodas. The hotel is a bit isolated from the rest of downtown by an undeveloped strip of land, but you can't beat the price.

2. NEAR UNION STATION

Only a mile from the Arch, Union Station is practically a city in itself with a myriad of diversions, making it a great place to stay for the entire family.

EXPENSIVE

HYATT REGENCY ST. LOUIS, Union Station, St. Louis, MO 63103. Tel. 314/231-1234, or toll free 800/233-1234. 522 rms, 20 suites. A/C TEL TV

$ Rates: $145 single; $170 double; Regency Club $30 extra. Extra person $20. Children under 18 stay free in parents' room, half price in separate room. Weekend packages available. AE, CB, DC, DISC, MC, V. Parking: $8.

This is one of the most talked-about hotels in St. Louis. Occupying part of Union Station, which was built in 1894, it boasts one of the most magnificent lobbies I've ever seen—six stories high with a barrel-vaulted ceiling, Romanesque arches, elaborate plasterwork highlighted in gold leaf, and stained glass. Once serving as the waiting room for train passengers, it's a feast for the eyes, and there's a lobby lounge where you can slowly take it all in.

Rooms are simple yet elegant, with standard rooms occupying a new free-standing structure right in the middle of the station. Each room features an extra cordless phone, a hairdryer, a small TV and clothesline in the bathroom, full-length mirrors, a TV with pay movies, and all the luxuries you'd expect from a first-class hotel. Regency Club rooms, which occupy the original rooms of the historic Terminal Hotel, offer turn-of-the-century charm along with a concierge, a free continental breakfast, complimentary evening cocktails, daily newspapers, and personalized matchbooks with each guest's name. Children love this hotel, not only for its many facilities but also because of the welcome packet they receive at check in and because of "Camp Choo Choo," a play room for children. A great place for a family vacation.

Dining/Entertainment: The Station Grille is housed in Union Station's original oak-paneled dining hall and offers steaks and seafood. Italian cuisine is featured in Aldo's. The Grand Hall in the lobby is open daily for an executive lunch as well as for evening cocktails.

Services: 24-hour room service, babysitting, concierge desk, laundry and dry-cleaning services.

Facilities: Outdoor swimming pool, health club, sauna, business center.

MODERATE

DRURY INN UNION STATION, 201 S. 20th St., St. Louis, MO 63103. Tel. 314/231-3900, or toll free 800/325-8300. 178 rms, 2 suites. A/C TEL TV

$ Rates (including continental breakfast): $68–$74 single; $78–$84 double; suites from $79 single, $88 double. Extra person $8. Children under 18 stay free in parents' room. Free cribs available. Corporate rates available. AE, CB, DC, DISC, MC, V. Parking: Free.

Drury Inn does it again with this imaginative use of what was once a YMCA, built in 1907 to serve transient railroad workers. Located beside Union Station, it has been lovingly restored utilizing many of the building's original features, including its large fireplaces, leaded-glass windows, oak paneling, and interior columns with marble bases. Rooms are clean and comfortable, with everything you might need. Some face inside with views over the pool; others face outside. Some of the suites are stocked with refrigerators and microwaves. A complimentary breakfast includes everything from doughnuts and muffins to fruit, juice, and coffee.

This hotel is one of St. Louis' best-kept secrets.

Dining/Entertainment: In the basement is David Slay's La Veranda, one of the city's best restaurants, boasting the creative dishes of a talented young chef.

Services: Free local phone calls.

Facilities: Indoor swimming pool, whirlpool.

3. CENTRAL WEST END

Located near Forest Park and only a 10-minute drive from downtown, the Central West End is a fun part of town to be in, with its many restaurants, shops, and bars stretched along Euclid Avenue. But it's also a quiet residential area, with large stately homes on tree-lined streets.

MODERATE

THE FOREST PARK HOTEL, 4910 West Pine Blvd., St. Louis, MO 63108. Tel. 314/361-3500, or toll free 800/622-4910; in Missouri, toll free 800/622-4913. Fax 314/361-3260. 200 rms and suites. A/C TEL TV

$ Rates: $60–$88 single; $70–$100 double. Extra person $5. Children under 19 stay free in parents' room. AE, CB, DC, DISC, ER, MC, V. Parking: Free.

Built in 1923 and listed on the National Register of Historic Places, this is an old-fashioned hotel with character—from the art nouveau mirrors in the lobby to the ancient elevators that require operators to run them. The atmosphere is laid back, and although some of the rooms look a bit tired and could do with a bit of sprucing up, I suspect that most guests who opt to stay here like it exactly the way it is. Each room is slightly different from the others, so if you don't like the one you're in, ask to see another. Some are paneled and tend to be dark. Each so-called minisuite comes complete with two beds, a kitchenette with sink and refrigerator (and microwave on request); each maxisuite is a two-room suite with a kitchenette at the higher prices listed above. Hotel guests receive free entry to a health club two blocks away. The hotel is located just off Euclid Avenue, the center of activity in the Central West End.

Services: Free in-house movies, room service until midnight, same-day laundry and dry-cleaning services.

Facilities: One restaurant, one lounge, outdoor swimming pool.

BED-AND-BREAKFAST

COACHLIGHT, 4612 McPherson Ave., St. Louis, MO 63108. Tel. 314/367-5870. 3 rms (all with private bath). A/C TEL TV

$ Rates (including continental breakfast): $65–$80 for two persons. Extra person $15. AE, MC, V. Parking: On the street.

Dating back to 1904 when the St. Louis World's Fair was held in nearby Forest Park, this brick home has been lovingly restored by a personable couple in their 30s, Susan and Chuck Sundermeyer. Susan, who used to work as director of sales for The Hotel Majestic and thus is very familiar with the hotel business, has decorated her home and guest rooms with antiques, soft down comforters, and Laura Ashley prints but also has installed such modern conveninences as private bathrooms, telephones, ceiling fans, and color TVs. Breakfast is a generous array of home-baked breads, muffins, fruit, coffee, and tea. Children ages three and older are welcome. Because there's a dog in residence, however, no pets are allowed.

4. CLAYTON

Since Clayton is a nucleus for business offices in St. Louis, most hotels here cater to the business traveler. However, only 15 to 20 minutes

Caverly Farm
  and Orchard **1**
Coral Court Motel **2**
Daniele Hilton **3**
Henry VIII Hilton **4**
Holiday Inn Airport West **5**
Huckleberry Finn
  Youth Hostel **6**
Hyatt Regency St. Louis **7**
Knights Inn **8**
Lafayette House **9**
Motel 6 **10**
Oakland Park Inn **11**
Old Convent Guesthouse **12**
Radisson Hotel Clayton **3**
Sheraton Plaza Hotel **13**
Sheraton West Port Inn **13**
Super 8 Motel **8**

from downtown and 10 minutes from the airport, it's also a convenient spot from which to explore the rest of the city.

EXPENSIVE

DANIELE HILTON, 216 N. Meramec, St. Louis, MO 63105. Tel. 314/721-0101, or toll free 800/HILTONS. 82 rms, 6 suites. A/C TEL TV

ST. LOUIS AREA ACCOMMODATIONS

$ Rates: $109–$139 single; $119–$149 double. Extra person $10. Children at any age stay free in parents' room. Corporate rates available. AE, CB, DC, MC, V. Parking: Free.

It's easy to see why business travelers keep coming back to this small hotel with its friendly and outgoing staff. Although the Daniele has recently been renovated and is modern in every sense of the word, it still manages to create a European-style atmosphere, in part because of its intimate size and in part because of its subdued and tasteful decor. The lobby is cozy, while the guest rooms are very pleasant, done in soothing mint green and cool pink. Each room has a separate vanity area, and each bathroom has a large counter with lots of room to spread out. In short, this is a good choice for those who shun large hotels but demand quality in service and accommodations.

Dining/Entertainment: The London Grill and Wine Bar features white tablecloth service in its presentation of English specialties, from prime meats and fresh seafood to traditional English sweets.

Services: Free shuttle to airport and Clayton vicinity, laundry service, room service until 11pm.

Facilities: Outdoor swimming pool.

THE RITZ-CARLTON, 1 Ritz Carlton Drive, St. Louis, MO 63105. Tel. 314/863-6300. Fax 314/863-7486. 268 rms, 33 suites. A/C MINIBAR TEL TV

$ Rates: $130–$165 single to triple occupancy; Ritz-Carlton Club executive floors $190; suites from $320. Children stay free in parents' room. Weekend and other packages available. AE, CB, DC, DISC, MC, V. Parking: Free.

The fine tradition of the Ritz-Carlton was brought to St. Louis with the 1990 opening of this spectacular property, featuring $5 million worth of original 18th- and 19th-century fine art and antiques. Filling the hotel are 52 chandeliers as well as fantastic bouquets of Hawaiian imports. The lobby is elegant with its marbled floor and chandeliers yet is comfortable and intimate with its overstuffed chairs and Persian rugs. Because of its quiet location on the edge of Clayton's business district, the Ritz-Carlton is spared the foot traffic that sometimes plagues downtown hotels. And, of course, the service here is excellent in every detail.

Each guest room, handsomely decorated with mahogany furniture and plush chairs, features TV with remote control, a two-line phone, an in-room safe, a vanity table with lighted makeup mirror and hairdryer, and all the amenities that you'd expect from a first-rate hotel. All rooms open up onto small balconies—those facing west have a view of an outdoor fountain and Clayton; those facing east have a view of the downtown skyline. If you feel like splurging, the Ritz-Carlton Club on the 17th and 18th floors provides guests with an exclusive lounge, private concierge service, a complimentary continental breakfast, cocktails, and hors d'oeuvres.

Dining/Entertainment: Besides cocktails, the Lobby Lounge serves afternoon tea daily from 2:30 to 5pm, featuring delicate sandwiches, scones, chocolates, and strawberries with Devonshire cream served on Wedgwood china to the accompaniment of classical music. The Grill serves grilled specialties for lunch and dinner. The signature restaurant, called simply The Restaurant, features continental and American cuisine.

Services: 24-hour room service, twice-daily maid service, babysitting, laundry and dry cleaning.

Facilities: Indoor swimming pool, Jacuzzi, fitness and exercise center, business center, gift shop.

SEVEN GABLES INN, 26 N. Meramec, St. Louis, MO 63105. Tel. 314/863-8400, toll free outside Missouri 800/433-6590. Fax 314/863-8846. 26 rms, 6 suites. A/C TEL TV

$ Rates (including continental breakfast): $105–$135 single; $120–$155 double; suites from $160. Extra person $30. Weekend rates available. AE, CB, DC, DISC, MC, V. Parking: Free.

This may well be the smallest hotel in St. Louis, and it achieves even more distinction by virtue of its two well-known restaurants. With only 32 rooms and suites, this inn was built in the 1920s as an apartment complex and was designed to resemble Nathaniel Hawthorne's *The House of Seven Gables,* from which the hotel takes its name. It has since become a landmark with its white-washed timbered facade and is listed on the National Register of Historic Monuments. Catering largely to business travelers who come back regularly, the Seven Gables offers rooms on three floors (there is no elevator), each room different but outfitted with a TV with remote control and a two-line phone.

Entertainment/Dining: Some St. Louisans consider Chez Louis the best restaurant around for traditional and innovative French cuisine. Bernard's, decorated like a turn-of-the-century French bistro, offers more casual dining, and in summer there's even outdoor seating in an inner courtyard.

MODERATE

CHESHIRE INN AND LODGE, 6300 Clayton Rd., St. Louis, MO 63117. Tel. 314/647-7300, or toll free 800/325-7378. 107 rooms and suites. A/C TEL TV

$ Rates: $88–$130 single; $98–$140 double; Fantasy Suites $190–$275. Extra person $10. Children under 19 stay free in parents' room. AE, CB, DC, DISC, MC, V. Parking: Free.

This lodging, located between Forest Park and the Clayton business district, will appeal to the child in all of you. Walk into its English Tudor–style building, and you leave St. Louis far behind. The decor is heavy English, almost medieval, with a lot of dark woods, reds, and kitsch. But the real treasures here are the so-called nine Fantasy Suites, each one designed on a different theme—all weird, whimsical, and wonderful. The Tree House suite, for example, the hotel's most popular room, features a waterfall in the room, along with a Jacuzzi, a king-size waterbed, and numerous mirrors and plants. The Safari Country suite boasts a king-size four-poster bed and decor that looks like an attraction at Disneyland. The decorator must have had fun here. The hotel's regular rooms carry on the theme with dark reds and more kitsch, and some of those on the first floor have doors leading outdoors directly to the swimming pool. However, if you can afford it and appreciate corniness, opt for one of the Fantasy Suites. They're in a class all themselves, certainly not your usual hotel experience.

IMPRESSIONS

St. Louis, as you approach it, shows like all the other French towns in this region, to much the greatest advantage at a distance. The French mode of building, the white coat of lime applied to the mud or rough stone walls, gives them a beauty at a distance. . . .
—*TIMOTHY FLINT, 1826*

Services: Free shuttle to downtown and Clayton, free newspaper, room service to 10pm, free local calls.

Facilities: One restaurant, two pubs, a deli, covered year-round swimming pool with sunning patio, sauna, whirlpool, health club, gift shop.

RADISSON HOTEL CLAYTON, 7750 Carondelet Ave., St. Louis, MO 63105. Tel. 314/726-5400, toll free 800/333-3333. 204 rms, 8 suites. A/C TEL TV

$ Rates (including continental breakfast): $85 single; $99 double. Extra person $10. Children under 18 stay free in parents' room. Corporate rates and other packages available. AE, CB, DC, DISC, MC, V. Parking: Free.

Formerly the Clayton Inn, the Radisson Hotel Clayton recently underwent a complete renovation, from the reception area and lobby to the guest rooms. It provides a wide range of facilities. Guest rooms, including those on no-smoking floors, are comfortable—each with a refrigerator, a TV with remote control, an alarm clock, and a full-length mirror.

Dining/Entertainment: The popular Joe Hanon's restaurant specializes in steaks and seafood.

Services: Free shuttle to airport, one-day laundry and valet, room service to 11pm, free happy hour hors d'oeuvres and cocktails.

Facilities: One restaurant, two bars, indoor and outdoor swimming pools, health club, whirlpool, sauna, steam room, tanning spa, exercise room, massage, hair salon, gift shop.

5. IN & AROUND SOULARD

Only minutes from downtown, Soulard and its vicinity are known for Soulard Market, the Anheuser-Busch Brewery, Antique Row on Cherokee Street, and a number of live music houses.

INEXPENSIVE BED-AND-BREAKFAST

LAFAYETTE HOUSE, 2156 Lafayette Ave., St. Louis, MO 63104. Tel. 314/772-4429. 4 rms (with and without pvt. bath), 1 apt. A/C

$ Rates (including breakfast): $45 double without bath, $55 double with bath; $65 apt. double with bath. Extra adult $10, extra child $7. No credit cards accepted. Parking: Street parking only.

Overlooking Lafayette Park, this bed-and-breakfast is an 1876 Queen Anne brick mansion built by James Eads (of Eads Bridge fame) for his daughter, Martha. Now owned by Sarah and Jack Milligan, who have run it since 1983, Lafayette House is a bit cluttered with mementos of a lifetime and is home to five cats. Sarah is friendly and helpful with advice on what to see and do, and, for a small fee, you'll be fetched from the airport or bus or train depot. Families will find the third-floor apartment with its own kitchen, living area with TV, and private bathroom especially appealing. A refrigerator on the second floor is stocked with soda, wine, and beer free to guests, and there's a communal lounge with a VCR. Sarah serves a full breakfast, including her famous cinnamon-raisin French toast.

THE OLD CONVENT GUESTHOUSE, 2049 Sidney St., St. Louis, MO 63104. Tel. 314/772-3531. 5 rms (with and without bath). A/C

$ Rates (including breakfast): $45 double without bath, $55 double with bath, $75–$95 double with bath and Jacuzzi. No credit cards accepted. Parting: Street parking only.

⭐ This bed-and-breakfast takes its name from the fact that it served as quarters of the Sisters of St. Joseph from the early 1900s until 1971. Built in 1881 by a cooper who made beer barrels, it contains an incredible 64 windows, 6 coal-burning fireplaces (no longer used), walnut and maple floors, and high ceilings. Light, open, and airy, it has been tastefully redecorated in a modern style that utilizes the best of the past. Each guest room is different from the others, ranging from the French room to the art nouveau room to the Oriental room. A couple rooms even have their own Jacuzzi. The hosts are Paul and Mary LaFlam; breakfasts here are especially good, a reflection of the fact that Paul worked as a professional chef for 20 years. Almost half of the people who stay here are local St. Louisans getting away for a weekend.

A BUDGET YOUTH HOSTEL

HUCKLEBERRY FINN YOUTH HOSTEL, 1904–1906 S. 12th St., St. Louis, MO 63104 (tel. 314/241-0076). 36 beds. **Bus:** 73, 21 or 5 to 12th & Russell.

$ Rates: $10 a night for members, $13 for nonmembers. Sheets $1. Discounts for stays of a week or longer. No credit cards accepted.

If all you're looking for is an inexpensive place to lay down your head at night, this youth hostel should suit your needs. The dormitory-style rooms, accommodating men and women separately, are lined with bunk beds. Facilities include lockers, a kitchen stocked with pots and pans, and a communal room with cable TV, public phone, and piano. Air-conditioning may have been installed by the time you read this. Walk-ins are welcome. If you wish to make a reservation, only written reservations with a check or money order are accepted. Check in is after 6pm. The Huckleberry Finn is located in three brick buildings built in the 1870s, about a mile south of the Arch.

6. NEAR LAMBERT AIRPORT

These hotels are convenient if you wish to be close to the airport or if you're arriving in St. Louis on I-70 from Kansas City and don't wish to drive all the way downtown.

MODERATE

HENRY VIII HOTEL, 4690 N. Lindbergh, St. Louis, MO 63044. Tel. 314/731-3040, toll free 800/325-1588; in Missouri toll free 800/392-1660. Fax 314/731-4210. 195 rms, 190 suites. A/C TEL TV

$ Rates: $90 single; $100 double; suites from $115. Extra person $10. Children under 18 stay free in parents' room. Weekend and corporate rates available. AE, CB, DC, DISC, MC, V. Parking: Free.

Situated on 50 acres just minutes from the airport near I-70 and I-270, this large hotel is built in mock Tudor style. In keeping with its Henry VIII theme, it has a timber-frame facade, stained-glass windows, a suit of armor in the lobby, chandeliers, and gleaming polished wood. Striving to appeal to business travelers, tourists, and convention groups, this hotel offers a wide range of facilities, from a game room for the kids to a quarter-mile jogging and nature trail. Each room has a refrigerator and a TV with remote control, while each suite offers an additional phone and a TV in both the bedroom and the living room.

Services: Free shuttle to and from airport, room service to 11pm.

Facilities: One restaurant, one Irish pub, game room, indoor and outdoor swimming pools, fitness equipment, sauna, whirlpool, tennis courts, jogging trail.

HOLIDAY INN AIRPORT WEST, I-270 at St. Charles Rock Rd., Bridgeton, MO 63044. Tel. 314/291-5100, or toll free 800/325-1395. 250 rms. A/C TEL TV

$ Rates: $80–$90 single or double. Extra person $8. Children under 18 stay free in parents' room. Weekend and special packages available. AE, CB, DC, DISC, MC, V. Parking: Free.

This Holiday Inn is similar to other hotels in this chain across the country, including its inner, spacious Holidome recreation center. Kids love the facilities here, which means that the hotel is packed with families. Rooms are clean and comfortable and face toward either the indoor pool or the outside of the building.

Services: Free shuttle to and from airport.

Facilities: One restaurant, one lounge, indoor pool, sauna, whirlpool, workout equipment, video-game room, indoor putting green, billiard table, Ping-Pong tables, business center.

OAKLAND PARK INN, 4505 Woodson Rd., St. Louis, MO 63134. Tel. 314/427-4700, or toll free 800/426-4700. 140 rms, 10 suites. A/C TEL TV

$ Rates: $82 single; $92 double; $100–$230 suites. Extra person $5. Children under 12 stay free in parents' room. Weekend and corporate rates available. AE, CB, DC, DISC, ER, MC, V. Parking: Free.

If you shun chain hotels, you'll love this family-owned hotel just 15 miles from downtown. Its walls serve as a gallery for 300 paintings, most done by the owner of the hotel. The Oakland Park strives for a European flavor and style, providing its mostly business clientele with a cozy home away from home. Its success is proved by the fact that it has survived for decades, even though it doesn't advertise. Rooms, 20% of which are reserved for nonsmokers, each feature a cable TV with remote control, full-length mirrors, bedtime mints, and such amenities as shampoo and sewing kits.

Services: Free shuttle to the airport and immediate vicinity, free coffee, free newspaper, laundry services.

Facilities: One restaurant, one pub, outdoor swimming pool, whirlpool, sauna, exercise room.

INEXPENSIVE

MOTEL 6, 4576 Woodson Rd., St. Louis, MO 63134. Tel. 314/427-1313. 106 rms. A/C TEL TV

$ Rates: $32.95 single; $38.95 double. Extra person $6. Children under 18 stay free in parents' room. AE, CB, DC, DISC, MC, V. Parking: Free.

Located across the street from the Oakland Park Inn above (south of I-70, a half-mile east of the 236 exit), Motel 6 provides modest accommodations at bargain prices. Rooms are simple but comfortable and provide individual air-conditioning and heating controls and showers. In addition, local phone calls and in-house movies are free. There are also an outdoor swimming pool and soda-vending machines.

7. WEST COUNTY

These accommodations are located just off I-270 in the western part of St. Louis.

EXPENSIVE

SHERATON PLAZA HOTEL, 900 West Port Plaza, St. Louis, MO 63146. Tel. 314/434-5010, or toll free 800/822-3535. 204 rms, 5 suites. A/C TEL TV

$ Rates: $97–$115 single; $108–$130 double; from $135 suite. Extra person $10. Children under 18 stay free in parents' room. Weekend and other packages available. AE, CB, DC, DISC, MC, V. Parking: Free.

The Sheraton Plaza Hotel and the Sheraton West Port Inn (below) are located on opposite ends of a shopping-and-entertainment complex called West Port Plaza, just off I-270 and Page Avenue. Each of the hotels has an individual character: The West Port Inn is in the style of a country chalet and overlooks a lake; the Plaza is a modern high-rise that caters to corporate businesspeople. The view at the Inn may be better, but I prefer the rooms at the Plaza, which are large, bright, and cheerful, with breezy rattan furniture and Asian-influenced artwork. Some even have small balconies. Be sure to walk through West Port Plaza, an open-air complex designed like an Alpine village and boasting 16 restaurants and numerous shops and boutiques. Guests of both Sheratons can use a nearby health club free of charge.

Services: Free shuttle to and from the airport, complimentary morning coffee, complimentary morning newspaper, concierge desk, laundry service, room service to 1am, free local phone calls.

Facilities: One restaurant, one bar, indoor swimming pool, whirlpool, sunning deck, sauna.

SHERATON WEST PORT INN, 191 West Port Plaza, St. Louis, MO 63146. Tel. 314/878-1500, or toll free 800/822-3535. 291 rms, 9 suites. A/C TEL TV

$ Rates: $107–$115 single; $108–$130 double; from $175 suite. Extra person $10. Children under 18 stay free in parents' room. Weekend and other packages available. AE, CB, DC, DISC, MC, V. Parking: Free.

Built in the style of a country lodge, the West Port Inn feels like a resort hotel. Its lobby, casual and intimate, emphasizes the Alpine theme with stone walls and wooden beams, while the outdoor pool overlooks an artificial lake complete with ducks. Rooms, all with balconies, are in two buildings—the main building and an adjoining tower with newer and slightly more expensive rooms. Regardless of where you stay, it's worth paying more for a lakeside room. The suites are particularly roomy, each with a large living area, a bar area and sink, two TVs, two phones, two bathroom sinks, and a clothesline and a hairdryer in the bathroom. Hotel guests have free use of a nearby health club.

Services: Free shuttle to and from the airport, complimentary morning coffee, complimentary morning newspaper, concierge desk, laundry service, room service to 1am, free local phone calls.

Facilities: One restaurant, one bar, outdoor swimming pool, jogging track.

AN INEXPENSIVE BED-AND-BREAKFAST

CAVERLY FARM AND ORCHARD, 389 N. Mosley Rd., St. Louis, MO 63141. Tel. 314/432-5074. 3 rms (1 with pvt. bath). A/C

$ Rates (including breakfast): $40 single without bath, $45 single with bath; $45 double without bath, $50 double with bath. Extra person $5. Children stay free in parents' room. No credit cards accepted. Parking: Free.

Originally built as a farmhouse in the 1880s but added on to through the years, this red-clapboard house is located in a very quiet and wooded residential area called Creve Coeur. Owned by David and Nancy Caverly, the Caverly is decorated in a casual country style, with rooms that are cheerful and comfortable. Breakfast includes berries from the backyard as well as homemade breads, eggs, and jam and jelly made from fruit of the small orchard out back. This is a good choice for families because there's a lot of room for children to run free and play. Two friendly dogs are in residence.

8. SOUTH COUNTY

These three accommodations, located in the south part of St. Louis, offer inexpensive lodgings.

INEXPENSIVE HOTELS

CORAL COURT MOTEL, 7755 Watson Rd., St. Louis, MO 63119. Tel. 314/962-3000. 74 rms. A/C TEL TV

$ Rates: $35 one bed; $40 two beds; $46 three beds. AE, MC, V. Parking: Free.

★ Nostalgic for the days of Route 66 and highway motels? This is a classic—located on Highway 50 and (of course) the original Route 66—a motel of yellow tile and glass brick, very art deco, spread like a village underneath a canopy of oak trees. Construction on the motel began around 1940, was halted because of World War II, and then began again in the 1950s. The Coral Court has changed little since then. Most units have attached garages complete with garage doors. The rooms themselves are a bit worn around the edges, are a bit too dark, and have furniture that looks like its been there since the 1950s including Murphy beds in some units. Even though the motel looks better on the outside than it does on the inside, for a bit of novel Americana straight from the past, you can't beat this place. Rates are based on the unit and the number of beds it contains, not on the number of people.

KNIGHTS INN, 6500 S. Lindbergh Blvd., St. Louis, MO 63123. Tel. 314/892-3664. 117 rms. A/C TEL TV

$ Rates: $37.50–$48.50 single; $44.50–$55.50 double. Extra person $3. Senior-citizen and weekly and monthly rates available. AE, MC, V. Parking: Free.

Located just off I-55, this hotel is convenient if you're coming into town from the south. Only 20 minutes from downtown, it offers large rooms containing just the basics decorated in mock English Tudor style, with dark wooden beams overhead. The most expensive rooms have kitchenettes with refrigerators, dishes, and microwave ovens. Local telephone calls are free. Complimentary coffee, tea, and hot chocolate are served in the lobby. All rooms are on the ground floor, so you can park right in front of your room. There are also an outdoor pool and a family-style restaurant next to the hotel.

SUPER 8 MOTEL, 6602 S. Lindbergh Blvd., St. Louis, MO 63123. Tel. 314/894-9449, or toll free 800/848-8888. 98 rms. A/C TEL TV

$ Rates: $39.88–$65.88 single; $48.88–$65.88 double. Extra person $2. AE, CB, DC, DISC, MC, V. Parking: Free.

S Just down the street from the Knights Inn, this Super 8 offers slightly better rooms, although they're still pretty basic. Local calls here also are free. Complimentary coffee and juice are served in the lobby. The TV offers cable and HBO as well as pay movies. If you feel like splurging, the most expensive room offers a king-size bed and a whirlpool bathtub.

9. CAMPING

ARCHWAY MANOR, 7474 St. Charles Rock Rd., St. Louis MO 63133. Tel. 314/726-6992. 40 trailer sites, 5 tent sites.
$ Rates: $15–$20. MC, V. **Season:** Year round.
Located in the northwest part of the city just off the 170 Inner Belt Expressway and only 30 minutes from downtown, this small 4.5-acre campground offers mainly RV hookups, including electricity, water, and sewage disposal.

KOA OF ST. LOUIS SOUTH, 8000 Metropolitan Blvd.,

Barnhart, MO 63012. Tel. 314/479-4449. 80 trailer sites, 20 tent sites.

$ Rates: $12–17. MC, V. **Season:** Mar 1–Nov 1.

This KOA campground is located south of St. Louis near Barnhart, Missouri, off I-55 at the 185 exit. About a half-hour from downtown St. Louis, it offers such facilities as a store, flush toilets, hot showers, fireplaces and firewood, a swimming pool, and a game room.

PINEWOODS CAMP AND FISHING PARK, 1500 Pinewoods Dr., Wentzville, MO 63385. 305 trailer sites, 86 tent sites.

$ Rates: $10–$14. MC, V. **Season:** Mar 1–Nov 30.

Located off I-70 in Wentzville about 30 minutes from downtown St. Louis, this 100-acre campground has such recreational facilities as a swimming pool, a game room, a playground, and fishing.

RV PARKING, 2nd and Poplar, St. Louis, MO 63101. Tel. 314/241-7777. 70 trailer sites.

$ Rates: $5–$7. No credit cards accepted. **Season:** Year round.

Conveniently located just south of the Gateway Arch underneath the Poplar Street Bridge, this RV park offers only electric hookup—nothing else.

ST. LOUIS RV PARK, 900 N. Jefferson, St. Louis, MO 63106. Tel. 314/241-3330. 100 trailer sites.

$ Rates: $25.50–$27.50. MC, V. **Season:** Mar 1–Nov 1.

Located in the heart of St. Louis near the crossroads of Jefferson and Martin Luther King Boulevard, this RV park with full hookups offers such facilities as a convenience store, a laundry room, a swimming pool, and a game room.

CHAPTER 6

ST. LOUIS DINING

1. **DOWNTOWN**
2. **NEAR UNION STATION**
3. **ON OR NEAR THE HILL**
4. **CENTRAL WEST END & FOREST PARK**
5. **UNIVERSITY CITY**
6. **CLAYTON & MID-COUNTY**
7. **IN & AROUND SOULARD**
8. **SPECIALTY DINING**

Nowhere does St. Louis' ethnic diversity express itself more joyously and thoroughly than in its cuisine. Italian food reigns supreme, and hardly a visitor passes through the city without consuming at least one pizza or pasta or veal dish. The Hill is the old Italian enclave, filled with family-owned restaurants that range from neighborhood mom-and-pop diners to plush establishments with valet parking. All St. Louis natives have their favorite Italian restaurant, but exactly which is the best is a hotly debated topic. Be sure to try the appetizer unique to St. Louis: toasted ravioli, consisting of ravioli filled with ground beef and vegetables and then deep-fried to a crispy golden brown.

In addition to Italian food, St. Louis boasts a great variety of other cuisine—from French, German, and Mexican to seafood and steaks. The past decade has ushered in a whole new generation of young chefs who aren't afraid to experiment with regional and ethnic foods, resulting in innovative and surprising combinations. No longer is St. Louis a backwater when it comes to dining; and even best is the fact that eating out here costs a fraction of what it costs in other parts of the country.

When choosing a restaurant, keep in mind that many establishments offer different lunch and dinner menus, which means that you can save money by eating your big meal at noon. You should make reservations for the more expensive and moderately priced restaurants, especially on weekend nights. Note that many close from about 3 to 5pm and that a 5.9% sales tax will be added to your bill. Tips are generally 15% to 20% of the total bill. And, finally, very much in fashion at St. Louis' expensive restaurants is valet parking, for which attendants expect a $1 or $2 tip, even if they drive your vehicle only 20 feet.

The following restaurants have been divided according to location and then further subdivided according to price. Note that restaurants located in hotels, however, have been grouped under a separate heading in the "Specialty Dining" section. Expect to pay more than $30 per person in the expensive restaurants, while the moderately priced establishments should run you about $20 to $30, excluding drinks. Recommendations listed in the inexpensive category should average you about $8 to $20, depending on your choice of entree, while budget establishments are those that offer dining for less than $8. A circled dollar sign by a listing denotes good value for money spent; a circled star signifies one of my particular favorites.

In addition to the restaurants listed here, be sure to check Chapter 10 for bars and entertainment establishments that also serve food.

1. DOWNTOWN

All the restaurants listed here are within walking distance of the Arch. Keep in mind that because many of them cater to office workers in the area, they tend to be closed on Sunday.

EXPENSIVE

AL'S STEAK HOUSE, 1200 N. 1st St. Tel. 421-6399.

Cuisine: STEAK/SEAFOOD **Reservations:** Recommended. Valet parking.

$ Prices: Entrees $22–$37. MC, V.

Open: Mon–Sat 5–11pm. **Closed:** Sun and holidays.

Located north of Laclede's Landing in a riverfront industrial area, Al's has been a longtime favorite ever since it opened its doors in 1926. There is no printed menu; rather, a tray of what's available is brought to each table, laden with steak, veal, rack of lamb, and fresh seafood, and the waiter elaborates on how each dish is prepared. This restaurant is a favorite destination for St. Louisans celebrating special occasions. Jackets and ties are required for men.

ANTHONY'S, Equitable Building, 10 S. Broadway. Tel. 314/231-2434.

Cuisine: CONTINENTAL **Reservations:** Preferred. Valet parking.

$ Prices: Appetizers $6; entrees $22–26. AE, CB, DC, DISC, MC, V.

Open: Mon–Sat 5:30–10:30pm.

Considered one of St. Louis' most romantic dining establishments, Anthony's has a reputation for efficiency, excellent service, and dependably good food. That, together with its downtown location in the midst of office buildings, makes it popular for business meals as well as for romantic encounters. Owner Tony Bommarito is usually present to assure that everything runs smoothly, and he insists that only the freshest of ingredients are used in dishes that are designed to appeal to a wide variety of individual tastes.

The menu, which changes seasonally, is traditional, with few culinary surprises. Past menus, for example, have included lobster with wild mushrooms and basil, veal Marsala with roasted pepper, and breast of pheasant with Madeira and red currants. Appetizers may include mussels with mustard and tarragon in a light cream sauce and grilled sweetbreads, while entrees range from steaks and seafood to roasted duckling and rack of lamb.

CAFÉ DE FRANCE, 410 Olive St. Tel. 231-2204.

Cuisine: TRADITIONAL FRENCH. **Reservations:** Imperative. Valet parking.

$ Prices: Appetizers $7.50; entrees $19–$24. AE, CB, DC, DISC, MC, V.

Open: Mon–Thurs 5:30–10pm, Fri and Sat 5:30–11pm.

Many consider this their favorite French restaurant in St. Louis. From the minute you walk into this intimate and elegant dining establishment, with its chandeliers and fresh flowers on the tables, you're whisked away to the adventures of another continent, a different cuisine, and a whole new way of looking at food. Owner/chef Marcel Keraval, born in France, is well known for the artful presentation of his dishes, which are so beautiful to look at that you almost hate to eat them.

But who could resist hot smoked salmon with dill sauce, veal scaloppine stuffed with crab and glazed with lobster and hollandaise, lamb with honey-ginger sauce, or duckling with honey? There are always daily specials not listed on the menu, as well as fixed-price three- or four-course meals. Although Keraval describes his cuisine as being traditional French, some of his creations border on nouvelle. Start your meal with gooseliver pâté, but be sure to leave room for the fantastic homemade French pastries. Jackets and ties are required for men.

TONY'S, 826 Broadway. Tel. 231-7007.
  Cuisine: ITALIAN. **Reservations:** Necessary. Valet parking.
$ **Prices:** Appetizers $7–$11; pasta $7–$9; entrees $18–$28; fixed-price dinners $44. AE, CB, DC, DISC, MC, V.
  Open: Mon–Sat 5–11:30pm. Closed: Sun and hols.

I could write an entire article on Tony's alone, as indeed many have. Although there may be a few rebel dissenters, most St. Louisans agree that this is the city's finest restaurant, as reflected in the fact that it's one of only two restaurants in the entire United States to hold both a 5-Star *Mobil Travel Guide* Award and an AAA Five Diamond Award. One reason is that diners are never disappointed—the food is always fantastically good. What's more, diners are treated with deference whether they're famous or just folks from out of town. Finally, the restaurant has had since 1949 to perfect its style.

Part of that calculated style is reflected in the way customers are shown to their tables—the maître d' leads the way, walking backward up the stairs, so that he never turns his back on his customers. That's only the beginning of the attentive yet unobtrusive service. As for the food, it's sublimely superb. I've never been the same since trying the cappellini primavera. Equally good are the smoked salmon filled with imported Italian cheese, the lobster Albanello (perhaps the star dish), various veal dishes, and steaks. All pasta dishes are cooked to order, the veal chops are four inches thick and are the best you'll find anywhere, the beef is dry-aged by the restaurant, and the seafood is flown in fresh daily. Even basil grows fresh in the kitchen. In fact, the kitchen is so spotlessly clean, orderly, and amazing that it should be on a tour. The kitchen floors are swept every hour and mopped every two hours, the silver is polished twice a week, and even the ceilings are washed down according to a strict schedule. I've never seen anything like it. All things considered, Tony's gets my vote as the best restaurant in town. Jackets are required for men.

MODERATE

LT. ROBERT E. LEE, 100 S. Leonor K. Sullivan Blvd. Tel. 241-1282.
  Cuisine: AMERICAN **Reservations:** Recommended.
$ **Prices:** Lunch buffet $5.95, entrees $6.50–$9.50; dinner entrees $12.25–$20. AE, DC, DISC, MC, V.

ST. LOUIS
Downtown

Al's Steak House

Anthony's

Café de France

Caleco's

Charlie Gitto's

Dierdorf & Hart's

Key West

Fedora Café & Bar

Fourth Floor Food Court

La Sala

Lt. Robert E. Lee

Miss Hullings

Old Spaghetti Factory

Premio

Ruth's Chris Steak House

Tony's

Open: Lunch daily 11:30am–3pm; dinner Mon–Thurs 5–10pm, Fri and Sat 5–11pm; Sun brunch 10am–2pm.

Dine right on the Mississippi on this boat moored near the Arch, built to resemble the sternwheelers that once ruled the river. It offers various options in dining. The Seafood Deck is the main dining room, specializing in sandwiches and seafood for lunch and steaks and seafood for dinner. Try the Mississippi Seafood Platter for a taste of shrimp, scallops, oysters, and pecan-fried catfish filets, served with hush puppies. There's also trout from the Ozarks. On Sunday, there's a brunch featuring live jazz priced at $10.95 for adults and $4.95 for children. In addition, the lounge offers a lunch buffet Monday through Friday for a bargain $5.95. If you want to be entertained while you dine, you might consider spending an evening in the Natchez Room with the Showboat Jubilee variety show (see Chapter 10 for more information).

PREMIO, Gateway One Building, 701 Market St. Tel. 231-0911.

Cuisine: ITALIAN **Reservations:** Recommended for lunch.
$ **Prices:** Lunch pasta $5–$9, entrees $9–$14; dinner appetizers $5–$7, pasta $4–$8.50, entrees $14–$24. AE, DC, MC, V.
Open: Lunch Mon–Fri 11am–2:30pm; dinner Mon–Thurs 5–10pm, Fri and Sat 5–11pm.

Brought to you by the same folks who own four-star Dominic's on the Hill (see the "On or Near the Hill" section), Premio caters to the downtown business crowd with its light contemporary Italian cuisine and its prime location on Market Street behind the Old Courthouse. A modern restaurant that relies on plants as its main decoration, it offers outdoor seating (with a great view of the Arch) as well as a separate bar. Its main business is at lunch, when it offers eight different pasta dishes, including cannelloni, fettuccine with veal sauce, tagliatelle primavera, linguine with fresh seafood, and ravioli filled with ricotta cheese in tomato and basil sauce. Risotto dishes of Northern Italy also are on the menu, as are fresh seafood, chicken, and veal. The dinner menu offers the same pasta and appetizers but with additional entrees.

RUTH'S CHRIS STEAK HOUSE, 101 S. 11th St. Tel. 241-7711.
Cuisine: STEAK **Reservations:** Recommended on weekends.
$ **Prices:** Appetizers $5–$7.25; entrees $14.80–$23.50. AE, DC, DISC, MC, V.
Open: Daily 4:30–11pm.

Part of a chain of steak houses that originated in New Orleans, Ruth's Chris Steak House has achieved a devoted following by serving only the best U.S. prime, corn-fed Midwestern beef, cut by hand, broiled to perfection, and then served sizzling hot. An upmarket restaurant with white tablecloths and modern decor, this steak house is located in the basement of a striking brick building that once served as a warehouse. In addition to its steaks, it serves lamb chops, veal chops, chicken, and lobster. There are nine different selections of potato dishes, from cottage fries to potatoes au gratin served in cream sauce and topped with sharp cheddar.

INEXPENSIVE

CALECO'S, 420 Olive. Tel. 421-0708.
Cuisine: ITALIAN/AMERICAN
$ **Prices:** Appetizers $3.50–$5.50; entrees $5.25–$14. AE, CB, DC, DISC, MC, V.
Open: Mon–Fri 11am–3am, Sat and Sun noon–3am.

This is a local success story, beginning in 1974 with the opening of a college establishment that has now expanded to more than a half-dozen locations across the city. The downtown Caleco's, on the corner of Olive and Broadway, is a casual bar and grill that caters to local businesspeople, families, and tourists. Its menu includes a bit of everything—such as pizza, fajitas, chicken pasta salad, burgers, sandwiches, prime rib, veal, and stir-fried vegetables—but it's best known for its offerings of more than a dozen different kinds of pasta. There are daily lunch specials as well as a children's menu. On Friday and Saturday there's live rock-'n'-roll music after 10pm, for which there is no cover charge.

Other Caleco's locations include 14 Marilyn Plaza in the Central

**FROMMER'S SMART TRAVELER
—RESTAURANTS**

VALUE-CONSCIOUS DINERS SHOULD TAKE
ADVANTAGE OF THE FOLLOWING:

1. Lunch menus offering entrees at cheaper prices than those on dinner menus; save money by eating a big meal at noon.
2. Daily specials offered by many restaurants, which are not on the regular menus and may offer a main course and side dish at a good price.
3. Fixed-price meals, each of which includes an appetizer or soup, a main course, and a dessert, at prices much cheaper than ordering à la carte.
4. Inexpensive entrees, such as chicken or pasta, offered by some of the more expensive restaurants, where even budget travelers can dine in style by choosing carefully.
5. St. Louis' many Italian restaurants in all price categories.
6. A view of the Arch from a few of St. Louis' downtown restaurants—request a table by the window when making your reservation.
7. Food offered by many pubs, bars, and taverns, usually hearty portions at bargain prices.

QUESTIONS TO ASK IF YOU'RE ON A BUDGET

1. Does the entree come with a side dish such as a vegetable or potato? (If so, it may be all you want to order, unless you have a voracious appetite.)
2. Is there a special of the day or a fixed-price meal not listed on the regular menu?

West End (tel. 361-8512); 10567 Old Olive St. (tel. 567-6047) in Creve Coeur; and 3815 Laclede St. (tel. 534-7878) in Midtown.

LA SALA, 513 Olive. Tel. 231-5620.
Cuisine: MEXICAN
$ Prices: Appetizers $2.60–$4.90; entrees $5.75–$7.95. AE, DC, MC, V.
Open: Mon–Sat 11am–11pm.

La sala means "living room" in Spanish—and that's the atmosphere this cozy restaurant tries to evoke. Dimly lit and comfortable, it's been a longtime favorite with the locals, especially during happy hour offered Monday through Friday from 4:30 to 6:30pm, when large margaritas go for only $2. The menu includes nachos, enchiladas, tamales, tacos, mole verde, burritos, tostadas, quesadillas, chimichangas, chili rellenos, and taco salads. There's a variety of alcoholic concoctions made with tequila and Kahlúa.

BUDGET

CHARLIE GITTO'S, 207 N. 6th St. Tel. 436-2828.
Cuisine: ITALIAN

$ Prices: $4.50–$9.50. AE, DC, MC, V.
   Open: Mon–Thurs 11am–10:30pm, Fri and Sat 11am–11:30pm, Sun 3–9:30pm (Cardinal game days only). **Closed:** Sun when there are no games.

There's no better place to go on game days than this St. Louis institution, even though it may be packed and it accepts no reservations, except for large groups. It's been *the* sports place ever since it opened more than 15 years ago in a small brick building that today looks out of place amidst the surrounding high-rises. It's filled with photos and sports memorabilia and is popular with athletes. Tom LaSorda has his own table here, and he makes it a point to drop in whenever the Dodgers are in town. The specialty is pasta, for which there are more than 20 different offerings, most available in small or large servings. There are also sandwiches, lunch and dinner specials, and a few choices of low-calorie, low-fat dishes.

FOURTH FLOOR FOOD COURT, St. Louis Centre, between 6th and 7th and Washington and Locust Sts. Tel. 314/ 231-5522.
   Cuisine: VARIED FAST FOOD
$ Prices: $1.50–$5. No credit cards accepted.
   Open: Mon–Sat 10am–7pm, Sun noon–7pm.

If you're looking for a fast meal at a cheap price, your best bet downtown is the fourth floor of the St. Louis Centre shopping mall. Popular at lunch with local office workers and with shoppers, this Food Court consists of counters specializing in various foods—from tacos and quiche to barbecued food, stir-fried vegetables, gyros, pizza, and salads. O'Connell's, an Irish pub famous for its hamburgers, also has a concession here.

MISS HULLINGS, 1103 Locust St. Tel. 436-0840.
   Cuisine: AMERICAN
$ Prices: $3.70–$7. AE, DC, DISC, MC, V.
   Open: Mon–Sat 6am–8pm.

A St. Louis tradition since 1928, Miss Hullings is an old-fashioned cafeteria offering home-style cooking. Pink is its trademark—hence the pink walls, pink aprons worn by the staff, and pink napkins. It offers 4 different soups each day, 14 types of vegetables, 26 salads, and a variety of entrees that changes daily. Selections may include such main dishes as fried chicken, prime rib, and ham, along with such side dishes as hot creamed spinach, broccoli, and corn. There's also a wide selection of cakes, pies, and other desserts.

THE OLD SPAGHETTI FACTORY, 727 N. 1st St., Laclede's Landing. Tel. 621-0276.
   Cuisine: PASTA
$ Prices: $4.50–$7.50. No credit cards accepted.
   Open: Summer Mon–Thurs 4:30–10pm, Fri 4–11pm, Sat 3–11:30pm, Sun 3–10pm; winter Mon–Thurs 5–10pm, Fri 5–11pm, Sat 4–11:30pm, Sun 3:30–10pm.

Its name leaves little doubt about the specialty served in this casual, family restaurant located in the heart of Laclede's Landing. The Spaghetti Factory is in the basement of a beautiful six-story cast-iron-and-brick building that once housed a tobacco company. There are antiques throughout the restaurant, including a 1920 streetcar that now contains some dining tables and a nine-foot Tiffany window commissioned by a Chicago cattle baron. Approximately a dozen selections of spaghetti and pasta are offered, all of which come with a salad, French bread, a drink, and ice cream. There's also a children's dinner.

2. NEAR UNION STATION

In addition to the restaurants here, Houlihan's (listed in Chapter 10) serves a wide variety of American food.

MODERATE

DIERDORF & HART'S, Union Station, 18th and Market. Tel. 421-1772.
   Cuisine: STEAK/SEAFOOD **Reservations:** Recommended.
 $ Prices: Lunch entrees $6–$12; dinner entrees $17–$33. AE, CB, DC, DISC, MC, V.
   Open: Mon–Thurs 11am–11pm, Fri and Sat 11am–midnight, Sun 11am–10pm.
Established by former Cardinal football players Dan Dierdorf and Jim Hart, this posh establishment claims to offer the best steak in St. Louis (don't they all?). Its walls lined with sketches of sports celebrities, Dierdorf & Hart's boasts an extensive bar and wine list. It offers for lunch egg dishes, burgers, sandwiches, seafood, and steaks and for dinner New York Strip (how about a 26-ounce cut?), filet mignon, T-bone, fresh fish, lobster, and pork, veal, and lamb chops.

INEXPENSIVE

FEDORA CAFÉ & BAR, Union Station, 18th and Market. Tel. 436-0855.

(F)FROMMER'S COOL FOR KIDS
RESTAURANTS

Rigazzi's *(see p. 78)* This family-style Italian restaurant on the Hill is inexpensive, fun, and lively—just the kind of atmosphere kids love.

Lt. Robert E. Lee *(see p. 69)* What kid wouldn't enjoy dining on a riverboat? This sternwheeler is moored near the Arch and offers weekday buffets, a Sunday brunch, and sandwiches and burgers.

Busch's Grove *(see p. 87)* There's no better setting for a family outing than this long-standing institution, with private cabañas offering outdoor dining.

Cuisine: AMERICAN/INTERNATIONAL
$ Prices: Lunch entrees $5–$12; dinner entrees $5.50–$20. AE, DC, DISC, MC, V.
Open: Lunch Mon–Sat 11:30am–3pm, Sun 11am–3pm; dinner Mon–Thurs 5:30–11pm, Fri and Sat 5pm–midnight, Sun 5–10pm.

Located near the information booth in Union Station, this stylish café with an open facade is a great place for people-watching. Its menu is fun and inventive, keeping up with the latest trends in the preparation of pastas, salads, Asian dishes, rotisserie foods, and entrees. Lunch offers such light meals as large salads, soups, pasta, pizza, and sandwiches. Dinner also features salads, pasta, and pizza, along with such selections as grilled quail and barbecued shrimp quesadilla, veal sweetbreads, steak, and duck. Watch out for the daily specials, which may range from a curry pasta dish to fresh seafood.

BUDGET

KEY WEST, Union Station, 18th and Market. Tel. 241-2566.
Cuisine: SEAFOOD/AMERICAN
$ Prices: $5.25–$10. AE, DC, MC, V.
Open: Daily 11am–1:30am.

Key West favorites—including conch fritters, fish sandwiches, Florida rock shrimp, and even alligator marinated in a spicy Cajun mixture and then grilled in garlic-lemon butter—at this combination bar/restaurant. There are also a dozen different versions of hamburgers with toppings and hot dogs. Happy hour is Monday through Friday from 4 to 7pm, when oysters are offered at half price and drink specials are available. There's a wide selection of domestic and imported beer.

3. ON OR NEAR THE HILL

The Hill, located just west of the Missouri Botanical Gardens, is St. Louis' Italian district, famous for its many restaurants.

EXPENSIVE

DOMINIC'S, 5101 Wilson. Tel. 771-1632.
Cuisine: ITALIAN **Reservations:** Preferred, necessary on weekends. Valet parking.
$ Prices: Appetizers $4–$10; entrees $16–$25. AE, CB, DC, DISC, MC, V.
Open: Mon–Sat 5pm–midnight. **Closed:** Sun and holidays.

Any discussion of the Hill's best Italian restaurants will include Dominic's, a formal affair where the waiters wear bow ties and black suits and the decor includes statues reminiscent of those in old Rome, chandeliers, and enough paintings on the walls to make the restaurant look like a museum. It's borderline pretentious—but all is forgiven due to the careful and exact service, subdued lighting, and, most important, great Italian food. After your meal, you'll think you've dined and gone to heaven. The menu includes both Italian and

American selections, including fresh seafood, chicken, beef tenderloin, steaks, rack of lamb, and veal. The veal saltimbocca and the chateaubriand are especially recommended. The wine list is extensive, and there's also a bar where you can come for only a drink if you wish. Jackets and ties are required for men.

GIOVANNI'S, 5201 Shaw. Tel. 772-5958.

Cuisine: ITALIAN **Reservations:** Strongly recommended, especially on weekends. Valet parking.

$ Prices: Appetizers $6.50–$7.50; pasta $14; entrees $16–$30. AE, DC, MC, V.

Open: Mon–Sat 5pm–midnight. **Closed:** Sun and holidays.

Giovanni's has a slight edge over Dominic's (above), by virtue of the fact that it was asked to prepare a pasta dish for former President Reagan's inaugurations in 1981 and 1985. In fact, Giovanni's may well have the best pasta in town, which is no mean feat considering the competition. Winner of four stars in the *Mobil Travel Guide* for the past decade, it is certainly a top contender for the best Italian restaurant in town. Elegant and romantic in the style of the Italian Renaissance, it's a great place for a splurge.

You'll probably want to include pasta with your meal. If you want what Reagan had, order the Presidential Farfalline Al Salmone, pasta in a rich cream sauce with fresh salmon. For an entree, you might choose veal saltimbocca or picante veal cooked with wine and lemon. There are also chicken breast cooked with champagne, fresh seafood, filet mignon, and rack of lamb. Jackets and ties are required for men.

MODERATE

GIAN-PEPPE'S, 2126 Marconi. Tel. 772-3303.

Cuisine: ITALIAN **Reservations:** Advised on weekends. Valet parking.

$ Prices: Lunch entrees $6.80–$12; dinner entrees $15–$23, pasta $12. AE, CB, DC, MC, V.

Open: Lunch Tues–Fri 11am–2pm; dinner Tues–Sat 5–11pm.

Quickly closing in on the two restaurants listed above in the fierce battle of best Italian eatery, this relative newcomer is more youthful in clientele and decor. Its dining room is small, intimate, chic, and comfortable, with crisp white tablecloths and fresh flowers on every table. The staff is friendly and efficient, and the customers tend to be regulars. You might wish to come for lunch, when you can choose a half order of pasta and have it as an entree or opt for one of the many veal dishes. For dinner, too, the pasta is not to be missed, and you can order it as a main dish or as a side dish. Fresh fish, veal piccata, an intriguing selection of chicken dishes, rack of lamb, and steaks round out the menu. Jackets are required for men.

INEXPENSIVE

CUNETTO HOUSE OF PASTA, 5453 Magnolia. Tel. 781-1135.

Cuisine: ITALIAN

$ Prices: Lunch $5–$9; dinner $7–$12. AE, DC, MC, V.

Open: Lunch Mon–Fri 11am–2pm; dinner Mon–Thurs 5–10:30pm, Fri and Sat 5–11:30pm.

✪ Ⓢ This family-style restaurant has been immensely popular for more than 15 years, in part because of its great prices but mostly because of its great Italian food. In fact, this place is so popular that you're guaranteed a wait—no reservations are accepted for dinner. No matter, head for the bar. The food is worth the wait, with more than two dozen selections of pasta alone. The dinner menu is more extensive and includes no-cholesterol, low-salt pasta, sirloin steaks, fish, veal, and chicken selections.

LOU BOCCARDI'S, 5424 Magnolia. Tel. 647-1151.

Cuisine: ITALIAN
$ Prices: Lunch $4–$7; dinner $5.25–$12. MC, V.
Open: Mon–Thurs 11am–12:30am, Fri and Sat 11am–1:30am.

Ⓢ This is a very unpretentious neighborhood restaurant that has changed little since it opened in 1972. Occupying three levels of an old house, with hand-painted murals on some of the walls, Boccardi's is best known for its thin-crust pizza, great if you prefer to fill up on topping rather than crust. In fact, people get so hooked on the pizza that some have ordered it delivered by Federal Express after they've left town. In addition to pizza, it also serves pasta, sandwiches, fish, steaks, veal, and chicken dishes.

RIGAZZI'S, 4945 Daggett Ave. Tel. 772-4900.

Cuisine: ITALIAN
$ Prices: Lunch buffet $3.95; dinner entrees $6–$12. AE, MC, V.
Open: Mon–Thurs 7am–11:30pm, Fri and Sat 7am–12:30am.

✪ Ⓢ Another neighborhood tradition for more than 30 years, Rigazzi's is an informal family-style restaurant located in a simple brick building. Its red-and-white-vinyl tablecloths are often lined elbow-to-elbow with an enthusiastic dining public, who come for the lunch buffet or the dinner pasta specials. There are also sandwiches, burgers, meat dishes, pizza, and seafood. You won't want to pass up the specialty, the so-called "fishbowls" of beer, a full 32 ounces of the brew. No wonder everyone here looks so enthusiastic.

BUDGET

AMIGHETTI BAKERY, 5141 Wilson. Tel. 776-2855.

Cuisine: ITALIAN
$ Prices: $4–$6. No credit cards accepted.
Open: Tues–Thurs 9am–8pm, Fri 9am–8:30pm, Sat 7:30am–5:30pm. **Closed:** Sun, Mon, and holidays.

Ⓢ Located in the heart of the Hill district, on the corner of Wilson and Marconi avenues across from the St. Ambrose Catholic Church, this establishment first opened as a bakery in 1921 and still uses traditional ovens to bake its great breads. A St. Louis tradition, Amighetti's is presided over by Mrs. Amighetti herself, called Mrs. A by people who know her. She specializes in mouthwatering sandwiches, the best known of which is the Amighetti Special, made with ham, beef, salami, Swiss cheese, lettuce, tomato, pickle, onion, pepperoncini pepper, and Mrs. A's special dressing. There's also pizza, pasta, salads, and homemade gelato. Mrs. A has branches at 101 N. Broadway (tel. 241-3700) and at 1010 Market (tel. 241-8555), both downtown, and at 8000 Carondelet in Clayton (tel. 725-8081).

O'CONNELL'S PUB, Kingshighway and Shaw. Tel. 773-6600.
Cuisine: BURGERS
$ **Prices:** $2.50–$5. AE, MC, V.
Open: Mon–Sat 11:15am–midnight.

Popular and unanimous consensus names O'Connell's as having the best burgers in town. A simple pub with wooden floor, pressed tin ceiling, and wooden tables, it also serves sandwiches filled with roast beef, Italian sausage, ham, salami, and other fillings, and on tap there's Guinness and Watney's. If this place is too far to go for a burger, there's an O'Connell's concession on the fourth floor of the St. Louis Centre downtown.

4. CENTRAL WEST END & FOREST PARK

These restaurants, many of them inexpensive and catering to a young, upwardly mobile crowd, are convenient if you're window-shopping in the Central West End or visiting the many attractions in Forest Park.

MODERATE

CAFÉ BALABAN, 405 N. Euclid Ave. Tel. 361-8085.
Cuisine: FRENCH/CONTINENTAL **Reservations:** Accepted until 7pm.
$ **Prices:** Café entrees $5.75–$17; dining hall entrees $18–$24. AE, MC, V.
Café open: Lunch Mon–Fri 11am–3pm, Sat 8am–11am, Sun 10:30am–3pm; café dinner Mon–Thurs 6–11:30pm, Fri and Sat 5:30–11:30pm, Sun 5–10:30pm. **Dining hall open:** Mon–Thurs 6–10:40pm, Fri and Sat 5:30–11:15pm.

Open since the early 1970s, this café/restaurant sets the pace for the Central West End, serving gourmet food to a discerning clientele. It's actually two restaurants in one, each with its own menu and atmosphere. The café, with a bistrolike feel to it, extends along the front of the building, with windows overlooking the sidewalk, and serves inexpensive food in a casual setting. Lunch includes pasta, roasted pepper and pesto pizza, hamburgers, chicken curry, and fresh Missouri trout, while dinner adds a few more items, such as steak.

The dining hall, on the other hand, is open only for dinner and is a lot more artsy, with brick walls, a wooden floor, and a more innovative menu. Fresh seafood is the restaurant's forté—from seared yellowfin tuna with citrus beurre blanc and kumquats to Mussels from Maine. Beef Wellington with a golden raisin sauce has been popular for years, and there are also sweetbreads with shiitake mushrooms and sauvignon blanc sauce, half roast duckling with wild rice and bing-cherry sauce, and grilled tournedos of beef. All in all, Café Balaban is a fun, laid-back, and eclectic place. A separate bar is open throughout the day and night.

Al Baker's ●1
Amighetti Bakery ◆2
An American Brasserie ◆3
Bar Italia ◆4
Blueberry Hill ◆5
Burrito Brothers ◆5
Busch's Grove ◆6
Café Balaban ◆4
Cardwell's ●1
Culpeppers ◆4
Cunetto House of Pasta ◆2
Dominic's ◆2
Duff's ◆4
Empanadas ◆4
Fio's La Fourchette ◆1
Gian-Peppe's ◆2
Giovanni's ◆2
L'Auberge Bretonne ◆1
Lou Boccardi's ◆2
Museum Café ◆7
Nantucket Cove ◆8
O'Connell's Pub ◆2
Pasta House Company ◆4
Redel's ◆9
Rigazzi's ◆2
Sunshine Inn ◆4

NANTUCKET COVE, 40 N. Kingshighway Blvd. (enter on West Pine). Tel. 361-0625.
Cuisine: SEAFOOD. **Reservations:** Recommended. Valet parking.
$ Prices: Appetizers $5–$7; entrees $12–$27. AE, CB, DC, MC, V.
Open: Mon–Sat 5:30–10pm. **Closed:** Sun and holidays.
Yes, you can have fresh seafood even in the Midwest, thanks to air

travel. Nantucket Cove has been serving what many St. Louisans consider to be the best seafood in the city for more than 30 years, so it must be doing something right. It's decorated to resemble what you might find on the New England coast—rustic with wooden walls and ceiling, galley lamps, boat fixtures, and antiques collected from the days when Nantucket Island was the whaling center of the world. Fresh lobster, flown in daily from Maine and kept alive in a tank until you choose the one you want, is a specialty, but there's also blackened redfish, charcoal-broiled fresh fish, fried catfish, shrimp stuffed with crab legs, scallops, and Alaskan king crab legs. For landlubbers there's steak. There are also an extensive white wine list and a bar where you can wait for your table or enjoy happy hour specials on oysters. Nantucket Cove is located just off Kingshighway Boulevard on West Pine, northeast of Forest Park.

INEXPENSIVE

AN AMERICAN BRASSERIE, 255 Union at Lindell. Tel. 361-2220.
   Cuisine: AMERICAN/FRENCH
$ **Prices:** $5–$11. AE, DC, MC, V.
   Open: Tues–Thurs 11am–11:30pm, Fri 11am–midnight, Sat noon–midnight, Sun 5–11pm.
   Located just north of Forest Park, An American Brasserie is a welcome newcomer to the St. Louis dining scene, housed in a historic former hotel. The cozy bar retains its original walnut panels, and since no reservations are accepted for groups of fewer than 10, you'll probably have a drink here first, where you'll be serenaded by live jazz Wednesday through Saturday evening. The dining hall has been completely redesigned—with a stained-glass ceiling that was once in a church, pillars of bright green and white, and potted palms. Also, there are tables on the outdoor patio. The food, French and American cuisine spiced with Italian influences, matches the breezy and somewhat eclectic decor. The menu, identical for lunch and dinner, changes every few days but usually includes a few choices of pasta, sandwiches, quiche, and such interesting entrees as pork chop with caramelized onions, grilled Merguez sausages in couscous, and orange roughy with peppercorn sauce. Good food at inexpensive prices.

BAR ITALIA, 4656 Maryland Ave. Tel. 361-7010.
   Cuisine: ITALIAN
$ **Prices:** Appetizers $5–$7; entrees $9.50–$16.50. AE, CB, DC, DISC, MC, V.
   Open: Tues–Thurs 11:30am–9:30pm (last order), Fri and Sat 11:30am–10pm, Sun 10am–9pm.
The Bar Italia originally opened as a sidewalk café for espresso, gelato, vino, and desserts, but it now serves authentic and nouvelle Italian cuisine. Resembling a European café with outdoor seating and a glass-enclosed front room, it offers such entrees as tortellini; seafood linguine; pasta with a sauce of eggplant, tomato, olives, and capers and topped with ricotta cheese; chicken breast poached with vegetables and wine and served with parsley, walnut, garlic, and olive oil; and veal stuffed with herbs, garlic, cheese, and pine nuts and sauced with puréed bell pepper coulis. Leave room for the home-made gelato, richer and denser than American ice cream but lower in butter fat and sugar, of which there are a dozen different kinds. There are also tempting pastries and coffees.

DUFF'S, 392 N. Euclid Ave. Tel. 361-0522.
   Cuisine: CONTINENTAL
$ **Prices:** Lunch $5.25–$7.50; dinner entrees $12–$16.50. AE, CB, DC, DISC, MC, V.

Open: Lunch Tues–Thurs 11am–4pm, Fri 11am–4pm, Sat 10am–4pm; dinner Tues–Thurs 5:30–10pm, Fri and Sat 5:30pm–midnight; Sun 10am–10:30pm.

Opened in 1972 in a building dating back to 1907, this is a casual, friendly, and earthy place, with an exposed brick wall, wooden floor, and ceiling fans. A venue for once-a-month poetry readings and occasional story readings, Duff's offers an interesting menu that changes with the seasons. A summertime lunch menu, for example, is likely to include light fare such as quiche, pizza, salads, and sandwiches, and a dinner menu may feature raspberry chicken, brandied duck with peaches, ginger lime scallops, and chicken marsala.

EMPANADAS, 32 N. Euclid Ave. Tel. 367-1300.
   Cuisine: INTERNATIONAL
$ Prices: Lunch $3.75–$4.50; dinner $6–$15; Sun brunch $8.25. AE, CB, DC, DISC, MC, V.
   Open: Lunch Mon–Fri 11am–3pm; dinner Mon–Thurs 5–9pm, Fri and Sat 5–10pm; Sun brunch 10:30am–2pm.

This is a funky and very pleasant place, devoted to the empanada but serving a variety of cross-cultural international food as well. One of its rooms features potted ferns and glass doors that open out onto the sidewalk, through which you can watch the world go by. There's also outdoor sidewalk seating. Lunch is served cafeteria-style with selections that change daily, but past items have included Wellington steak, Italian calzone, French poulet Dijonnaise, Greek spanokopita, and a Spanish empanada (beef in a tomato-base sauce, vegetables, olives, and raisins wrapped in a flaky pie crust). Dinner is more formal, featuring table service, dim lighting, and candles on the tables, with a limited menu that may include fresh salmon with dill, barbecue lamb ribs, and sautéed ribeye steak. The food is not only great but also healthy.

MUSEUM CAFÉ, St. Louis Art Museum, Forest Park. Tel. 721-5325.
   Cuisine: CONTINENTAL
$ Prices: Lunch $5.50–$8; dinner entrees $8.50–$9.95; Sun brunch $11.50. AE, MC, V.
   Open: Lunch Tues and Fri 11am–5pm; Wed, Thurs, and Sat 11am–3pm; dinner Tues and Fri 5–8:30pm; Sun brunch 10am–2pm.

If you're in Forest Park visiting all of the wonderful attractions, you can't find a more cheerful place to eat than this restaurant located inside the St. Louis Art Museum. It certainly looks like a museum café, bright and cheery, with a view of the courtyard's artificial waterfall and sculpture. Its menu ranges from the ordinary cheeseburger to more exotic fare, such as turkey and mushroom quesadillas and grilled rainbow trout with pineapple salsa. Dinner is available two nights a week; the great Sunday brunch features a spread varied enough to please the adventuresome and the traditionalist.

REDEL'S, 310 DeBaliviere Ave. Tel. 367-7005.
   Cuisine: AMERICAN
$ Prices: $3.80–$16. AE, MC, V.
   Open: Lunch Mon–Fri 11:30am–2:30pm; dinner Mon–Wed 5:30–11pm, Thurs–Sat 5:30–11:30pm, Sun 5–10pm.

This avant-garde restaurant met with instant success when it opened a few years ago. Its decor is a zany mix of the American Southwest and the classical, with a cactus placed beside a Greek pillar, a changing exhibition of artwork on the walls, and glass bricks. The effect is breezy and very upmarket, and the clientele is young. The menu includes such sandwich standbys as the BLT, club sandwich, and Reuben, but there's also fresh seafood, baby-back ribs, pasta, chicken teriyaki, and very popular pizzas with toppings you can choose yourself. Reservations are accepted only for parties of five or more, but there's a bar where you can wait, and at each table are crayons you can use to draw the evening away.

BUDGET

CULPEPPERS, 300 N. Euclid Ave. Tel. 361-2828.
   Cuisine: BAR FOOD
$ Prices: $4.75–$6.50. AE, MC, V.
   Open: Mon–Sat 11am–midnight (last order), Sun noon–11pm.
This is a simple neighborhood watering hole that may have looked pretty hip at one time but now seems outdated with its brown walls and decor. But it's still a place to be seen—and almost everyone who comes here can't resist the dish Culpeppers is famous for: spicy chicken wings (less than $5 for a pound). Other bar food includes cold shrimp, melts, hamburgers, tuna salad, and sandwiches. No children under 12 allowed.

THE PASTA HOUSE COMPANY, 309 N. Euclid Ave. Tel. 361-7811.
   Cuisine: PASTA
$ Prices: $3.90–$10. AE, DISC, MC, V.
   Open: Sun–Thurs 11am–11pm, Fri and Sat 11am–1am.
This is an enormously successful pasta chain begun in 1974 that now has 25 locations throughout the St. Louis metro area each offering more than two dozen inexpensive pasta dishes. The Central West End location occupies the lobby of a former hotel, with high stucco ceilings, pillars, and green-checked tablecloths. One of the rooms is huge, with windows that overlook Euclid Avenue, and there's also a long, full-service bar. Everything from toasted ravioli and rigatoni to flat noodles with asparagus is offered, as well as a couple selections of pizza and sandwiches; there's also a children's menu and carry-out. The Special Salad can't be beat. Other locations include 6214 S. Lindbergh (tel. 894-9161) in South County and 295 Plaza Frontenac (tel. 569-3040) in Mid-County.

SUNSHINE INN, 8½ Euclid Ave. Tel. 367-1413.
   Cuisine: AMERICAN/VEGETARIAN
$ Prices: Lunch $4–$9; dinner $4.75–$9. AE, CB, DC, DISC, MC, V.
   Open: Tues–Thurs 11am–10pm, Fri 11am–10:30pm, Sat 8am–10:30pm, Sun 10am–2:30pm and 5–9pm.
Opened on Valentine's Day in 1974, this laid-back, simple establishment paved the way for natural foods in St. Louis and has since expanded from vegetarian foods to fish and chicken selections as well. Still, no red meat and no preservatives is Sunshine Inn's motto in the preparation of its wholesome and nutritious dishes. It remains best known for its salads with great house dressings (including a tofu

herb dressing); many of its entrees include salad in either a small or a large portion. Other items include a vegetarian burrito, a vegetarian burger made with soy beans, a mushroom curry pita-pocket sandwich, Szechuan tofu, and grilled salmon steak.

5. UNIVERSITY CITY

Both these restaurants are located on Delmar Boulevard, on a stretch known as The Loop.

BUDGET

BLUEBERRY HILL, 6504 Delmar Blvd. Tel. 727-0880.
Cuisine: BAR FOOD
$ Prices: $3.50–$5.50. AE, DISC, MC, V.
Open: Mon–Sat 11am–midnight (last order), Sun 11am–11pm.

Blueberry Hill rates as a St. Louis attraction and is worth a visit even if you don't eat here. Dedicated to rock-'n'-roll, it's packed with memorabilia relating to Chuck Berry and Elvis, Howdy Doody, Pee Wee Herman, the Beatles, and much more; also, there are seven dart boards. Its juke box, which has a library of more than 30,000 records, has been rated the best in the country. So gaze and listen as you munch on a burger, a sandwich, or soup.

BURRITO BROTHERS, 6600 Delmar Blvd. Tel. 726-2767.
Cuisine: MEXICAN
$ Prices: $2–$4.40. No credit cards accepted.
Open: Sun–Thurs 11am–10pm, Fri and Sat 11am–midnight.

This self-serve fast-food joint is about as casual as you can get. Eat at one of the booths indoors or sit outside and watch the action along The Loop. Burrito Brothers offers tacos, fajitas, quesadillas, enchiladas, tostadas, burritos, and chimichangas—all available with red or green sauce and with vegetarian, pork, roast beef, chicken, steak, or seafood fillings.

6. CLAYTON & MID-COUNTY

EXPENSIVE/MODERATE

All the restaurants here could cost you more than $30 per person for dinner if you go all out. If you're careful, however, and stick to an appetizer and a less expensive entree, you can dine at one of these highly recommended establishments for $20 or $25.

AL BAKER'S, 8101 Clayton Rd. Tel. 863-8878.
Cuisine: ITALIAN/CONTINENTAL **Reservations:** Recommended. Valet parking.
$ Prices: Appetizers $4.50–$7.50; pasta dishes $12–$15; entrees $13–$25. AE, CB, DC, DISC, MC, V.
Open: Mon–Sat 5pm–midnight.

In a world of increasing trendiness where sparse decor is all the rage, Al Baker's remains steadfastly comfortable. Its corridor is lined with photographs of people who have dined here and its dining room is richly decorated in deep red, with flickering sconces along the walls. An institution since 1965, it's still the place to go for a special occasion, with attentive service, many dishes prepared tableside, and live music nightly.

Al Baker's is well known for its pasta dishes, so you may wish to start with one of its dozen offerings. Among its entrees, the Veal Oskar (breaded veal and whole lobster tail garnished with asparagus and topped with a cream sauce), Greek-style rack of lamb, and stuffed tenderloin are outstanding. There's also fresh fish and a low-cholesterol menu kind to your heart (and approved by the Cardiovascular Risk Reduction Center at St. Louis University). Its wine cellar is probably the best in the city, with approximately 20,000 bottles. Jackets are required for men.

CARDWELL'S, 8100 Maryland. Tel. 726-5055.

Cuisine: NEW AMERICAN. **Reservations:** Recommended.

$ Prices: Lunch $8–$12; dinner entrees $12–$24; fixed-price dinners about $16. AE, MC, V.

Open: Mon–Thurs 11:30am–10pm, Fri and Sat 11:30am–11pm.

This upstart restaurant hit it off big in St. Louis and is already considered one of the great establishments in the city. The dining area is cooly comfortable and elegant, with a tiled floor, polished wood ceiling beams, palm trees, and artwork on the walls. French doors open onto an outdoor patio in summer. Because of its prime location in the business district of Clayton, it's a favorite place for a business lunch.

The menu changes often, reflecting what's available and fresh. Thus, homegrown tomatoes offered by a local farmer or perhaps fish from a special delivery from Boston may suddenly appear on the night's menu. Past selections have included a chilled gazpacho with pepper vodka and crispy corn tortilla chips; pan-roasted breast of pheasant prepared with muscat wine, green peppercorn, and fresh peach sauce; and grilled herb-marinated naturally raised chicken with summer-squash salsa, basil butter, and crispy potato straws. On Monday through Thursday there's a fixed-price dinner that includes a salad or soup, an entree, and a dessert. Don't pass up the souffle for dessert.

FIO'S LA FOURCHETTE, 1153 St. Louis Galleria. Tel. 863-6866.

Cuisine: NOUVELLE FRENCH **Reservations:** Recommended.

$ Prices: Appetizers $7–$8; entrees $20–$22; fixed-price dinners $40. AE, DC, MC, V.

Hours: Tues–Sat 6–10pm.

Don't let its location in a mall deter you because the food is fun, avant-garde, and imaginative. The owner/chef, Fio Antognini, isn't afraid to experiment by blending traditional French haute cuisine with international and nouvelle cuisine and adding his own personal touches.

Entrees may include Norwegian salmon stuffed with shiitake mushrooms and fresh herbs, served with grilled peppers and lemon sauce; and grilled medallions of beef tenderloin with a roast garlic sauce. There's also a selection of entrees with reduced fat for those watching calories. But the restaurant is most famous for its six-course fixed-price menu that might include, for example, a free-range veal-and-pistachio pâté on decorated herb sauce, followed by chilled smoked Missouri trout and Louisiana crawfish Napoleon, grilled Hawaiian swordfish, salad, dessert, and coffee or espresso with petits fours.

L'AUBERGE BRETONNE, 200 S. Brentwood. Tel. 721-0100.

    Cuisine: TRADITIONAL FRENCH **Reservations:** Recommended, especially on weekends.

$ **Prices:** Lunch $6.50–$15; dinner entrees $15–$26. AE, CB, DC, MC, V.

    Open: Lunch Mon–Fri 11:30am–3pm; dinner Mon–Sat 5:30–10:30pm.

Formerly located in Frontenac until its recent move to Clayton, L'Auberge Bretonne was St. Louis' pioneer French restaurant and is still highly recommended for its traditional classic cuisine. The service is impeccable and the comfortable dining room is a great place for lunch or dinner because the dark windows screen out harsh sunlight providing a romantic atmosphere even at high noon. The lunch menu is basic, consisting of sandwiches, salads, pasta, burgers, steaks, seafood, and omelets; at dinner traditional French food might include appetizers like snails in garlic butter or angel-hair pasta with scallops and basil, followed by baked boneless breast of duckling with a port wine sauce, tenderloin, rack of lamb, veal with lobster and asparagus, or lobster Wellington.

INEXPENSIVE

BUSCH'S GROVE, 9160 Clayton Rd., Ladue. Tel. 992-0011.

    Cuisine: AMERICAN **Reservations:** Imperative outdoors, recommended indoors. Valet parking.

$ **Prices:** Lunch $6.50–$9.50; dinner entrees $11.50–$20; fixed-price dinners $19. AE, CB, DC, MC, V.

    Open: Tues–Thurs 11am–11pm, Fri and Sat 11am–midnight.

A great place for outdoor dining with its screened cabañas, individual shelters with ceiling fans and table service. It's so popular that reservations sometimes must be made two weeks in advance. The indoor dining hall is not nearly as interesting, but it's often full as well. Located in the community of Ladue on the crossroads of Clayton and Price roads, this place has been a local institution for a hundred years.

    The food is simple American cooking, a bit predictable, and the younger generation will enjoy the children's menu. Lunch offers

---

IMPRESSIONS

I have spent many years out of America, but the Missouri and Mississippi rivers have made a deeper impression on me than any other part of the world.
—T. S. ELIOT, 1948

everything from burgers to lemon-pepper catfish filet, including sandwiches, chicken, seafood, and steak. For dinner there's chicken, veal, beef, and seafood selections. Whatever you choose, include a bowl of the homemade soup and some cottage fries. There's a nightly fixed-price dinner, the most popular being Wednesday's barbecue ribs and Saturday's prime rib.

CAFÉ NAPOLI, 21 S. Bemiston St.

Cuisine: ITALIAN

$ Prices: Lunch $4.50–$7; dinner pasta $8.25, entrees $10.95–$15. AE, MC, V.

Open: Lunch Mon–Fri 11am–2pm; dinner Mon–Thurs 5–10pm, Fri and Sat 5–11pm.

This relatively new Italian restaurant has already gained a loyal following due to its dependably good food at very reasonable prices and its friendly service. Casual and usually crowded, Café Napoli is a small place with tables so close together that diners receive little privacy, especially during lunch, when the room is packed with business people. At dinner the establishment is transformed by white tablecloths, candles, and lots of small white lights on the ceiling that twinkle like distant stars. The menu offers various pasta, chicken, veal, beef, and fish selections; the wines are affordable. You can't go wrong here.

SCHNEITHORST'S HOFAMBERG INN, Lindbergh and Clayton Rds. Tel. 993-5600.

Cuisine: GERMAN

$ Prices: Lunch $5.95–$16.50; dinner entrees $12–$18. AE, CB, DC, MC, V.

Open: Lunch Mon–Sat 11am–4pm; dinner Mon–Thurs 5–10pm, Fri and Sat 5–11pm, Sun 2–8pm; Sun brunch 10am–1:30pm.

Schneithorst's first opened in 1917 and has been in this location since 1957, under the same family management. A huge establishment with four dining rooms and eight private banquet rooms, all decorated to resemble a Bavarian lodge, it boasts the largest beer stein in the world. The "Pig-skin Room," featuring genuine pigskin wallpaper and wood carvings, is the most popular room while the main dining room containing a beer stein collection and booths along one wall is romantic. Most customers, however, are family groups and senior citizens.

Although the menu contains some German specialties, it offers much more than sauerbraten (marinated beef) and wiener schnitzel, including steaks, country fried chicken, pork tenderloin medallions, and catfish. There are also nightly specials, and if it's available, I'd suggest you order the German Sampler—sauerbraten, bratwurst, and beef roulade—along with a side order of crisp potato pancakes. The wine list is extensive Schneithorst's 60-item Sunday brunch, is enormously popular ($10.95 for adults and $5.95 for children).

BUDGET

YEN CHING, 1012 S. Brentwood Blvd. Tel. 721-7507.

Cuisine: CHINESE

$ Prices: Lunch $4.50; dinner entrees $6.50–$9. AE, DC, MC, V.

Open: Lunch 11:30am–2pm; dinner Mon–Thurs 5–9:30pm, Fri and Sat 5–10:30pm, Sun 4:30–9pm.

Located across from the Saint Louis Galleria and in operation since the early 1970s, this Chinese restaurant specializes in Peking and Szechuan food. Considered by many to be the best Chinese restaurant in the city, its decor is restrained, with only its red tablecloths, Chinese lanterns, and a bit of Chinese artwork to give it away. At lunch a dozen selections include spicy-hot chicken wings, broccoli beef, and a vegetable combo, all of which come with hot-and-sour soup, an egg roll, fried rice, and tea. Dinner is much more extensive, with more than 60 entrees of pork, poultry, beef, seafood, and vegetables. Recommended dishes include the twice-cooked pork braised with vegetables and hot peppers, the snow-white breasts of chicken cooked with mushrooms and peas, the Peking duck ($20.75—order in advance), sliced beef marinated in garlic sauce, and deep-fried prawns.

7. IN & AROUND SOULARD

These restaurants are convenient if you're visiting the Soulard Market, the Anheuser-Busch Brewery, Antique Row, and other sights in Soulard south of downtown.

INEXPENSIVE

PARK AVENUE CAFÉ, 1923 Park Ave. Tel. 241-9122.
Cuisine: CONTINENTAL/NEW AMERICAN
$ Prices: Lunch $7–$9.50; dinner entrees $14–$19. CB, DC, DISC, MC, V.
Open: Lunch Mon–Sat 11am–2:30pm; dinner Wed–Sat 6–11pm.

Located across the street from Lafayette Park, this is a very fashionable and chic café, with a polished wooden floor, white tablecloths, fresh flowers, modern lighting, and a black bar with black stools. Park Avenue's white walls serve as an art gallery. Lunch features such salads and sandwiches as a cashew chicken salad, an American crab sandwich on English muffins with tomato sauce, and a broiled chicken sandwich on French bread with brie. For dinner there are approximately 10 entree choices, which may include sesame chicken, sea scallops grilled with pineapple and papaya in a ginger sauce, and lamb chops with rosemary in a brandy-mint sauce.

PATTY LONG CAFÉ, 1931 Park Ave. Tel. 621-9598.
Cuisine: AMERICAN/CONTINENTAL
$ Prices: Lunch $7–$8.30; dinner $13.20–$19. AE, DC, DISC, MC, V.
Open: Lunch Mon–Sat 11:30am–2pm; dinner Fri and Sat 6–10pm; Sun brunch 10am–2pm.

Located next to the Park Avenue Café (above), this establishment is more earth-bound than the Park Avenue, with exposed-brick walls and daily specials written on a chalkboard—but it's still classier than the usual café due to the artwork on the walls and the white tablecloths and flowers. The lunch menu may include curry chicken salad, quiche, rainbow trout, smoked-turkey sandwich, and grilled salmon. Dinner entrees, most served with a salad, seasonal vegetables, and rice or potato, change often and range from fresh seafood to a vegetable cannelloni.

BUDGET

DE MENIL MANSION RESTAURANT, 3352 De Menil Place. Tel. 771-5829.
  Cuisine: AMERICAN
$ **Prices:** $6–$8. AE, MC, V.
  Open: Tues–Sat 11am–2pm.
Located in the former carriage house of a stately mansion now restored and open to the public, this is a very pleasant place for lunch. If the weather's fine, you'll want to dine outside in the garden. The lunch fare, primarily salads and sandwiches, is light and healthy. There's the California Sunshine whole-wheat sandwich with avocado, bacon (well, maybe not so healthy, but bacon is that food you hate to love), American cheese, tomato, and alfalfa sprouts; bratwurst on rye bread; and a vegetable garden salad. There are also a wide selection of desserts, including cheesecakes and such alcoholic concoctions as strawberry-mint lemonade and chocolate-almond cream, the latter made with Amaretto, Irish Cream, and hot chocolate (perfect for winter).

NORTON'S CAFÉ, 808 Geyer. Tel. 436-0828.
  Cuisine: AMERICAN
$ **Prices:** $4–$10. CB, DC, MC, V.
  Open: Mon–Thurs 11am–11pm, Fri and Sat 11am–midnight.
A casual café in the heart of Soulard's nightlife district, housed in an ivy-covered brick building dating from the mid-1800s, it's popular for its hearty portions of Irish- and Cajun-inspired food. Norton's has sandwiches served with Irish potatoes and also a changing menu that may include blackened shark, raspberry chicken, steak, and pasta. The desserts are a must, especially the cheesecakes.

8. SPECIALTY DINING

HOTEL DINING

The restaurants listed here represent the best of St. Louis' hotel dining, with correspondingly high prices. Jackets usually are required for men, as are reservations.

DOWNTOWN

FAUST'S, Adam's Mark Hotel, Fourth and Chestnut. Tel. 241-7400.
  Cuisine: AMERICAN/CONTINENTAL **Reservations:** Recommended for lunch, imperative for dinner. Free valet parking evenings.
$ **Prices:** Lunch $7.50–$15; dinner entrees $17–$24. AE, CB, DC, DISC, MC, V.
  Open: Lunch Mon–Fri 11:30am–2pm; dinner Sun–Thurs 5:30–10pm, Fri and Sat 5:30–10:30pm.
The signature restaurant of this premier hotel, it's decorated like a

European baron's castle, with stone walls, wooden beams, and chandeliers. Rustic and elegant at the same time, it adjoins Pierre's Lounge, where you can relax with a cocktail before or after dinner and listen to piano music. A few tables have a view of the Arch but you should request one when making your reservation.

The creative menu changes often to reflect what's in season. For lunch you might start with bow-tie pasta au gratin with three cheeses and a vodka sauce, followed by Norwegian salmon grilled with fresh thyme and ground lemon pepper. For dinner you might opt for an appetizer of smoked Missouri ham with an assortment of fruit or ragout of wild hare; for the main course you may choose pheasant and venison seared with a rosemary, juniper, and game glaze or jumbo shrimp and abalone. Suits and ties are required for men.

RICHARD PERRY RESTAURANT, Hotel Majestic, 1019 Pine St. Tel. 436-2355.

    Cuisine: AMERICAN **Reservations:** Strongly recommended.

$ **Prices:** Lunch $6–$10; dinner entrees $15–$23; fixed-price dinner $38. AE, CB, DC, DC, MC, V.

    Open: Lunch Mon–Fri 11am–2:30pm; dinner Sun–Thurs 5:30–10pm, Fri and Sat 5:30–11pm.

This restaurant, which resembles a bistro with its large windows, plushly cushioned booths, palm tree, and tall ceilings, occupies the original lobby of the Hotel Majestic. Under the direction of Richard Perry, it serves meals that celebrate its Midwestern heritage by using local specialties in creative new ways. Past menus have included crabcakes coated in a Midwestern-style breading, black Angus sirloin steak, and veal chop T-bone. There's also plenty of seafood. But what makes this restaurant especially interesting is its Taster's Menu (about $38 per person), which gives diners small portions of several items from the current menu, including a sampling of four desserts. Absolutely sinful.

UNION STATION

DAVID SLAY'S LA VERANDA, Drury Inn Union Station, 201 S. 20th St. Tel. 231-3900.

    Cuisine: NEW AMERICAN/ITALIAN **Reservations:** Recommended.

$ **Prices:** Pizza from $8.50; pasta $14–$16; entrees $14.75–$26. AE, MC, V.

    Open: Mon–Thurs 5–10pm, Fri and Sat 5–11pm.

A success story if there ever was one, although with David Slay's talent there's no luck involved. He started by offering pizza and pasta as carry-out while he was still too young to apply for a liquor license, and then he expanded into a tiny hole-in-the-wall with only 12 tables. His present restaurant belies its humble beginnings, chic and dignified and very New York in style and appearance. Unfortunately for St. Louis, David Slay is opening a new restaurant in Los Angeles but he promises it won't affect La Veranda.

Slay's success lies in his nouvelle Italian-American cuisine. His pizza and pasta are still as good as ever, and highly recommended are the pizza of smoked salmon and cream cheese with sliced tomato and red onion and penne rigati with lobster and seafood and a spiced cream sauce. Entrees range from grilled sea scallops atop a light roasted-garlic zabaglione to calves' liver with caramelized onions, prosciutto ham, and mushrooms in a sweet marsala sauce. The pastry is out of this world.

STATION GRILLE, Hyatt Regency St. Louis, Union Station at 18th and Market Sts. Tel. 231-1234.
　　Cuisine: STEAKS/SEAFOOD **Reservations:** Recommended.
$ Prices: Appetizers $6.25–$7.50; entrees $18–$30. AE, CB, DC, DISC, MC, V.
　　Open: Mon–Thurs 5:30–10:30pm, Fri and Sat 5:30–11pm.
Housed in Union Station's original oak-paneled dining hall, once occupied by the famous Fred Harvey restaurant, this is the Hyatt Regency's signature restaurant. It's an elegant place to dine and still reminiscent of the railroad era with art deco motifs, brass, lots of warm woods, an open copper grill, plants, and white tablecloths. The waiters and waitresses wear crisp black-and-white uniforms, much like they did back in the 1890s when the Station first opened.

　　Dinner at the Station Grille could begin with a selection from its raw bar, including cherrystone clams, Chesapeake Bay oysters, mussels, shrimp, and Alaskan king crab—all flown in daily. Other appetizers include blackened carpaccio and wild boar sausage. Entrees are mainly seafood and steaks, as well as such dishes as veal chop with roasted pepper and sweet garlic sauce, Long Island duck, and spit-roasted chicken.

CLAYTON

CHEZ LOUIS, Seven Gables Inn, 26 N. Meramec. Tel. 863-8400.
　　Cuisine: FRENCH **Reservations:** Recommended.
$ Prices: Lunch $6.50–$11; dinner entrees $15.50–$27. AE, CB, DC, DISC, MC, V.
　　Open: Lunch Mon–Fri 11am–2pm; dinner Mon–Sat 5–10pm.
This place looks so French that you almost expect a "Bonjour" when you walk through the door—there are white curtains that cover only the bottom half of the window, crisp linen tablecloths, artwork on the walls, and fresh flowers. But even better is the fact that the food lives up to the restaurant's image. *The New York Times* once named Chez Louis one of the best hotel restaurants in the country.

　　The food is classic French, beautifully presented, with an eye on current trends emphasizing health without sacrificing taste. The lunch menu changes daily but always includes a large selection of salads, a crêpe du jour, egg dishes, and fish. Listed alongside the entrees are recommended wines that best complement the food. For dinner, you might start with frog's legs cooked with butter, garlic, and lemon or perhaps escargots in a rich garlic cream sauce with puff pastry. For the main course, choose from medallions of veal with morels, rack of lamb with a hazelnut-and-rosemary gratin, or grilled snapper or duck breasts in a hoisin sauce with raisins.

THE RESTAURANT, The Ritz-Carlton, 100 Carondelet Plaza. Tel. 863-6300.
　　Cuisine: AMERICAN/CONTINENTAL **Reservations:** Recommended.
$ Prices: Lunch $8.25–$20; dinner entrees $18–$35. AE, CB, DC, DISC, MC, V.
　　Open: Lunch Mon–Sat 11:30am–2:30pm; dinner 6–11pm daily.
The Restaurant is everything you'd expect from the Ritz-Carlton's

best dining hall: richly enameled walls adorned with 18th- and 19th-century art, a crystal chandelier, fantastic flower arrangements, and food served under silver domes on scalloped Hutschenreuther china. Even lunch is an experience in luxury: you can begin with the sautéed soft-shell crab appetizer or the Missouri corn chowder and proceed to such entrees as blackened swordfish, veal rib-eye steak, or chicken breast filled with leek, prosciutto, spinach, and grain mustard sauce. Dinner is even more elaborate, with such appetizers as Beluga caviar; smoked lamb loin, artichoke, and feta cheese in a peppered garlic vinaigrette; and baked rabbit loin with spinach and a mushroom-mustard glaze and cardamom sauce. The dinner selection offers such specialties as sautéed Dover sole with crabmeat; Maine lobster with black pepper and basil fettucini in rosemary sauce; broiled prime New York strip with red wine and truffles; and roasted milk-fed lamb loin with caraway ratatouille and pinot noir sauce. For the health-conscious, there are dishes offered for lunch and dinner that are low in fat, cholesterol, sodium, and calories—in accordance with guidelines set by the American Heart Association.

DINING WITH A VIEW

TOP OF THE RIVERFRONT, Clarion Hotel, 200 South 4th St. Tel. 241-9500.

   Cuisine: AMERICAN **Reservations:** Recommended.

$ Prices: Lunch $4–$10, fixed-price lunches $8.50; dinner entrees $14–$23; Sun brunch $12.95. AE, DC, DISC, MC, V.

   Open: Lunch Mon–Fri 11am–2pm; dinner daily 5–11pm; Sun brunch 9am–2pm.

Although this hotel restaurant doesn't measure up to the quality of those listed above, it does have something the others don't—a bird's eye view of the Arch. St. Louis' only revolving restaurant, it's located downtown and makes a complete turn every hour. There's piano music Tuesday through Saturday evening. Besides salads and sandwiches, lunch offers such entrees as fresh fish; crab, shrimp, and avocado quiche; and St. Louis Bake, which is smoked breast of turkey with broccoli and mushrooms served on a croissant with sharp Cheddar-cheese sauce. There are also set-price lunches for about $8.50. Dinner is a lot fancier, with a menu that offers such main courses as a St. Louis pepper steak, roast duck, scampi and linguini, and grilled swordfish.

COOL FOR KIDS

There's more to pasta than spaghetti, and you cannot find a better place than St. Louis to introduce your kids to the wonders of Italian cuisine. The city has a great many casual Italian restaurants that cater to children either with special children's dishes or with such low prices that the whole family can afford to dine out. Family restaurants specializing in pizza and pasta dishes include **Caleco's** and **The Old Spaghetti Factory** downtown, while the Italian district of the Hill is home to **Cunetto House of Pasta, Lou Boccardi's, Rigazzi's,** and **Amighetti Bakery.** In the Central West End there's the **Pasta House Company.**

   Children would also love the drama of dining on a riverboat, so head down to the Mississippi near the Arch for the **Lt. Robert E. Lee,** which offers sandwiches and salads for lunch and a Sunday brunch. If your children insist on a hamburger, there's even a

McDonald's and Burger King next to the Lt. Robert E. Lee, both occupying riverboats. Finally, there's room to move about at **Busch's Grove,** where there are screened cabañas for outdoor dining.

For more information on each of these listings, refer to the individual descriptions above and below and to the "Frommer's Cool for Kids" box earlier in this chapter.

LIGHT, CASUAL, AND FAST FOOD

MCDONALD'S, 322 South Leonor K. Sullivan Blvd. Tel. 231-8895.
   Cuisine: HAMBURGERS
$ Prices: 60¢–$2.25. No credit cards accepted.
   Open: Sun–Thurs 7am–midnight; Fri and Sat 7am–1am.
Fast-food chains are not what guide books are all about, but you won't find a McDonald's more unusual than this one—a riverboat on the Mississippi under the shadow of the Arch. There are even tables outside so you can enjoy the view. Nearby are other riverboats for Burger King and Tombstone Pizza.

TED DREWES, 6726 Chippewa St. Tel. 481-2652.
   Cuisine: FROZEN CUSTARD
$ Prices: $1.25–$2.60. No credit cards accepted.
   Open: Daily 11am–midnight.
A St. Louis tradition! When evening comes, the crowds start lining up at the windows of this roadside parlor specializing in frozen custard. Begun by the present owner's father 60 years ago with a small cart on Chippewa, Ted Drewes now packs them in with its dips (called Concretes), shakes, malts, sundaes, and sodas in flavors ranging from chocolate chip and strawberry to Heath Bar and Oreo. For many fans, it's the perfect way to complete a night on the town. There's a second stand set up during summer only at 4224 S. Grand (tel. 352-7376), but most people patronize the crowded Chippewa location just for the experience in camaraderie.

SUNDAY BRUNCH

All the hotels in the expensive and moderate ranges have restaurants that serve breakfast. A standout is the **Pullman's Country Breakfast** served in the Grand Hall Lounge of the Hyatt Regency in Union Station every Sunday from 9am to 2pm. For $8.95 per person, diners can feast on various dishes in the incredibly ornate former waiting hall of this St. Louis landmark. Another great view, this one outdoors, is afforded by **Top of the Riverfront,** a revolving restaurant atop the Clarion Hotel downtown. Sunday brunch here, served from 9am to 2pm, costs $12.95. And if money is no object, dine in sinful luxury at the Ritz-Carlton's **The Restaurant** on Sunday between 6:30am and 2:30pm—$22 for adults and $12 for children.

Another personal favorite is the Sunday brunch aboard the **Lt. Robert E. Lee,** moored downtown on the Mississippi, which offers a lineup of breakfast goodies from 10am to 2pm—$10.95 for adults and $4.95 for children—all to the accompaniment of live jazz. **The Museum Café,** located in the St. Louis Museum of Art, is a bright and airy venue for Sunday brunch served from 10am to 2pm, where $11.50 gives you breakfast and lunch items and a view of an artificial waterfall. **Schneithorst's,** a German restaurant in Clayton, was the first in town to offer Sunday brunch and still does so from 10am to 1:30pm, when approximately 60 items are offered—$10.95 for adults and $5.95 for children. Finally, **Café Balaban,** located in the Central West End, is a great place to rub elbows with the natives and dine on anything from smoked trout with dill sauce or cheese blintzes to eggs Benedict. Prices for individual dishes here range from about $5 to $7. Hours are Sunday from 10:30am to 3pm.

For more information on the locations and addresses of these establishments, refer to the individual listings earlier in this chapter.

AFTERNOON TEA

This English tradition is carried on in St. Louis at two of its most impressive hotels, the Adam's Mark Hotel and the Ritz-Carlton. At the **Adam's Mark,** located downtown across from the Arch, tea is served in the lobby lounge's Tiffany Rose on Monday through Saturday from 2 to 5pm; this tea features pastries and desserts for $2.50 to $8.95, along with music provided by a jazz trio and a pianist.

It would be difficult to find a fancier setting than the **Ritz-Carlton's** Lobby Lounge for afternoon tea, served daily from 2:30 to 5pm and costing $10.50. Included in the price are delicate sandwiches, crumpets, scones, chocolates, and strawberries with Devonshire cream served on Wedgwood china—all to the strains of classical music.

PICNIC FARE AND WHERE TO EAT IT

LAFAYETTE GOURMET, 1915 Park Ave. Tel. 436-7177.
   Open: Mon–Sat 10am–6pm.
Located across from Lafayette Park not far from the historic Soulard district, this combination shop/café specializes in gourmet carry-out and box lunches, including sandwiches, salads, cheeses, breads, and wines. Because tables are set up in a patio out back and the big Lafayette Park is across the street, you don't have far to go to consume your goodies.

KOPPERMAN'S, 386 N. Euclid Ave., Central West End. Tel. 361-0100.
   Open: Sun–Thurs 7:30am–9pm, Fri and Sat 7:30am–10pm.
This grocer's has been serving the surrounding Central West End neighborhood since 1897 and is well stocked with breads, rolls, cheeses, salads, vegetables, fruit, wines, and spirits. Half the store serves as a casual cafeteria, where such items as homemade chili, hickory-smoked chicken wings, baby-back ribs, sandwiches, seafood, and desserts are offered for takeout or for immediate consumption at the indoor or sidewalk tables. Box lunches also are available.

ST. LOUIS BREAD COMPANY, 4651 Maryland Ave., Central West End. Tel. 367-7636.
   Open: Mon–Thurs 6:30am–10pm, Fri and Sat 6:30am–11pm, Sun 7:30am–6pm.
The place to go for breads, this clean and bright place sells everything from French loafs to sourdough, rye, cinnamon raisin, pumpernickel, and more. It also offers approximately a dozen versions of the muffin, as well as a variety of sandwiches. You can carry-out or eat your purchases here at the tables. There's another convenient location in University City on The Loop at 6309 Delmar Blvd. (tel. 726-6644).

SOULARD MARKET, bounded by 9th, 7th, Carroll, and Lafayette Sts.
Open: Wed–Sat 6am–4pm.

Saturday is the big day for St. Louis' city market, with stalls selling fruit, vegetables, meat, eggs, fish, deli meats, and even live chickens. Pick up your basics here or wander through for the atmosphere.

The best place to eat your purchases is the biggest park in town: Forest Park, less than a 10-minute drive west of downtown. There are acres here to spread a blanket and relax, and after eating you can visit such cultural attractions as the St. Louis Art Museum and the zoo. Other parks worth a picnic are Lafayette Park near Soulard and Laumeier Sculpture Park on Geyer and Rott roads, which features a sculpture garden. Of course, you can simply sit down beside the Mississippi at the Jefferson National Expansion Memorial Park and watch the river float by.

CHAPTER 7

WHAT TO SEE & DO IN ST. LOUIS

1. **THE TOP ATTRACTIONS**
2. **MORE ATTRACTIONS**
3. **COOL FOR KIDS**
4. **ORGANIZED TOURS**
5. **SPORTS & RECREATION**

One of the great things about St. Louis is that it offers such a wide range of things to see and do. You can go up the Arch, shop at Union Station, stroll through one of the nation's best botanical gardens, visit the zoo, sample beer at a brewery, watch the Cardinals at Busch Stadium, and much, much more. Many of its attractions are absolutely free, making St. Louis a perfect destination for a family vacation.

SUGGESTED ITINERARIES

To help you get the most out of your visit, here are some suggested itineraries to guide you to the most important attractions.

IF YOU HAVE ONE DAY

Get up early in the morning and head straight for the Gateway Arch, the Midwest's most well known landmark, which symbolizes the expansion of America to the West. Since the tram to the top of the Arch is sometimes so packed that there's a two- or three-hour wait in summer and on the weekend, buying your tram ticket should be your first priority. Then you can stroll through the Museum of Westward Expansion and watch the 35-minute *Monument to the Dream,* a film about the construction of the Arch. If time permits, visit the nearby Old Courthouse, with a museum tracing the history of St. Louis.

For lunch, you might wish to dine at Top of the Riverfront, a revolving restaurant with a bird's-eye view of the Arch, or on the Lt. Robert E. Lee, a riverboat moored on the Mississippi. Spend the afternoon at the Missouri Botanical Garden, the oldest botanical garden in the United States, or at the St. Louis Art Museum, ranked as one of the top art museums in the country. If you have children in tow, you may wish instead to go to the St. Louis Zoo or to Grant's Farm, which includes a small-game preserve, a zoo, and a ride on a trackless train in its tour.

By late afternoon, you should make your way to Union Station. Built in the 1890s and once the largest and busiest passenger terminal in the world, it now houses a wonderland of shops, restaurants, bars, and other diversions. Eat dinner at Union Station or go to the Hill, St. Louis' Italian district, for some of the best Italian food in

? DID YOU KNOW . . . ?

- The 1904 St. Louis World's Fair offered a number of firsts, including the first hot dog, the first ice-cream cone, and the first iced tea.
- The first Olympics held in the United States was in St. Louis in 1904.
- The St. Louis Cardinals have won the World Series nine times, more than any other National League team.
- The Gateway Arch, the nation's tallest monument at 630 feet, is as wide as it is tall.
- In 1895, when there were only four gasoline-powered vehicles in all of the United States, two of them collided in St. Louis.
- St. Louis is the home of the nation's second-oldest orchestra and the first university founded west of the Mississippi River.

the country. For evening entertainment, take a stroll through Laclede's Landing, a 19th-century warehouse district just north of the Arch that now serves as one of the city's top nightlife spots.

IF YOU HAVE TWO DAYS

Day 1 Spend the morning at the Gateway Arch as outlined above, adding Busch Stadium with its Sports Hall of Fame, the Old Courthouse, the Eugene Field House and Toy Museum, or perhaps the St. Louis Centre shopping mall to your itinerary. After lunch, head south to the Anheuser-Busch Brewery, where you can tour one of the world's largest brewers and sample its products. Afterward, visit the historic De Menil Mansion (you may wish to come here first to eat lunch in its carriage house) and then stroll down nearby Cherokee Street with its many antique shops.

By late afternoon, head for Union Station as described above. Stay for dinner or head straight for Laclede's Landing for dining, music, and entertainment.

Day 2 You may wish to start the morning at the Missouri Botanical Garden, especially if it's summer and the weather is hot. Afterward, head directly north for the Central West End, a fashionable neighborhood of shops, galleries, restaurants, and cafés. Stop here for lunch. After you feel replenished, go to the St. Louis Art Museum for a look at one of the country's great collections. In the evening, attend the theater or a musical production at one of the many venues outlined in Chapter 10.

IF YOU HAVE THREE DAYS

Days 1 and 2 Follow the itinerary outlined above.

Day 3 Pursue your own special interests: a trip to the St. Louis Zoo; the Laumeier Sculpture Park; one of the city's historic homes now open to the public; or an offbeat museum, such as the Dog Museum or the National Bowling Hall of Fame. If you have children, there are many other options also available—including the Magic House, with its hands-on approach in explaining wonders of the world; the St. Louis Science Center, with its workshops for kids; and Grants Farm, with its animals and a cabin built by Ulysses S. Grant. In addition, Six Flags Over Mid-America, located about 30 miles southwest of St. Louis, is an enormous theme park with roller coasters and other amusement rides. Enjoy the evening at one of the popular live-music spots in historic Soulard.

IF YOU HAVE FIVE DAYS OR MORE

Days 1 through 3 Follow the itinerary outlined above.

Day 4 Head farther afield. Hermann, Missouri, for example, an old German settlement famous for its wineries, can be visited in a day. Cahokia Mounds is an archeological site once occupied by a large population of Native Americans and now containing a museum with a replica village.

Day 5 If you feel like taking an overnight excursion, good destinations outside St. Louis include Hannibal, Missouri, hometown of Mark Twain, and Springfield, Illinois, former home of Abraham Lincoln with a number of historical attractions. For more information on excursions outside St. Louis, refer to Chapter 11.

1. THE TOP ATTRACTIONS

GATEWAY ARCH, Jefferson National Expansion Memorial Park, between Memorial Drive and Leonor K. Sullivan Blvd., (Downtown). Tel. 425-4465.

Perhaps no monument is as well known in the Midwest as the Gateway Arch, America's tallest monument, a graceful rainbow of shining steel soaring 630 feet into the air. Located beside the Mississippi River in the heart of the city, it was erected to honor the westward expansion of America through the 1800s. St. Louis is an appropriate site for such a monument, because it was from here that Lewis and Clark set out to explore the riches of Thomas Jefferson's Louisiana Purchase. In addition, throughout the 19th century St. Louis served as a gateway to the west for explorers, pioneers, immigrants, cowboys, and entrepreneurs setting out to seek their fortune. In 1990 the Arch celebrated its 25th birthday and now welcomes 2.5 million visitors a year.

For most visitors, the most thrilling experience is riding the small tram to the top, where an observation room provides a panoramic view toward the east and west. The tram—not for the claustrophobic—consists of eight tiny capsules, each of which holds only five passengers and is designed to stay vertical throughout the four-minute ride to the top. Be sure to purchase your tram ticket immediately upon your arrival at the Arch, since tickets are for a specific time and often booked solid for two or three hours in advance in the summer and on the weekend.

While waiting for your trip up the Arch, be sure to go underneath the arch to visit the **Museum of Westward Expansion,** which traces the westward journey of Lewis and Clark, who were followed by pioneers, immigrants, and others traveling west. Displays spread in a semicircle from the entrance, cleverly giving the illusion of expansion. Be sure, too, to watch the 35-minute film *Monument to the Dream,* which depicts the construction of the Arch from its conception to the placement of its last section. Movies are shown every 45 minutes.

ST. LOUIS
Downtown

Busch Stadium **11**
Campbell House Museum **5**
City Hall **14**
Dental Health Theatre **2**
Eads Bridge **3**
Eugene Field House **16**
Gateway Arch **9**
Laclede's Landing **1**
Mercantile Money
  Museum **4**
Museum of
  Westward Expansion **10**
National Bowling
  Hall of Fame **13**
Old Cathedral **8**
Old Courthouse **7**
St. Louis Sports
  Hall of Fame **12**
Soldiers' Memorial
  and Museum **6**
Union Station **15**

Admission: $1 National Park entrance fee for adults, free to senior citizens 62 and older and children under 17. Tram ride costs $2.50 for adults, 50¢ for children 3 through 12. Movie tickets cost $1 for all visitors 3 years and older.

Open: Tram rides daily Memorial Day to Labor Day 8:30am–9:10pm (last ride), winter 9:30am–5:10pm (last ride). **Closed:** Thanksgiving, Christmas, New Year's Day.

DOWNTOWN ST. LOUIS SIGHTS

UNION STATION, 18th and Market Sts. (Downtown). Tel. 421-4314.

First opened in 1894, Union Station soon became the largest and busiest passenger-rail terminal in the United States. More than twice the size of its nearest competitor, it served more than 100,000 passengers per day before finally closing in 1978 as people began choosing other forms of transportation.

Since it's reopening in 1985, Union Station has become as popular a destination for visitors as the Gateway Arch. In fact, I know one family who came to Union Station's Hyatt Regency for a vacation and ended up staying there the entire time. While that seems a bit demented considering everything else that St. Louis has to offer, it does illustrate the fact that Union Station is practically a city in itself. In addition to a hotel, it contains more than 80 specialty shops, more than two-dozen food outlets and restaurants in all price categories, a 10-screen cinema, and even a small lake. Throughout the station are 22 plaques describing its architecture and what life was like when the rails were king and also display cases containing memorabilia relating to the Station donated by former employees and travelers. For more information on Union Station and a brochure of its shops and services, stop by the Information Booth in Union Station, located near the 18th St. entry.

Admission: Free to Union Station; Memories Theater admission 75¢.

Open: Shops open Mon–Thurs 10am–9pm, Fri and Sat 10am–10pm, Sun 11am–7pm. Restaurants open later, usually weekdays until 11pm and weekends until midnight.

MISSOURI BOTANICAL GARDEN, 4344 Shaw. Tel. 577-5100.

The Missouri Botanical Garden is the oldest botanical garden in the nation, opened to the public in 1859 and located less than a 10-minute drive from downtown. Locals refer to it as Shaw's Garden, after the wealthy businessman, Henry Shaw, who conceived, designed, and directed the garden until his death in 1889 at the age of 89.

Covering 79 acres, the botanical garden is divided into various individual gardens, including two rose gardens with more than 6,000 roses, an iris garden, a daylily garden, and an azalea/rhododendron garden. The 14-acre Japanese Garden is the largest one in North America and contains a lake with huge carp (just like in Japan, where there isn't a pond without carp), a tea house, stone lanterns, and traditional bridges. In the Scented Garden are plants chosen for their strong fragrance or textured leaves, and visitors are encouraged to touch and smell, with signs also in Braille.

There are also greenhouses, the most interesting of which is the Climatron, the world's first geodesic-domed greenhouse, containing beautifully landscaped tropical vegetation that includes orchids. Throughout the Botanical Gardens are sculpture pieces, including works by Henry Moore and Swedish Carl Milles. A 25-minute tram ride winds through the park and stops at the Japanese Garden. There's also a restaurant open for breakfast and lunch with indoor and outdoor seating.

By the summer of 1991, a new facility called the William T. Kemper Center for Home Gardening will be open, dedicated to providing the public with practical gardening information. In addition to thematic garden plots and displays, staff will be on hand to answer gardening questions from the public.

Admission: $2 for adults, $1 for senior citizens 65 and older, free for children under 12. Tram ride $2, children under 6 free.

Open: Memorial Day to Labor Day daily 9am–8pm; winter daily 9am–5pm. **Closed:** Christmas.

ST. LOUIS ART MUSEUM, Forest Park. Tel. 721-0067.

✪ Occupying the crest of a hill in Forest Park, a 10-minute drive from downtown, the St. Louis Art Museum is housed in the only permanent building constructed for the 1904 World's Fair, built in the American Renaissance style. It was the first art museum in the world created by a citizens' vote to finance it through taxation. Now ranked as one of the top museums in the country, it contains collections from every significant period of art history—from ancient Egypt and Asia through the Middle Ages, the Renaissance, and 19th-century Europe, up to modern American art. Its pre-Columbian and German Expressionist collections are considered among the top in the world.

Highlights of the museum's many excellent paintings include works by George Caleb Bingham, van Gogh, Gauguin, Cezanne, Monet, Picasso, Kandinsky, Rodin, Lovis Corinth, Matisse, Georges Braque, Oskar Kokoschka, Paul Klee, Joan Miro, Thomas Hart Benton, and Georgia O'Keeffe. Among the German Expressionists represented are Max Beckmann, Emil Nolde, Max Ernst, and Ernst Ludwig Kirchner.

Other galleries show Islamic and ancient art; the museum's exceptional Asian collection; and art from Africa, Oceania, and the Americas. The Egyptian collection's newest acquisition is a mummy. There also are displays of Chinese, European, and American decorative arts, including furniture, vases, ceramics, silver, and armor. Finally, there's a museum shop, as well as the Museum Café serving meals and a Sunday brunch.

Admission: Free to the permanent collection. Temporary exhibitions charge admission Wed–Sun, free on Tues.

Open: Tues 1:30–8:30pm; Wed, Thurs, Sat, and Sun 10am–5pm; Fri 10am–8:30pm. **Closed:** Thanksgiving, Christmas, New Year's Day.

BUSCH STADIUM AND ST. LOUIS SPORTS HALL OF FAME, 100 Stadium Plaza. Tel. 421-FAME. For ticket information, tel. 421-3060.

Baseball and beer are what summers in St. Louis are all about—and of course that means watching the Cardinals at Busch Stadium. (In fact, Busch gets its name from Anheuser-Busch, and the St. Louis Cardinals are part of the Anheuser-Busch Company.) What makes this stadium special is that it's located in the heart of downtown—in fact it probably *is* the heart of downtown to Cardinal fans. If you're a true-blooded sports fanatic, you'll want to visit Busch Stadium's St. Louis Sports Hall of Fame, located between gates 5 and 6 on Walnut Street. In addition to displays of the Cardinals' greatest players, there are exhibits relating to all sports played in St. Louis, including soccer, hockey, tennis, and even amateur sports. A 25-minute movie shows the Cardinals in action (the Cardinals have won 9 World Championships and 15 National League pennants), and a trivia quiz game tests what you've learned in the museum. On evenings when there are games, the museum is open only to those who have tickets to the game.

Next to the Sports Hall of Fame is a gift shop where you can purchase everything imaginable with "Cardinals" written on it, from hats to nightlights to keychains to T-shirts. At the gift shop you can also purchase tickets for a 45-minute tour of Busch Stadium, with visits to the press box, the umpire's corridor, the dugout, and a portion of the field (only if there's no practice—otherwise you can watch some of the practice).

Admission: Free to gift shop. St. Louis Sports Hall of Fame $2 for adults, $1.50 for children 5 to 15. Stadium tours cost $2.50 for adults, $2 for children. Combination tickets for both Sports Hall of Fame and stadium tour are $4 for adults, $3 for children.

Open: Sports Hall of Fame daily 10am–5pm (to 11pm on game days, open only to spectators with game tickets). Stadium tours in summer daily at 10:15am, 11am, 1pm, 2pm, and 3pm; in winter daily at 11am and 2pm (cancelled in bad weather). No tours on days when games are played in the afternoon.

ANHEUSER-BUSCH BREWERY TOUR, 13th and Lynch. Tel. 577-2153.

The Anheuser-Busch Brewery claims to be the largest beer brewer in the world, with plants stretching from Tampa, Florida, to Fairfield, California. The St. Louis brewery is the company's largest facility and is also where the story of Anheuser-Busch began. Its 100 acres are an architectural delight, with old brick buildings—some of them very ornate, with turreted tops and detailed facades—and streets lined with shade trees. The oldest building dates from 1868; the brew house was built in 1892.

To see the brewery and sample its brew, visitors are invited to join a tour, which takes approximately 1¼ hour and covers eight blocks of walking. The tour begins with the complicated brewing process, and visitors see the huge vats, follow the fermentation process, and watch the packaging lines in action. Tour groups also see the famous Clydesdale horses in their stable (which must be one of the prettiest stables in the world). The tour culminates with complimentary samples of beer, including Busch, Budweiser, Michelob, and Bud Light.

Admission: Free, on a first-come, first-served basis.

Open: Tours leave every 10 minutes May–Oct Mon–Sat 10am–5pm; in winter every 20 minutes Mon–Sat 9am–4pm. **Closed:** Sun and holidays.

2. MORE ATTRACTIONS

LAUMEIER SCULPTURE PARK, Geyer and Rott Rds. Tel. 821-1209.

Located in South County on the southwestern edge of St. Louis, near I-44 and I-270, this is one of only two contemporary outdoor sculpture parks in the United States. The park, covering 96 acres, contains the largest single collection of works by sculptor Ernest Trova, as well as pieces by more than 30 other artists, including Alexander Liberman, Carl Milles, Richard Serra, and Alice Aycock. Among the most interesting pieces are Aycock's *The Hundred Small Rooms,* a 30-foot-tall wooden sculpture painted white, and Liberman's *The Way,* a 100-foot-long piece made of storage tanks

FROMMER'S FAVORITE
ST. LOUIS EXPERIENCES

Enjoying the Mississippi Riverfront   Ride a tram to the top of the Gateway Arch for a view of the Mississippi and all of St. Louis. Stroll along the riverfront. Take a riverboat sightseeing cruise. In the evening, head for the restaurants, clubs, and bars of Laclede's Landing.

A St. Louis Cardinal's Game   Summer in St. Louis means baseball and beer at Busch Stadium with the St. Louis Cardinals.

A Drink at a Sidewalk Café   The Central West End, settled at the turn of the century by St. Louis' upper class, offers a lively mix of unusual clothing stores, galleries, antiques shops, restaurants, outdoor cafés, and bars, making it a great place for window-shopping and people-watching.

A Saturday at Soulard Market   The city's oldest open-air market is one of the best free shows in town on Saturday, when vendors sell everything from fruit and vegetables to live chickens.

Antique Row   Even if you don't buy something, it's interesting browsing in the many antiques shops here—and who knows, you might find a treasure.

Afternoon Tea at the Ritz-Carlton   For an afternoon of indulgence, feast on finger sandwiches, crumpets, scones, chocolates, and strawberries with Devonshire cream, served on Wedgwood china—to the accompaniment of classical music.

An Italian Meal   No visit to St. Louis would be complete without at least one meal in the Italian district, the Hill, which is packed with Italian restaurants in all price categories.

A Night with the Blues   St. Louis offers some of the best blues in the country, much of it for free, so spend an evening in Soulard or Laclede's Landing at one of the many live music houses.

Frozen Custard at Ted Drewes   When the late-night munchies hit, head for Ted Drewes' custard stand and join the multitude of others who come here religiously to cap off a night on the town.

welded together and painted red. Included in the park are hiking trails, picnic sites, a museum shop, and a gallery for changing exhibitions.
   Admission: Free.
   Open: Park daily 8am–dusk; gallery Wed–Sat 10am–5pm, Sun noon–5pm.

HISTORIC BUILDINGS

OLD COURTHOUSE, 11 N. 4th St. at Market St. Tel. 425-4465 or 425-4468.

Just two short blocks from the Gateway Arch is the Old Courthouse, one of the oldest buildings left standing in downtown St. Louis. First built in the 1820s and then reconstructed and added on to through the next few decades, the present courthouse stems from 1862. Built in Greek Revival style with a 150-foot dome, it is best known as the site of the 1847 Dred Scott trial, in which a slave sued for freedom and ultimately lost. On the ground floors of the courthouse is a museum dedicated to the history of St. Louis from its early years in the 1700s to the present. On the second floor are restored courtrooms, and on the fourth floor is an observation area around the rotunda. The building is under the administration of the National Park Service, which also maintains a gift shop selling books relating to St. Louis.

Admission: Free.

Open: Daily 8am–4:30pm. **Closed:** Thanksgiving, Christmas, New Year's Day.

CAMPBELL HOUSE MUSEUM, 1508 Locust St., Downtown. Tel. 421-0325.

In the decades following the Civil War, Lucas Place was an exclusive residential street, buffered from downtown by a park. The sole survivor of Lucas Place is the Campbell House, built in 1851, residence of Robert Campbell and his family from 1854 to 1938. What makes it especially unique, however, is that, with the exception of only a few items, everything in the house is original, giving insight into the Campbell family's taste and lifestyle. That taste was decidedly French, financed by wealth acquired through fur trading, banking, and real estate. The Campbells had 13 children, only 3 of whom reached maturity. Visitors walk through the house on guided tours given continuously throughout the day.

Admission: $3 for adults, $1 for children.

Open: Tues–Sat 10am–4pm, Sun noon–5pm. **Closed:** Jan and Feb and holidays.

CHATILLON–DE MENIL MANSION, 3352 De Menil Place. Tel. 771-5828.

Located three blocks south of the Anheuser-Busch Brewery, just off Cherokee Street, this historic home was first built in 1848 as a four-room farmhouse by Henri Chatillon, a fur trapper and wilderness guide. It was later acquired by Dr. Nicholas De Menil, a Frenchman who completely renovated the house in Greek Revival style and added nine rooms. Today it contains antiques dating from the latter part of the 1800s, as well as two oil portraits by famed Missouri artist George Caleb Bingham. Tours, lasting about half an hour, are given continuously throughout the day. There's a gift shop in the basement, while in the carriage house is the De Menil Mansion Restaurant, open for lunch Tues–Sat 11am–2pm.

Admission: $2.50 for adults, 50¢ for children under 12.

Open: Tues–Sat 10am–3:30pm (last tour). **Closed:** Jan and holidays.

ST. LOUIS CATHEDRAL, 4431 Lindell Blvd., Central West End. Tel. 533-2824.

Three blocks east of Forest Park, the St. Louis Cathedral is nothing short of incredible, a magnificent piece of architecture and art. Begun in 1907 and combining Byzantine and Romanesque architecture, its claim to fame is that it contains the largest collection of mosaics in the world, some 145 million pieces of stone and glass covering 83,000 square feet of ceilings, domes, arches, and wall panels. These mosaics portray scenes from the Old and New Testaments, events in the life of St. Louis IX, and men and women prominent in the history of the Catholic Church. The cathedral's main dome is higher than a 22-story building, and marble used in the construction of the cathedral comes from almost every marble center in the world. A must see.

Admission: Free.

Open: Daily 6am–6pm.

CUPPLES HOUSE, 3673 West Pine Blvd., St. Louis University Campus. Tel. 658-3025.

Located on a pedestrian-only lane between Grand Boulevard and Spring Avenue on the campus of St. Louis University, the Cupples House was the home of Samuel Cupples, a self-made millionaire who made his fortune as a wood merchant. His mansion, built in 1889 at a cost of $500,000 (which would be the same as $10 to $15 million today), is in the Romanesque Revival style and is constructed of pink Missouri granite and Colorado sandstone. As many as 18 servants were employed to take care of the 42-room home, which has 20 operative fireplaces. Today Cupples House is filled with beautiful antiques and decorative objects, which visitors can view on their own. In the basement, in what was formerly a bowling alley, is the McNamee Gallery, which features changing exhibits from both the University's own collection of modern paintings and pieces lent by other institutions.

Admission: $1 for adults, 50¢ for senior citizens over 60, free to children under 13.

Open: Cupples House Mon–Fri 10am–3pm, Sun 2–4pm; gallery Mon–Fri noon–3pm, Sun 2–4pm.

MORE MUSEUMS

ST. LOUIS HISTORY MUSEUM, Jefferson Memorial Building, Forest Park. Tel. 361-1424.

Built in 1913 as the nation's first national monument to Thomas Jefferson, the Jefferson Memorial Building houses both the Missouri Historical Society and the St. Louis History Museum. The museum traces important events in the history of St. Louis, the state of Missouri, and the American West, and also houses memorabilia from the people who played indispensable roles in St. Louis' development, including Charles Lindbergh, Daniel Boone, and Lewis and Clark. You can learn about the 1904 St. Louis World's Fair and Lindbergh's historic flight across the Atlantic in *The Spirit of St. Louis.* You'll see early firefighting equipment, toys, and guns and sabers used in the Civil War.

Admission: Free.
Open: Tues–Sun 9:30am–4:45pm. **Closed:** Thanksgiving, Christmas, New Year's Day.

THE EUGENE FIELD HOUSE AND TOY MUSEUM, 634 S. Broadway (Downtown). Tel. 421-4689.

This was the childhood home of Eugene Field, known as the "children's poet" for such works as *Wynken, Blynken and Nod* and *Little Boy Blue*. Built in 1845, the oldest residence still standing in downtown St. Louis, the Eugene Field House today contains a large collection of antique toys and dolls spanning 300 years, all donated by individuals.

Admission: $2 for adults, 50¢ for children under 12.
Open: Tues–Sat 10am–4pm, Sun noon–4pm. **Closed:** Mon and holidays.

NATIONAL MUSEUM OF TRANSPORT, 3015 Barrett Station Rd. West County. Tel. 965-7998.

Located west of I-270 between Big Bend and Manchester, this 50-acre outdoor museum contains one of the largest collections of locomotives in the country, along with railway cars, automobiles, streetcars, buses, trucks, horse-drawn vehicles, and aircraft.

Admission: $3 for adults, $1 for children 5 to 12, $1.50 for senior citizens 65 and older.
Open: Daily 9am–5pm. **Closed:** Thanksgiving, Christmas, New Year's Day.

NATIONAL BOWLING HALL OF FAME, 8th and Walnut, (Downtown). Tel. 231-6340.

Located across from Busch Stadium, this museum salutes a sport played by millions of Americans. The history of bowling is traced from medieval Europe (even monks got into the action then), when it was played at country festivals, village dances, and even baptisms. Variations of the game also are presented, along with explanations of how it spread through the New World colonies and was eventually taken up also by women. A highlight is the eight-lane bowling alley in the basement, four lanes of which are automated and four of which are operated by pin setters. The museum also houses the American Bowling Congress and Women's International halls of fame.

Admission: $3 for adults, $2 for senior citizens, $1.50 for children.
Open: Summer Mon–Sat 9am–7pm, Sun noon–7pm; winter Mon–Sat 9am–5pm, Sun noon–5pm. **Closed:** Thanksgiving; Dec 24, 25, and 31; New Year's Day.

THE DOG MUSEUM, Queeny Park, 1721 S. Mason Rd. Tel. 821-3647.

Dedicated to man's best friend, the Dog Museum contains works of art and literature depicting the dog throughout history, in an effort to promote understanding about the canine. It's housed in the Jarville House, built in 1853 in Greek Revival style, and also contains a library for research on various breeds. This is probably one of the only museums in the world that encourages visitors to bring their dogs.

Admission: $2 for adults, 50¢ for children 5 to 14, free to dogs.
Open: Mon–Sat 9am–5pm, Sun 1–4pm. **Closed:** Easter Sunday, Thanksgiving, Christmas, New Year's Day.

3. COOL FOR KIDS

SIX FLAGS OVER MID-AMERICA, Allenton Rd., Eureka, MO. Tel. 314/938-5300 or 938-4800.

Amusement rides, arcade games, shows, food, and fun are featured in this theme park, located 30 miles southwest of St. Louis on I-44 at the Allenton exit. Among its many attractions are a dolphin show, the Screaming Eagle roller coaster (reputedly one of the longest, tallest, and fastest in the world), the NINJA roller coaster with its 360-degree loop, an old-fashioned carousel, and much more. The park is divided into six sections, each one representing one of the six countries that have flown their flags over the Midwest through the centuries. Allow a whole day to tour the park.

Admission to all attractions: $18.50 for adults, $14.50 for children 3 to 11.

Open: June–Aug Sun–Thurs 10am–9pm, Fri 10am–midnight, Sat 10am–10pm; Apr, May, Sept, and Oct usually Sat and Sun only 10am–7 or 8pm. Because the park occasionally closes for private functions, telephone for verification of hours prior to planning your trip.

ST. LOUIS ZOO, Forest Park. Tel. 781-0900.

Like the St. Louis Art Museum, the St. Louis Zoo was the first zoo in the world that was supported by a citizens' vote to tax themselves, and it remains one of the few free zoos in the world. Covering 83 acres in beautiful Forest Park, it's home to 2,800 animals—including apes, lions, tigers, jaguars, birds, penguins, and reptiles. The Herpetarium and the Primate House date from the 1920s, while the Bird Cage dates from the 1904 World's Fair as the Smithsonian Institution's walk-through bird cage.

Particularly outstanding is the newly opened Living World, designed to teach visitors about how nature works and what happens when humans upset the balance of nature, in the belief that it is no longer enough for zoos simply to display exotic animals. Approximately 150 animals are on display at Living World, chosen for their diversity, from bats and sponges to the tarantula and microscopic creatures (magnified to the size of house cats). Throughout are high-tech equipment, such as computers, videodisk presentations, and sound systems, to explain and entertain. A must see.

Admission: Free.

Open: Daily 9am–5pm. **Closed:** Christmas and New Year's Day.

GRANT'S FARM, 10501 Gravois Rd. Tel. 843-1700.

In 1856, several years before he became the 18th president of the United States, Ulysses S. Grant built himself a log cabin not far from St. Louis and farmed the surrounding land. Today that log cabin and that farm are part of the 281-acre estate of August A. Busch, Jr. (as in Anheuser-Busch), and they are open free to the public. There's also a game preserve where buffalo, longhorn sheep, deer, horses, and other animals roam free; a small zoo; a beer garden; and a stable of Clydesdale horses.

Although free, tours must be reserved in advance and are for a specific time. Lasting approximately two hours, tours start with a

MISSOURI

St. Louis ★

Busch Stadium **7**
Cupples House **6**
The Dog Museum **11**
Forest Park **3**
Grant's Farm **12**
Missouri Botanical
    Gardens **8**
National Museum
    of Transport **10**
St. Louis Art Museum **2**
St. Louis Cathedral **5**
St. Louis Carousel **9**
St. Louis History Museum **1**
St. Louis Zoo **4**

trackless train ride to the Tiergarten—a small zoo with deer, camels, elephants, bears, goats, and other animals—along with shows starring birds or elephants. After wandering through the zoo at your leisure, you're invited to visit the Bauernhof, built in 1913 as Busch's home and now housing his collection of horse-drawn carriages dating from the 1800s, and to sample a free glass of beer. Then it's back on the trackless train for a ride through the game preserve and past Grant's cabin. All in all, this is a great outing for the family.

Admission: Free, but advance reservations required.

Open: Jun–Aug Tues–Sun 9am–3pm (last tour); Apr 15–May 31 and Sept–Oct 31 Thurs–Sun 9am–3pm. Tours depart on the hour.

ST. LOUIS SCIENCE CENTER, Forest Park. Tel. 289-4444.
This is a great learning experience for children (and adults), with hands-on displays and equipment. Outdoors there's Science Park, 24 playground-type exhibits involving kids in experiments with light, sound, motion, and energy, including a giant lever that allows children to lift their families. Indoors there's the star of the science

center, the McDonnell Star Theater, which features a Digistar Planetarium Projector for a variety of changing shows. More hands-on exhibits are inside, including what it feels like to be in an earthquake or how exercise changes your heart beat.

There also are three supervised play rooms: The Discovery Room allows children to dress in Native American costumes, explore a Missouri cave, or look at items under a microscope; the Science Lab encourages children to use computers and other tools in science; and the Science Showplace features audience-participation demonstrations on various topics of science and technology. By 1992 the Science Center will expand into a nearby facility across Highway 40 (connected by a bridge) and will focus on the ecology, people, technology, and space sciences.

Admission: Free to Science Park and indoor exhibits. McDonnell Star Theater $2.50 per person, free to children under 5. Discovery Room, Science Lab, and Science Showplace $1 per person.

Open: Mon–Thurs 9:30am–5pm, Fri and Sat 9:30am–9pm, Sun 11am–5pm. **Closed:** Thanksgiving, Christmas, New Year's Day.

MAGIC HOUSE, 516 S. Kirkwood Rd. Tel. 822-8900.

Located one mile north of I-44 on Lindbergh, the Magic House is filled with exhibits that encourage kids to use their senses to discover the world's wonders. There's an electrostatically charged ball that makes your hair stand on end, a human-size maze, a three-story spiraling slide, simple computers that teach letters and numbers, and room upon room packed with things to do. Children can test their reaction times, identify smells, watch the pupils in their eyes grow larger or smaller with corresponding light, or test for color blindness. There's also a special play room for children younger than 7.

Admission: $2.50 per person.

Open: Summer (Memorial Day to Labor Day) Tues–Thurs 9:30am–5:30pm, Fri 9:30am–9pm, Sat 9:30am–5:30pm, Sun 11:30am–5:30pm; Winter Tues–Thurs 1–5:30pm, Fri 1–9pm, Sat 9:30am–5:30pm, Sun 11:30am–5:30pm.

ST. LOUIS CAROUSEL, Faust County Park, Olive St., West County. Tel. 889-3356.

Located north of I-64/Highway 40 in West St. Louis County, 98-acre Faust County Park is the home of the St. Louis Carousel, built about 1920 by the Dentzel Co. of Pennsylvania and one of only 10 still in existence. It features 60 hand-carved, colorfully painted horses, 4 reindeer with real antlers, and 2 chariots.

Admission: $1 for adults, 50¢ for children.

Open: Wed–Sun noon–5pm.

BOB KRAMER'S MARIONETTES, 4143 Laclede Ave., Mid-County. Tel. 531-3313.

Bob Kramer began making puppets when he was five years old, and he has since designed and constructed more than 800 marionettes and rod puppets. You can visit his workshop for a one-hour studio demonstration of how his puppets are made and how they work and also a brief history of puppetry. Marionette shows change with the season, ranging from a Christmas variety show to classics, such as *Peter and the Wolf*. Reservations for the demonstration or the show are a must.

Admission: Studio demonstration $3.50 for adults, $3 for children. Shows $4.50 for adults, $4 for children. Combination tickets for demonstration and show $6 for adults, $5.50 for children.

Open: Studio demonstration Mon–Sat 10am and 1pm; shows Mon–Sat 11:15am and 2:15pm. **Closed:** Sun and holidays.

DENTAL HEALTH THEATRE, 727 N. 1st St., Laclede's Landing. Tel. 241-7391.

This is a small theater, designed to teach kids what teeth are, why they are important, and how to take care of them. Demonstrations take place using three-foot-high fiberglass teeth that light up as an educator explains each function and how to brush and floss. Also included in the one-hour show is a film with Charlie Brown, Snoopy, and Lucy, as well as the use of puppets to further explain our teeth.

Admission: Free, but reservations required.

Open: Mon–Fri 9am–4pm. Telephone beforehand to inquire about showtimes.

4. ORGANIZED TOURS

BOAT CRUISES

St. Louis owes its existence to the mighty Mississippi, and you can be part of its river traffic by joining a one-hour cruise with **Gateway Riverboat Cruises,** which operates three replica paddlewheelers called the *Huck Finn, Tom Sawyer,* and *Becky Thatcher.* Moored near the Arch on the riverfront, the boats are in operation daily April through December, with departures every 45 minutes between 10:15am and 5pm during the summer months, less frequently during the rest of the year. The cost is $6.50 for adults and $3.50 for children ages 3 to 12.

There are also dinner-and-dancing cruises, which cost $23.30 Sunday through Thursday, $25.46 on Friday, and $27.61 on Saturday. The price for children any night of the week is $16.22.

Finally, there are Sunday brunch cruises, with departures throughout the year at 10:30am, 11:30am, 12:30pm, and 1:30pm. Featuring live music, these cruises last only 45 minutes, but diners are allowed to remain on board for the next sailing. The cost of Sunday brunch is $12.95 for adults and $4.95 for children.

For more information regarding Gateway Riverboat Cruises, times of departure, and prices, call 621-4040.

BUS TOURS

Although the purpose of this book is to guide you through St. Louis on your own, for orientation purposes you may wish to join a tour upon your arrival in the city, returning later to explore sights at leisure. The **Gray Line** offers a 3½-hour Grand Tour, which includes a trip through the downtown area, Forest Park, and the Central West End, with stops at the Missouri Botanical Gardens and the New Cathedral. Departing from major hotels in St. Louis, the tour costs $15.50 for adults and half price for children ages 6 through 12. Tours are offered from April 1 to October 31, every afternoon. For more information on exact departure times from each hotel, call 241-1224 in St. Louis, or toll free 800/542-4287.

5. SPORTS & RECREATION

SPECTATOR SPORTS
BASEBALL

For baseball fans, St. Louis is synonymous with the St. Louis Cardinals, who have won 9 World Championships and 15 National League pennants. Home games are played at **Busch Stadium,** located right in the heart of downtown, a ball's throw from the Arch. Baseball season runs from April through September, with approximately 80 home games. Tickets range from $4 for bleacher seats to $11 for box seats. For tickets and general information, call 421-3060. The Individual Ticket Charge Line is 421-2400. You can also order tickets by mail at St. Louis Cardinals Ticket Office, P.O. Box 8787, St. Louis, MO 63102, for which there's an extra $3 handling-and-postage charge.

HOCKEY

The St. Louis Blues Hockey team plays for the **National Hockey League at the Arena,** 5700 Oakland, south of Forest Park. The season runs from October through April, with about 40 home games each season. Ticket prices range from $10 to $21. For more information, call 781-5300.

HORSE RACING

Fairmont Park is a horse-racing track in Collinsville, Illinois, just a 15-minute drive from the Arch. Thoroughbreds are raced from March to November, while harness racing takes place from November to the end of December. Approximately five races are held each week. General admission to the grandstand costs $2, while admission to the Club House costs $3. On Tuesday, admission to the grandstand or Club House is only $1. To reach Fairmont Park from downtown St. Louis, cross the Mississippi River on the I-70/Highway 55 Bridge, go to the Black Lane Exit, then turn left on Route 40. For more information on horse racing and schedules, call 436-1516 in St. Louis or 618/345-4300 in Illinois.

RECREATION

The lungs of St. Louis is **Forest Park,** established in the early 1870s with nearly 1,300 acres. At one time well outside city limits, it is now completely enveloped by the city and is only a 10-minute drive from downtown. The site of the 1904 World's Fair, it contains a number of the city's most famous attractions, including the St. Louis Art Museum and the St. Louis Zoo. It also has a number of recreational facilities, including three golf courses, a tennis center, handball courts, a Perrier fitness parcourse, a playground, and biking and jogging trails. The **Forest Park Municipal Golf Course** (tel. 367-1337) has an 18-hole, 70-par public course, with green fees costing about $10. Golf Clubs are available for rent for $14.

For more information on recreational facilities in St. Louis, contact the **St. Louis Convention and Visitors Commission** (tel. 421-1023).

CHAPTER 8

STROLLING AROUND ST. LOUIS

1. DOWNTOWN
2. CENTRAL WEST END

As with many major U.S. cities, particularly those in the Midwest, St. Louis is best traversed by car. However, even though its many attractions are spread throughout the metropolitan area, St. Louis does have a few areas that warrant exploration on foot, the best of which are downtown and the Central West End.

WALKING TOUR 1 — Downtown

Start: Gateway Arch, between Memorial Drive and Leonor K. Sullivan Boulevard.

Finish: Union Station, 18th and Market streets.

Time: Allow approximately two hours, not including museum and shopping stops.

Best Times: Weekdays, when downtown is livelier.

Worst Times: Weekends, when the Arch is crowded, particularly in the afternoon.

A stroll around St. Louis' downtown brings you to the city's most famous attractions, including the Gateway Arch, Union Station, and Busch Stadium, as well as the best of St. Louis shopping. Although the total walking time of this tour is about two hours, you'll want to spend much longer—perhaps the entire day—exploring downtown's many offerings.

FROM THE GATEWAY ARCH TO LACLEDE'S LANDING

1. **The Gateway Arch.** The Arch would be difficult to overlook—630 feet tall, it towers high above the St. Louis skyline and is the nation's tallest monument. Erected to honor the westward expansion of America, the Arch rises from the Jefferson National Expansion Memorial Park, an expanse of lawns and artificial lakes. For the trip to the top of the arch, try to arrive as early in the morning as possible, since trams are sometimes so full that there's a two-hour wait. Be sure to visit the **2. Museum of Westward Expansion,** located underground beneath the Arch, and to watch the introductory film *Monument to the Dream,* about the construction of the Arch. (*See p. 99 for complete information*).

There are steps leading down from the Arch to the Mississippi riverfront, which is where St. Louis' history began. Among the several boats moored here, the *Huck Finn, Tom Sawyer,* and *Becky Thatcher,* operated by **3. Gateway Riverboat**

Cruises, leave every 45 minutes for an hour's cruise along the river. (*See p. 113 for more information.*)

REFUELING STOPS If the trip up the Arch and the riverboat cruise have worn you out, refresh yourself with a meal aboard the **4. Lt. Robert E. Lee,** a boat moored near the Arch offering steaks and seafood in an atmosphere reminiscent of the old sternwheelers that once ruled the river. If you're looking for something less formal, there are even fast-food chains occupying boats moored along the riverfront, including **5. McDonald's, Burger King,** and **Tombstone Pizza.**

The northern end of Jefferson National Expansion Memorial Park is bounded by ancient-looking **6. Eads Bridge.** It was built in 1874 by James Eads and was the first bridge to span the entire Mississippi River at the middle of its run towards the Gulf. It was also the first arched steel-truss bridge in the world. Cross under the bridge, and you'll find yourself at Laclede's Landing. **7. Laclede's Landing.** This is a neighborhood of restored 19th-century brick warehouses and cobblestone streets. One of St. Louis' most well known entertainment nightspots, it also has some shops; restaurants; and the **8. Dental Health Theatre,** at 727 N. 1st St., a small theater designed to teach children the importance of teeth and how to take care of them. (*See p. 113 for complete information.*) Take your time wandering along North Second Street, North First Street, and Lucas and Morgan streets.

REFUELING STOPS Most establishments in Laclede's Landing don't open until late afternoon, but one that opens earlier for lunch is **9. Kennedy's 2nd Street Co.,** 612 N. 2nd St., located in a restored warehouse with brick walls, tall ceilings, and wood-and-brick floors. It offers burgers, salads, and sandwiches for lunch and beer throughout the day. Live alternative and progressive music are featured in the evening.

FROM LACLEDE'S LANDING TO BUSCH STADIUM From Laclede's Landing, take Morgan Street inland, passing underneath the highway overpass, past the Days Inn hotel, to Sixth Street. Turn left, where you'll soon see the **10. St. Louis Centre,** which opened in 1985 as the largest urban enclosed shopping mall in the United States. Covering two city blocks between Sixth and Seventh streets and Washington and Locust, it offers four levels of shopping and dining. Its Food Court, by the way, is on the fourth floor.

After walking through the St. Louis Centre and exiting through the Famous-Barr department store, one of its anchors, you'll find yourself on Olive Street, where you should take a left. Olive Street is one of downtown's most important thoroughfares and is lined with office buildings. Walk two blocks to Fourth Street, then take a right, and within a few minutes you'll find yourself at the **11. Old Courthouse,** 11 N. 4th St. Built in 1862 in Greek Revival style, it's managed by the National Park Service and contains a museum dedicated to the history of St. Louis as well as a gift shop with books on St. Louis. (*See p. 106 for complete information.*) Leave the Old Courthouse through its

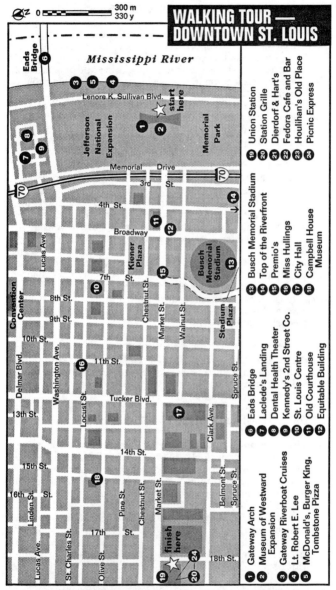

300 m
330 y

Mississippi River

Lenore K. Sullivan Blvd.

start here

Jefferson
National
Expansion

Memorial
Park

Memorial   Drive

3rd   St.

4th St.

Broadway

Kiener
Plaza

Busch
Memorial
Stadium

Convention Center

7th St.

8th St.

9th St.

10th St.

11th St.

Tucker Blvd.

13th St.

14th St.

15th St.

16th St.

17th St.

18th St.

Eads
Bridge

Market St.

Walnut St.

Chestnut St.

Stadium
Plaza

Spruce St.

Clark Ave.

Belmont
Spruce St.

Locust St.

Washington Ave.

Lucas Ave.

Delmar Blvd.

Linden St.

Lucas Ave.

St. Charles St.

Chestnut St.

Market St.

Pine St.

Olive St.

finish here

1 Gateway Arch
2 Museum of Westward
Expansion
3 Gateway Riverboat Cruises
4 Lt. Robert E. Lee
5 McDonald's, Burger King,
Tombstone Pizza

6 Eads Bridge
7 Laclede's Landing
8 Dental Health Theater
9 Kennedy's 2nd Street Co.
10 St. Louis Centre
11 Old Courthouse
12 Equitable Building

13 Busch Memorial Stadium
14 Top of the Riverfront
15 Premio's
16 Miss Hullings
17 City Hall
18 Campbell House
Museum

19 Union Station
20 Station Grille
21 Dierdorf & Hart's
22 Fedora Cafe and Bar
23 Houlihan's Old Place
24 Picnic Express

back-door exit onto Broadway and take a left, crossing Market
Street. **12. The Equitable Building,** at 10 S. Broadway, is
where on the third floor you'll find the main office of the St. Louis
Convention and Visitors Commission. Stop here for brochures,
maps, and other information on St. Louis if you have not already
done so.

One block farther south on Broadway is Walnut Street, with its
unmistakable **13. Busch Memorial Stadium,** home of the St.
Louis Cardinals. Baseball fans know that the Cardinals have won

9 World Championships and 15 National League pennants, all captured in the St. Louis Sports Hall of Fame, located between gates 5 and 6 of Busch Stadium on Walnut Street. There's a gift shop here where you can purchase everything imaginable and unimaginable with the Cardinals logo on it. If you wish, you can also join a tour of Busch Stadium. (*See p. 103 for complete information.*)

Across the street from Busch Stadium is another hall of fame honoring another American tradition, the National Bowling Hall of Fame, at 8th and Walnut, where you can even bowl an old-fashioned alley operated by pin setters. (*See p. 108 for complete information.*)

REFUELING STOPS   Although it's a five-minute walk away, **14. Top of the Riverfront** is a revolving restaurant providing the best view the city has to offer. Located atop the Clarion Hotel at 200 S. 4th St., it offers everything from sandwiches to fresh fish for lunch. A bit closer to Busch Stadium is **15. Premio's,** 701 Market St., a modern restaurant popular with downtown business clientele for its contemporary Italian cuisine. If the weather's fine, you may wish to dine on its outdoor patio, with an unobstructed view of the Old Courthouse and the Arch. For the budget-conscious, there's **16. Miss Hullings,** 1103 Locust St., a cafeteria serving homecooked foods. It's located about halfway between Busch Stadium and the next stop on your tour, the Campbell House.

FROM BUSCH STADIUM TO UNION STATION   From Busch Stadium, return to Market Street, on which you should head west, away from the Arch. On the left corner of 12th Street (also called Tucker Memorial Boulevard) is: **17. City Hall,** built as an exact copy of the Hotel de Ville in Paris. Take a right onto 12th Street and walk four blocks to Locust, on which you should take another left.

18. The Campbell House Museum. Within a few minutes you'll arrive at the Campbell House Museum, 1508 Locust St., built in 1851 as a private residence in what used to be one of St. Louis' most exclusive neighborhoods. The home contains almost all the original furnishings, providing valuable insight into life in the city in the 1800s. (*See p. 106 for complete information.*)

Follow 15th Street back to Market Street and continue walking west. After passing the main post office, you'll come upon **19. Union Station** on your left, at 18th and Market streets. There's no mistaking its fortresslike facade topped by a clock tower, behind which stretches what was once the largest and busiest passenger-rail terminal in the world. Today it houses a wonderland of shops, cafés, and restaurants, as well as a hotel and even an artificial lake. Since the shops stay open late here, it's a good place to end the day. (*See p. 101 for complete information.*)

FINAL REFUELING STOPS   There are so many places to eat and drink in Union Station that the problem is not in finding one but in deciding which one. For elegant dining there's the **20. Station Grille,** Union Station's former dining hall, as well as **21.**

Dierdorf & Hart's, both of which serve steaks and seafood. **22. Fedora Café and Bar** serves innovative American food, but you may just want to have a drink here and watch the crowds. **23. Houlihan's Old Place** serves beer, cocktails, and food, with outdoor seating beside the lake, and there's also the upper-level **24. Picnic Express,** with vendors selling a variety of fast foods.

WALKING TOUR 2 — Central
West End

Start: North Euclid Avenue at Lindell Boulevard.

Finish: North Euclid Avenue at McPherson.

Time: Allow approximately an hour, not including shopping and dining stops.

Best Times: Monday through Saturday in the afternoon, when shops are open.

Worst Times: Sunday, when galleries and most shops are closed.

Located a few miles west of downtown and bordered by Forest Park, the Central West End was settled at the turn of the century by the upper crust of St. Louis society. The elegant homes here still remain, now accompanied by a lively mix of unusual clothing shops, galleries, antique shops, restaurants, and bars, making it a great place for strolling and people-watching. Its center is Euclid Avenue and a few sidestreets.

FROM NORTH EUCLID AVENUE AT LINDELL BOULEVARD STREET TO MARYLAND AVENUE Head north on North Euclid Avenue, and within a minute you'll arrive at the first of many antique shops in the Central West End:

1. **Hirschfeld Galleries,** 234 N. Euclid Ave. Established in 1931, this family-owned shop offers rare books and antiques.

     The next intersection, Euclid and Maryland avenues, is the heart of the Central West End, with several sidewalk cafés perfect for whiling away an afternoon watching the world go by. If you turn right onto Maryland Avenue, you'll soon see:

2. **Four Seasons West,** 4657 Maryland Ave., dealing in French, English, and Chinese furniture and decorative objects from the 17th through 19th centuries. (*See p. 124 for more information.*) Almost next door is:

3. **St. Louis Bread Company,** 4651 Maryland Ave., considered St. Louis' best bakery, with a wide assortment of breads ranging from sourdough to rye and baguettes.

     Retrace your steps, cross back over Euclid Avenue, head in the other direction on Maryland Avenue, and you'll see:
     Maryland Plaza, a small roundabout with a fountain. Here you'll find one of St. Louis' foremost galleries:

4. **The Greenburg Gallery,** at 44 Maryland Plaza. A contemporary art gallery focusing on post–World War II American and European paintings, sculpture, and drawings, it has carried works by Andy Warhol, Georgia O'Keeffe, Alexander Calder, Roy Lichtenstein, Helen Frankenthaler, Joel Shapiro, and many more. (*See p. 126 for more information.*)

REFUELING STOPS **St. Louis Bread Co.,** described above, sells sandwiches using its delicious breads, which you can eat at one of its indoor or outdoor tables. Across the street is **5. Bar Italia,** 4656 Maryland Ave., serving authentic and nouvelle Italian cuisine, espresso, and gelato. Try to get a seat outdoors if weather permits.

6. **Culpeppers,** on the corner of Euclid and Maryland avenues, is a simple neighborhood bar famous throughout St. Louis for its spicy chicken wings. The nearby **7. Pasta House Company,** 309 N. Euclid Ave., offers more than two dozen inexpensive pasta dishes in a pleasant setting that was once the lobby of a hotel. It, too, has outdoor seating.

FROM MARYLAND AVENUE TO MCPHERSON

PERSHING AND HORTENSE PLACES Continuing north on Euclid, you'll soon come to Pershing Place and Hortense Place, two residential streets lined with elegant turn-of-the-century homes. Although they are marked with a gate that says "Private Road," you can stroll down them to see how the other half lived at the time of the 1904 World's Fair, with homes built in almost every style that socialites could imagine, from Italian Renaissance to Victorian.

Return to reality on Euclid Avenue and continue north to:

8. **Kopperman's,** 386 N. Euclid Ave., a grocer's that has been serving the needs of the neighborhood since 1897. Stock up on picnic supplies or enjoy a drink at one of its outdoor tables.

9. **Venus Adonis** is next door at 390 N. Euclid Ave., specializing in unique clothing from small companies in New York, Los Angeles, Chicago, and St. Louis, as well as from known designers, such as Betsey Johnson.

10. **Kerr-Oberbeck,** across the street at 391 N. Euclid Ave., is another fashion boutique, selling mainly accessories for the young and young at heart.

Near the corner of Euclid and McPherson is:

11. **Rothschild's Antiques,** 398 N. Euclid, packed full with furniture, lamps, stained-glass windows, watches, jewelry, and junk. Take a right onto McPherson, and there are more antique shops.

12. **West End Gallery,** 4732 McPherson, is actually three shops in one, housing an antique shop, a florist, and an art jeweler.

13. **McPherson Antique Gallery,** next door, offers four floors of antiques, collectibles, and curios, including furniture and brass hardware.

14. **Alice's Vintage Clothing,** across the street at 4703 McPherson, is crammed full with men's and women's clothes from 1900 to 1960. Back on Euclid Avenue, one more shop is worth checking out:

15. **Zigi,** 415 N. Euclid Ave., is another fashion boutique that strives to present St. Louisans with one-of-a-kind fashion statements, from the whimsical to the conservative, most imported from Los Angeles and New York. You'll find designs here long before they hit the other stores.

FINAL REFUELING STOPS **16. Café Balaban,** 405 N. Euclid Ave., was a forerunner in the Central West End's urban

Central West End □
ST. LOUIS

Washington Boulevard

finish here

North Euclid Avenue

Taylor Avenue

McPherson Avenue

Kingshighway Boulevard

Hortense Place

Lenox Place

Pershing Place

Maryland Plaza

Maryland Avenue

York Avenue

North Euclid Avenue

Taylor Avenue

Kingshighway Boulevard

start here

Lindell Boulevard

① Hirschfeld Galleries
② Four Seasons West
③ St. Louis Bread Company
④ Greenburg Gallery
⑤ Bar Italia
⑥ Culpeppers
⑦ Pasta House Company
⑧ Kopperman's
⑨ Venus Adonis
⑩ Kerr-Oberbeck
⑪ Rothschild's Antiques
⑫ West End Gallery
⑬ McPherson Antique Gallery
⑭ Alice's Vintage Clothing
⑮ Zigi
⑯ Cafe Balaban
⑰ Duff's
⑱ Dressel's Pub

revitalization, and it still sets the pace with its French and continental cuisine. Equally well known is **17. Duff's,** 392 N. Euclid Ave., a casual and friendly restaurant with a menu that changes with the seasons. For a beer with a difference, head for **18. Dressel's Pub,** 419 N. Euclid, a true Welsh pub with imported beers from Europe and such pub fare as Welsh vegetarian pie and Ploughman's Lunch. This is a great place to end the day and herald the evening.

CHAPTER 9

ST. LOUIS
SHOPPING

1. SHOPPING AREAS
2. ANTIQUES & ART

Shopping in St. Louis does not differ much from that in any other major U.S. city, with the same chains selling the same merchandise. However, in St. Louis it's *where* you shop that makes a difference: How many other cities have shopping centers that match the scale of Union Station? How many other cities have more than a dozen major shopping malls or a street devoted entirely to antiques shops? And if you're looking for something truly unique, you can find that, too—from arts and crafts produced by local artists and artisans to antiques and collectibles. In short, the best of St. Louis shopping is its shopping centers, such as Union Station; its many antique shops; and its art galleries.

Shopping hours throughout the city vary. Downtown shops are generally open Monday through Saturday from about 9 or 10am to about 5:30 or 6pm. Shopping centers stay open longer, from about 10am to 9 or 10pm Monday to Saturday and noon to 5 or 6pm on Sunday. A 5.925% tax will be added to the price of purchased goods.

1. SHOPPING AREAS

DOWNTOWN

ST. LOUIS CENTRE, Bounded by Locust, Seventh St., Washington and Sixth Sts. Tel. 231-5522.
Upon its opening in 1985, the St. Louis Centre was hailed as the largest downtown enclosed shopping mall in the country. It offers four levels, the fourth containing the Food Court popular with downtown office workers. All together there are more than 100 shops, with Dillard's and Famous-Barr serving as anchors. Interesting shops include Abercrombie & Fitch, with its upscale clothing, and The Sharper Image, with its pricy gadgets and gifts, but there also are bookstores, clothing boutiques, shoe stores, jewelry outlets, and much more.
   Open: Mon–Sat 10am–6pm, Sun noon–6pm.

UNION STATION, 18th and Market Sts. Tel. 421-4314.
Any city would be proud of Union Station, so successfully has it been transformed from the nation's largest rail terminal into a marketplace and showplace. It's big, light, airy, and packed with all kinds of things to do, from shopping to dining to nighttime entertainment. Union Station has more than 100 specialty shops and restaurants, including

such notable shops as the Disney Store, Eddie Bauer, Banana Republic, Crabtree and Evelyn, and the Great Train Store. The Nature Company and Brookstone always have lovely gift items on display. Missouri Peddlers has a small outlet here selling items crafted by Missouri artisans. It would be difficult to pass by the Fudgery, where employees sing, dance, and give entertaining demonstrations as they go about their work making fudge.

Open: Mon–Thurs 10am–9pm, Fri and Sat 10am–10pm, Sun 11am–7pm.

ELSEWHERE

ST. LOUIS GALLERIA, Clayton Rd. and Brentwood Blvd., Clayton/Richmond Heights. Tel. 863-5500.

This is one of St. Louis' newer, smarter shopping malls, with a 100-foot-high atrium, an Italian marble interior, and three levels of shops. Dillard's is the anchor shop (Famous-Barr and Lord & Taylor are expected to follow), backed by more than 90 specialty shops featuring fashion boutiques, home accessories, gifts, jewelry, books, and more.

Open: Mon–Sat 10am–9:30pm, Sun noon–6pm.

PLAZA FRONTENAC, Lindbergh Blvd. and Clayton Rd., West County. Tel. 432-0604.

Some call this the Rodeo Drive of St. Louis. At any rate, Plaza Frontenac contains some 70 stores, including Nieman Marcus, Saks Fifth Avenue, Gucci, Burberrys, Ralph Lauren, Waterford Wedgwood, Bruno Magli, Williams-Sonoma, Rodier of Paris, and The Coach Store—not to mention Banana Republic, Laura Ashley, Mondi, and Victoria's Secret.

Open: Mon–Fri 10am–9pm, Sat 10am–6pm, Sun noon–5pm.

NORTHWEST PLAZA, Lindbergh Blvd. at St. Charles Rock Rd. Tel. 298-0071.

Located only five minutes from Lambert Airport, this shopping center underwent complete renovation in the late 1980s and emerged as one of the largest in the city. It's the only St. Louis mall with four anchors—Dillard's, Famous-Barr, J. C. Penney, and Sears—and boasts more than 200 specialty shops. It also contains a family-

---

 FROMMER'S SMART SHOPPER

1. Use cash and traveler's checks when you possibly can; you will tend to overspend with a credit card.
2. Take advantage of "Sale" signs posted in windows, just as you would at home.
3. Look for discount shopping coupons in tourist booklets and newspapers.
4. Comparison shop before buying especially in shopping centers or malls where there are many stores under one roof.

entertainment center with video games, miniature golf, and a movie theater with nine screens.

Open: Mon–Sat 10am–9:30pm, Sun noon–5pm.

2. ANTIQUES & ART

ANTIQUES

ANTIQUE ROW, CHEROKEE STREET

Located south of downtown, not far from the Anheuser-Busch Brewery, Cherokee Street is St. Louis' premier hunting ground for antiques, known to locals as Antique Row. Surrounded by an older neighborhood of two- and three-story brick homes, it boasts nearly 5 blocks of more than 50 antiques shops, the oldest of which opened some 45 years ago. Most deal in 18th- to 20th-century collectibles and antiques, although some specialize in such items as furniture, art deco, neon, jewelry, and door handles and knobs.

Since there are so many shops, the best strategy is to cover first one side of the street and then the other. Be sure to pick up a free pamphlet on Antique Row, available at most Antique Row shops or at the St. Louis Tourist Office. It lists each shop's address, telephone number, and open hours.

Open: Hours vary, but most open Mon–Sat 10 or 11am–4 or 5pm, Sun noon–5pm. Some shops open daily, others closed Mon or Tues. Best shopping days are Thurs, Fri, and Sat.

CENTRAL WEST END

There are approximately a dozen antiques shops in the fashionable Central West End, most clustered along North Euclid Avenue or on such side streets as Maryland Avenue and McPherson. Among these are the following:

THE FOUR SEASONS WEST GALLERY, 4657 Maryland Ave. Tel. 361-2929.
This shop, in business since 1965, specializes in fine French, English, and Chinese furniture dating from the 17th century to the 19th

IMPRESSIONS

As compared with the world, St. Louis has the largest railroad station, hardware store, tobacco factories, lead works, brickyards and stove and range factories. As compared with the United States, St. Louis has the largest brewery, shoe factory, saddlery market, street-car factories, hardwood lumber market, and the finest street cars and botanical gardens . . .
—CHARLES T. LOGAN, 1897

century and also cut glass and such items as perfume bottles and paperweights—in all price ranges.

Open: Mon–Fri 1–4pm, Sat 10am–5pm.

MCPHERSON ANTIQUE GALLERY, 4728 McPherson. Tel. 361-0551.

Although a bit overpriced, the antiques, collectibles, and curios here cover four floors and include a large supply of furniture, china, glassware, and crystal.

Open: Mon–Sat 10am–5pm, Sun 11am–4pm.

ROTHSCHILD'S ANTIQUES, 398 N. Euclid Ave. Tel. 361-4870.

This shop is packed with an eclectic mix of antiques and junk, with lots in between. Furniture, watches, jewelry, lamps, mounted animal heads, old radios, stained-glass windows, paintings, and more vie for the shopper's attention. Worth a browse.

Open: Mon–Thurs 10am–6pm, Fri and Sat 10am–10pm.

WEST END GALLERY, 4732 McPherson. Tel. 361-1059.

This is actually three stores in one, containing an antique shop, a florist's shop, and a custom-made jewelry shop. The antiques are mostly from the 18th and the 19th centuries and include furniture, silver, china, and accessories.

ST. CHARLES

Located just to the northwest of St. Louis off I-70, St. Charles was the site of Missouri's first state capitol. Today it contains the state's largest National Register Historic District, with many mid-1800s buildings authentically restored. The center of St. Charles is Main Street, where you'll find a few antiques shops as well as the St. Charles Tourism Center at 230 S. Main, with its brochures and map of the city.

However, the real focal point of antiques shopping in St. Charles is Frenchtown, located a few blocks north of Main Street on North 2nd Street; it offers 10 blocks of antique shops selling American furniture, glassware, stoneware, quilts, baskets, jewelry, old toys, and collectibles.

Open: Most shops open daily 10am–4pm. Some closed Mon.

ART AND CRAFT GALLERIES

There are more than 60 art galleries listed with the St. Louis Gallery Association, covering everything from local talent to international greats. For a copy of the Association's *Gallery Guide,* published twice a year, contact the **St. Louis Gallery Association,** P.O. Box 24226, St. Louis, MO 63130. The list that follows includes some of St. Louis' most well known galleries, plus a few of my personal favorites.

ST. LOUIS ARTISTS COALITION GALLERY, Gateway One Building, Suite 1210, 701 Market St., Downtown. Tel. 241-1127.

Created in 1986 as a nonprofit organization to foster a supportive climate for the visual arts of St. Louis and regional artists, the St. Louis Artists Coalition lists more than 500 members, including professional artists, educators, designers, and art patrons. In addition to sponsoring each autumn a juried exhibition by St. Louis artists, it also stages changing exhibits by both established and emerging local

artists in its 12th-floor gallery. If you want to know about the art scene in St. Louis, this place is a good start.
Open: Mon–Fri 10am–4pm.

ATRIUM GALLERY, Old Post Office Building, 815 Olive St., Downtown. Tel. 621-1066.

Serving both the private sector and the corporate market, this commercial gallery represents contemporary artists who are active regionally and nationally. In addition to one-person shows and occasional group or theme shows, it maintains a large on-site inventory of canvases, oil and acrylic, mixed-media pieces, paper pieces, fabric works, prints, photography, and three-dimensional work.

CRAFT ALLIANCE, 6640 Delmar Blvd., University City. Tel. 725-1151.

Founded by six artisans in 1964, Craft Alliance is dedicated to exhibitions of contemporary crafts as well as to art education in the St. Louis area. Besides offering classes and workshops in everything from ceramics, weaving, painting, and metal working, it stages nine major exhibitions per year. The work of local, national, and international artists includes contemporary and avant-garde crafts made from ceramics, wood, glass, fiber, metals, and more, used to create everything from furniture and baskets to vases and jewelry. A beautiful gallery.
Open: Tues–Fri noon–5pm, Sat 10am–5pm.

THE FORUM, 555 Washington Ave., (Downtown). Tel. 421-3791.

The Forum was founded in 1980 by a group of civic and arts leaders to address arts and humanities issues with a variety of exhibits and programs. It is a multipurpose center for the arts, with an emphasis on contemporary, historic, and civic themes. With the goal of reaching as wide an audience as possible, it has dealt with a wide range of subjects—including fashion, photography, architecture, advertising art, and furniture. The Forum also sponsors musical, theatrical, and educational events.
Open: Mon–Fri 11am–6pm.

GREENBURG GALLERY, 44 Maryland Plaza, Central West End. Tel. 361-7600.

This is one of St. Louis' premier contemporary art galleries, focusing on postwar American and European paintings as well as drawings, sculpture, and ceramics. Dealing primarily with originals rather than with prints or graphics, it is a member of the Art Dealers Association of America and represents established artists of international stature, including Georgia O'Keeffe, Andy Warhol, Alexander Calder, Frank Stella, Willem DeKooning, Henry Moore, Helen Frankenthaler, Joel Shapiro, Roy Lichtenstein, and Ken Price. In addition to its Central West End location, it features young up-and-coming artists at its Greenberg Gallery Annex, 917 Locust St., located downtown.
Open: Tues–Sat 10am–5pm.

LITHOS', 6301 B. Delmar Blvd., University City. Tel. 862-0674.

This gallery features the works of top black artists from all over the country as well as artists from Africa and the Caribbean. All types of media are on display, including originals, prints, silkscreens, and even posters.

Open: Mon–Fri 10am–7:30pm, Sat 10am–6:30pm, Sun 1–5pm.

MJF ARTS STUDIO GALLERY, 1709 Washington St., (Downtown). Tel. 421-4402.

This gallery, located on the fourth floor, is an alternative exhibition space maintained for artists of St. Louis and the regional art community.

Open: Tues–Thurs 11am–5pm; opening receptions Sat 7–9pm. **Closed:** July and Aug.

RANDALL GALLERY, 999 N. 13th St., (Downtown). Tel. 231-4808.

Located one block west of the Post-Dispatch newspaper building, this is actually six gallery spaces under one roof, all in a renovated warehouse building. It features the works of regional, national, and international artists—including contemporary paintings, sculpture, drawings, prints, photographs, ceramics, and glass.

Open: Tues–Sat 10am–5pm.

PHILIP SAMUELS FINE ART, 8112 Maryland Ave., Clayton. Tel. 727-2444.

This upscale gallery carries American contemporary art, specializing in pop art. In addition to handling works by Andy Warhol, Alexander Calder, and other well-known artists, it serves as the international representative for St. Louis artists Ernest Trova and Michael Rubin.

Open: Mon–Fri 10:30am–5:30pm.

ST. LOUIS NIGHTS

No matter where your interests lie in evening entertainment, you're bound to find satisfaction in St. Louis' night scene: a Broadway production at the restored Fox Theatre, an outdoor concert underneath the stars at The Muny, or a performance of the St. Louis Symphony Orchestra. One of the most exciting developments in St. Louis' nightlife is the revitalization of North Grand Boulevard, once the heart of entertainment from the late 19th century to the mid-1950s and known as the "Broadway of the Midwest." Home of the Fox Theatre and Powell Symphony Hall, the district will eventually house nine theaters by the turn of the 21st century.

If blues are your style, you have a choice of more than two dozen clubs in St. Louis that feature blues or rhythm and blues on a regular basis, ranking the city behind only Chicago and New Orleans in terms of the availability and quality of live performances. In St. Louis you can also listen to jazz, traditional Irish music, alternative and progressive bands, and even the top 40. But the most astounding thing about St. Louis is that many of its clubs are absolutely free.

To find out what's happening where, consult the entertainment pages of the *St. Louis Post-Dispatch* morning newspaper. Two other great sources are the weekly *Riverfront Times,* distributed free at many restaurants and establishments, and the monthly *St. Louis* magazine, available at newsstands for $1.95.

1. THE PERFORMING ARTS

THEATERS

FOX THEATRE, 527 N. Grand Blvd. Tel. 534-1678; for information 534-1111; for tickets 652-5000.
When the Fabulous Fox opened in 1929, it was considered one of the three most lavishly beautiful movie houses in the country. Completely restored in 1982 to its former neo-Byzantine glory, it has 4,500 seats, a 106-foot-high ceiling with a 2,000-pound chandelier made from 2,264 pieces of jeweled glass, and a giant four-manual Wurlitzer

organ, one of five of its type ever built. The Fox features Broadway and off-Broadway productions as well as concerts by rock, pop, country and jazz performers. From September through May, it serves as the home of the Muny's Broadway musicals.

Tours: Tues, Thurs, and Sat by appointment at 10:30am; cost is $2.50 adults, $1.50 children under 12.

Prices: Usually between $5 and $35.

Open: Box office open Mon–Sat 10am–2pm; open until time of performance when there's a performance.

THE MUNY, Forest Park. Tel. 361-1900; for information 534-1111.

The Muny is a huge 12,000-seat open-air amphitheater in beautiful Forest Park. It stages Broadway musicals as well as rock and pop concerts. From September through May, The Muny presents a Broadway Series at the Fox Theatre.

Prices: Generally between $5 and $30.

Open: Box office Mon–Sat 9am–5pm; performances mid-June–Aug.

EDISON THEATRE, Mallinckrodt Center, Washington University Campus. Tel. 889-6543.

The Edison Theatre presents high-calibre performing artists in plays, dances, and concerts from throughout the country. It prides itself on presenting events that would not otherwise be brought to St. Louis, including contemporary and avant-garde theater productions and performances of the St. Louis Ballet.

Prices: Usually $16 adults, $12 senior citizens, $8 students.

Open: Box office Mon, Wed, Fri 10am–4pm, Tues and Thurs 10am–6pm, Sat 10am–2pm. Performances Sept–May. Call for exact times and schedule.

MAJOR PERFORMING ARTS COMPANIES

BLACK REPERTORY COMPANY, Administrative office, 634 N. Grand Blvd., 10th Floor, Suite F, Downtown. Tel. 534-3807.

The St. Louis Black Repertory Company was founded in 1976 to provide platforms for theater, dance, and other creative expressions from the African-American perspective, in an effort to heighten cultural awareness in its audience. Six main stage productions are

MAJOR CONCERT AND PERFORMANCE HALLS

Fox Theatre, 527 N. Grand Blvd. (tel. 534-1678)
The Muny, Forest Park (tel. 361-1900)
Edison Theatre, Mallinckrodt Center, Washington University Campus (tel. 889-6543)

offered each year, currently performed at the 23rd Street Theatre, 2240 St. Louis Ave. Note, however, that plans call for an eventual relocation to new facilities on North Grand Boulevard beside the Fox Theatre by 1992.

Prices: $5–$13.

Open: Box office at 23rd Street Theatre open from 7pm on night of performance; tickets also available at administrative office Mon–Fri 8am–6pm.

REPERTORY THEATRE OF ST. LOUIS, Loretto Hilton Center, 130 Edgar Rd., Webster University. Tel. 968-4925.
This professional, nonprofit live theatrical organization seeks to engage its audience in the thrill of live theater with its wide variety of classic and contemporary plays. Each season brings six full-length plays, of which three are new.

Prices: $7–$22.

Open: Season is Sept–Apr. Call for ticket and box office information.

THEATRE PROJECT COMPANY, Administrative office, 634 N. Grand Blvd., 10th Floor, Suite H, Downtown. Tel. 531-1301.
This professional theater company has emerged as the major off-Broadway theater of St. Louis. Dedicated to the employment of area theater artists and the revitalization of St. Louis, it presents innovative classics and new plays. Performances are held at the New City Theatre, New City School, 5209 Waterman, but note that future plans call for eventual relocation to North Grand Boulevard next to the Fox Theatre sometime in 1992.

Prices: $8–$15.

Open: Box office at administrative office open Mon–Fri 10am–5pm. Season runs end of Sept–May, performances 8pm, matinees 2pm.

OPERA

OPERA THEATRE OF ST. LOUIS, Loretto Hilton Center, 130 Edgar Rd., Webster University. Tel. 961-0171.
The Opera Theatre of St. Louis has been presenting opera, both classic and new, for more than 15 years. All productions are sung in English, accompanied by the St. Louis Symphony Orchestra. There are usually four operas per season.

Prices: $7–$45.

Open: Season runs May–Jun. Call for ticket and box office information.

CLASSICAL AND ORCHESTRAL MUSIC

ST. LOUIS SYMPHONY ORCHESTRA, Powell Symphony Hall, 718 N. Grand Blvd. Tel. 533-2500; box office 534-1700; toll free inside Missouri 800/231-1880, outside Missouri 800/232-1880.
Founded in 1880, The St. Louis Symphony Orchestra is the nation's second-oldest orchestra and is now under the dynamic direction of conductor Leonard Slatkin. A Grammy Award winner and recently named by *Time* magazine as one of the top two orchestras in the

country, it plays more than 240 concerts yearly—from classical to pop, chamber, and educational concerts.

Prices: Tickets vary; orchestral concerts start at $10.

Open: Box office open Mon–Sat 9am–5pm. Performances usually 8 or 8:30pm, Sun matinee 3pm.

DANCE

ST. LOUIS BALLET, Administrative office, 634 N. Grand Blvd., 10th Floor, Suite E, Downtown. Tel. 652-7711; box office 889-6543.

St. Louis Ballet is a professional company performing traditional and contemporary dance, under the artistic direction of Ludmila Dokoudovsky and Antoni Zalewski. Plans include the staging of many of the great but neglected ballets of the early and post-Diaghilev/Ballet Russe period with the help of artists who danced in these productions. Performances are given at Edison Theatre, Mallinckrodt Center, Washington University Campus, and other stages around town.

Prices: Usually about $13.

Open: Season is Sept–Apr. Call for box office and performance schedule.

DANCE ST. LOUIS, 149 Edgar Rd. Tel. 968-4341.

Dance St. Louis brings in national and international companies who perform traditional and contemporary ballet and modern dance. Past performances have featured the State Ballet of Missouri, the Alvin Ailey American Dance Theater, and the American Ballet Theatre. Performances are staged at Fox Theatre, Edison Theatre, and at other university theaters.

Prices: $10–$30.

Open: Season runs Oct–May. Call for exact schedule and box office hours.

DINNER THEATERS

BISSELL MANSION RESTAURANT, 4426 Randall Place. Tel. 533-9830.

Who's done it will keep you guessing as you participate in this Mystery Dinner Theater. Upon your arrival at the Bissell Mansion, built in the 1820s, you'll receive an identity, with murderers and suspects chosen randomly from the audience. The mystery unfolds as you partake a five-course dinner, including wine and your choice of three entrees. The shows change with the seasons, including, naturally, a Halloween show. Bissell Mansion is located off I-70 at the Grand Avenue exit, about 3½ miles from the Arch. Reservations are required. Incidentally, Bissell Mansion is also open for lunch and dinner throughout the week, when you can dine without having to wonder who did it.

Prices: Fri $27.95, Sat $30.95, Sun $25.95.

Open: Fri–Sun 7–10:30pm.

NATCHEZ RIVER REVUE, Lt. Robert E. Lee, 100 S. Leonor K. Sullivan Blvd. Tel. 241-1282.

In the tradition of the old riverboats, a music revue is featured aboard the Lt. Robert E. Lee, moored on the Mississippi River in the shadow of the Gateway Arch. The professional cast serves double time as the serving staff.

Prices: Show and dinner $18.95 adults, $9.95 children.
Open: Summer shows Tues–Sun, winter Thurs–Sat. Call for exact times.

---

2. THE CLUB & MUSIC SCENE

Live music every night of the week? No problem. Soulard and Laclede's Landing lead the way in terms of quantity and quality—and what's more, many performances are free. Several establishments offer dance floors in addition to live music.

DOWNTOWN

AJ'S, Adam's Mark Hotel, Fourth and Chestnut. Tel. 241-7400.

I usually encourage visitors to venture outside their hotels to immerse themselves in the city's night scene, but AJ's is so obviously popular and successful that to ignore it would be folly. Packed with both St. Louisans and out-of-towners, it boasts a dance floor with live entertainment nightly from 8:30pm, featuring top 40 tunes. There's a complimentary food buffet Monday through Friday from 4:30 to 8pm, as well as daily promotionals. On Wednesday there's AJ's own Wheel of Fortune, while Thursday is ladies' night, with reduced drink prices for females. Thursday is also when in-house phones are placed throughout the club, each marked with a balloon sporting a number: Simply single out the person you want to talk to and call him or her up. There are also backgammon tables, and the bathrooms are equipped with such high-class amenities as hairspray, makeup, and mouthwash. What will they think of next?
Prices: Beer from $2. **Admission:** Free.
Open: Mon–Fri 4:30pm–3am, Sat 7pm–3am.

KENNEDY'S 2ND STREET CO., 612 N. 2nd St., Laclede's Landing. Tel. 421-3655.

One of the few establishments at Laclede's Landing that is open for lunch and throughout the day, this locale also offers live music nightly from 10:30pm to 2:30am. Possessing a distinct warehouse atmosphere with its tall ceiling, brick walls, and wood floors, Kennedy's features original alternative and progressive music—from punk to metal, funk, blues, jazz, and Motown. As one employee said, top 40 hits are avoided here like the plague. There's a happy hour Monday through Friday from 4:30 to 6:30pm with cheaper prices for drinks, and Friday brings cheaper drinks for women all night long. The menu lists burgers, steaks, and sandwiches.
Prices: Beer from $2. **Admission:** From free to $3.
Open: Mon–Sat 11:30am–3am, Sun 11am–3am.

LUCIUS BOOMER, 707 Clamorgan Alley, Laclede's Landing. Tel. 621-8155.

Opened in 1978 and now one of the old-timers in Laclede's Landing, this club has never flagged in popularity, due in large part to the river of tourists that flood the Landing. Boomer's specialties are its exotically named drinks: The Mind Eraser sure does the job, mixing Kahlúa, vodka, and seltzer; I kind of like the sound of Sex on the

Beach with Sand in Your Crack, which is made with Chambord, Midori, vodka, and pineapple juice. A band plays nightly from 10pm to 2:30am, sticking to top-40 and recognizable tunes. There's also an outdoor patio.

Prices: Draft beer from $1.50, exotic drinks from $2.25. **Admission:** Free.

Open: Daily 8pm–3am.

MISSISSIPPI NIGHTS, 914 N. 1st St., Laclede's Landing. Tel. 421-3853.

This may be the best place in the city to hear live music, as everyone from Jimmy Cliff and Tracy Chapman to the Talking Heads have performed here. Only 1,000 people can squeeze through its doors, and the music gets so loud that earplugs are available at the front door. There's a dance floor, and when the big names aren't playing, the music is usually rock and alternative rock.

Prices: Beer from $2. **Admission:** Usually $3–5, as much as $14 for big names.

Open: Mon–Thurs 8pm–1am, Fri and Sat 8pm–3am.

MISSOURI JOE'S, Union Station, 20th and Market Sts. Tel. 231-6563.

This is a slick nightclub, with a large dance floor and two bars. It features live music nightly from 10pm to 2am, usually jazz and blues, and there's happy hour Monday through Friday from 4 to 7pm, with a food buffet and reduced drink prices. Ladies' nights are Wednesday and Thursday, with free admission and special drink prices.

Prices: Beer from $2.50. **Admission:** Sun–Thurs $1–$2, Fri and Sat $3.

Open: Daily 4pm–3am.

MUDDY WATERS, 724 N. 1st St., Laclede's Landing. Tel. 421-5335.

Dichotomy, the house band here, has been raising a ruckus for 15 years. Playing old rock-'n'-roll and country music, the band members are notorious for their comments between songs, which can only be classified as vulgar comedy, with most of the fun poked at the audience. Lord help any woman who gets up to go to the bathroom. But the audience seems to eat it up, and this place is packed most nights of the week. The band and crowd ridicule begin at 9:30pm. There's an outdoor patio; the house specialty is charbroiled catfish.

Prices: Beer from $2.25. **Admission:** Free.

Open: Mon–Sat 11am–3am, Sun noon–midnight.

SOULARD

HILARY'S, 1017 Russell Blvd., Soulard. Tel. 421-3126.

This is a great place to spend an evening listening to blues, jazz, or Motown; drinking; and dining on blackened redfish, filet mignon, or chicken chardonnay. It's a tiny place, but that doesn't stop people from pouring through its doors. Highly recommended.

Prices: Beer from $1.75, cocktails $2.75. **Admission:** Free.

Open: Mon–Thurs 7:30pm–1am, Fri and Sat 9pm–1am, Sun 7:30pm–midnight.

JOHN D. MCGURK'S, 1200 Russell Blvd., Soulard. Tel. 776-8309.

A simple establishment with brick archways and a wooden floor, this pub is true to its name by featuring live Irish music, either bands brought over from the old country or local bands that play Irish tunes. Sometimes a Scottish group slips through. Happy hour is daily from 5 to 7pm, with such food specials as tacos on Wednesday and chicken wings on Friday. A lively place.

Prices: Beer from $2.25. **Admission:** Free.
Open: Mon–Fri 11am–1:30am, Sat noon–1:30am, Sun 4pm–midnight.

MIKE & MIN'S, 10th and Geyer, Soulard. Tel. 421-1655.
Formerly a dry-goods store dating from 1850 but the site of a tavern for almost 60 years, this establishment specializes in import beers, with 30 different brands, along with a full-service bar. Its bands, which perform Thursday to Saturday from 9pm to 1am, play jazz and the blues. There are a happy hour Monday through Friday from 4 to 7pm and extensive lunch and dinner menus.

Prices: Draft beer from $1.25. **Admission:** Fri and Sat $1.
Open: Mon–Wed 11am–11pm, Thurs–Sat 11am–1:30am.

UNIVERSITY CITY

CICERO'S, 6510 Delmar Blvd., University City. Tel. 862-0009.
An informal place with a bar on the ground floor and a live-music hall in the basement, Cicero's is a venue for jazz, folk, funk, and rock. The ground-floor bar serves Italian pizza and pastas.

Prices: Beer from $1.75. **Admission:** $2 or $3.
Open: Ground-floor bar daily 11am–12:30am; music hall opens at 7:30pm, live music from 9pm.

COMEDY

FUNNY BONE COMEDY CLUB, 940 West Port Plaza, West County. Tel. 469-6692.
Located in the West Port Plaza shopping-and-dining complex just off I-270, the Funny Bone offers live comedy seven nights a week. On Monday it's The Best of St. Louis, featuring local comedians, while on Tuesday it's open mike. If you come before the show for dinner, you're guaranteed a reserved seat, but be sure to make a reservation beforehand. Entrees include seafood, pasta, chicken, and steak dishes. No one under 18 admitted.

Prices: Beer from $2. **Admission:** Mon–Thurs $3, Fri and Sun $6, Sat $9.
Open: Shows Mon–Thurs 8:30pm; Fri 8:30 and 10:45pm; Sat 7:45pm, 10pm, and midnight; Sun 8pm.

3. THE BAR SCENE

BLUEBERRY HILL, 6504 Delmar Blvd., University City. Tel. 727-0880.
If you're a rock-'n'-roll fan, chances are that you've already heard of

Blueberry Hill. It's a St. Louis institution, an attraction in its own right, and a treasure trove of memorabilia that includes a Howdy Doody collection and a compilation of record jackets nailed to the walls. It contains more memorabilia on Chuck Berry than any other place in the world, including his ES-350 Gibson, which he used to compose "Roll Over Beethoven." Other collections on display include Pee Wee Herman dolls, lunchboxes, the Smurfs, and papier-mâché animals. Blueberry Hill also boasts seven dart boards and a jukebox that has been rated the best in the country, with a selection of nearly 100 songs that are changed every two weeks from a library of more than 30,000 45's. There's live music Friday and Saturday night from 9pm downstairs in the Elvis Room, where the cover charge ranges from $3 to $5.

Prices: Beer from $1.75.

Open: Mon–Sat 11am–1:30am, Sun 11am–midnight.

DRESSEL'S, 419 N. Euclid Ave., Central West End. Tel. 361-1060.

This is one of my favorite pubs in St. Louis, a true Welsh pub that knows its beer and its grub. Dressel's walls are filled with portraits of writers and musicians, all done on commission by local artists or donated by friends and patrons of the bar. Beethoven, William Faulkner, Mozart, Count Basie, and Emily Dickinson are just some of those who stare down at you as you put away Welsh vegetarian pie or a Ploughman's lunch, washing it down with Welsh ale. Upstairs is The Pub Above, which features a bar created from antique moldings, a jazz quartet on Wednesday, and classical music on Saturday.

Prices: Wine from $2.50, Welsh ales $3.75.

Open: Dressel's Mon–Fri 11:30am–2pm and 5pm–1am, Sat noon–1am, Sun noon–midnight; The Pub Above Wed–Sun 5:30pm–1:30am.

HOULIHAN'S, Union Station, 18th and Market. Tel. 436-0844.

Houlihan's, which had its beginnings in Kansas City and has since spread like a prairie fire throughout the country, is a popular place for both drinking and dining. It features a happy hour on Monday through Friday from 4 to 7pm, with drink specials and a food buffet, as well as an extensive menu that ranges from quiche and fajitas to Cajun shrimp, fresh fish, sandwiches, and baby-back ribs. Across Union Station's artificial lake is an outdoor pavilion, Houlihan's Biergarten, with live music Thursday through Sunday evening in the

---

IMPRESSIONS

Meet me in St. Louis, Louis,
Meet me at the fair.
Don't tell me the lights are shining,
Any place but there.
We will dance the Hoochee Koochee,
I will be your tootsie wootsie,
If you will meet me in St. Louis, Louis,
Meet me at the fair.
—F. A. MILLS, 1904

summer. In addition, there's another Houlihan's located in the St. Louis Galleria, at Clayton Road and Brentwood Boulevard (tel. 863-9116).

Prices: Beer from $2.
Open: Mon–Sat 11am–1am, Sun 10am–11pm.

O'CONNELL'S PUB, 4652 Shaw, at Kingshighway, the Hill. Tel. 773-6600.

Located on the edge of the Italian Hill district, this Irish pub, named after a street in Dublin, is famous for its burgers. O'Connell's is a popular place also for a brew and has been in business since 1962. It's located in a hundred-year-old building with wooden floors and a pressed-tin ceiling.

Prices: Beer from $1.25.
Open: Mon–Sat 11:15am–1:30am.

4. MORE ENTERTAINMENT

MOVIES

THE CENTER OF CONTEMPORARY ARTS [COCA], 524 Trinity Ave., University City. Tel. 735-6555.

This center, devoted to the visual and performing arts, presents a year-round film series featuring international cinema.

Ticket prices: $4.

ST. LOUIS ART MUSEUM, Forest Park. Tel. 721-0067.

Films are shown Tuesday and Friday year-round at this great museum, usually on a certain cinematic theme—from French classics to film legends.

Ticket prices: $3 adults, $2 senior citizens and students.

TIVOLI PREMIER THEATRE, 6350 Delmar Blvd., University City. Tel. 725-0220.

Alternative films, both domestic and international, are featured here, primarily those that are never shown at the regular movie houses.

Ticket prices: $5 adults, $3 children and senior citizens.

CHAPTER 11

EASY EXCURSIONS

1. HANNIBAL
2. SPRINGFIELD, ILLINOIS

The destinations in this chapter are easy half-day, day, or overnight trips.

1. HANNIBAL

I wonder whether Mark Twain would recognize Hannibal today. As it is, Twain put Hannibal on the international map, and today it receives annually about a quarter of a million visitors who come to pay tribute to one of America's greatest authors and humorists. Twain's name is bestowed upon everything, from a campground and a motel to restaurants and sights. No doubt Twain would have given free reign to his thoughts about that, but even during his lifetime the town had changed. While on one of his visits, he noted with his usual dry wit, "Everything was changed, but when I reached Third or Fourth street the tears burst forth, for I recognized the mud." Yet despite the fact that the town capitalizes heavily on Mark Twain's name, Hannibal remains remarkably and refreshingly small town. True, it does have souvenir shops and all the trappings that go with them, but Hannibal is not nearly the tourist trap it could be—it's simply not sophisticated enough for that. It remains friendly, charming, and unassuming, still that "white town drowsing in the sun." It's a great family destination.

ORIENTATION

Hannibal, located about 120 miles from St. Louis, is easily reached via Highway 61. The **Visitors and Convention Bureau** is located at 320 Broadway in the heart of Hannibal (tel. 314/221-2477)—open Monday to Friday from 8am to noon and from 1 to 5pm. In addition, there's an **Information Booth** set up during the warmer months at 402 N. Main Street (tel. 314/221-8300)—open daily Memorial Day to Labor Day from 9:30am to 5:30pm and on some weekends during April, May, September, and October.

Most of the town's major attractions are located on Main and Hill streets, just a stone's throw from the Mississippi. The tourist offices distribute a pamphlet on Hannibal that contains a map.

THE *DELTA QUEEN* AND THE *MISSISSIPPI QUEEN*

Although you can drive to Hannibal from St. Louis in less than two hours, a much more relaxed and traditional way to travel there is by boat on the Mississippi. The *Delta Queen* and the *Mississippi Queen* are the only two steamboats left in America that offer the unique opportunity to live aboard a luxury steamer, dine and sleep in luxury, and watch the Mississippi valley roll by. The *Delta Queen*, built in 1926, is listed on the National Register of Historic Places and is also designated a National Historic Landmark. The *Mississippi Queen,* commissioned in 1976, is the largest steamboat the world has ever seen. Both boats make two round-trip journeys from St. Louis to Hannibal each summer, which includes three nights aboard ship and a day in Hannibal. Cabin prices as of 1990 ranged from $445 to $1,500. For information on sailing dates and current prices, call toll free 800/543-1949.

WHAT TO SEE AND DO

A town of approximately 20,000 people, Hannibal was founded in 1818 and is known worldwide as the boyhood home of Samuel Clemens, who lived here from 1839 to 1853 before going on to become a river pilot and a famous writer under the pen name of Mark Twain. Understandably, many of Hannibal's attractions relate to its most famous citizen.

MARK TWAIN BOYHOOD HOME AND MUSEUM, 208 Hill St. Tel. 314/221-9010.

Judge John Clemens moved his family to this small white-clapboard home in 1844, when Sam Clemens was four years old. Only two blocks from the Mississippi River, the home is featured in Twain's *The Adventure of Tom Sawyer* as the residence of Aunt Polly, Tom Sawyer, Sid, and Mary. It's a simple home that was recently restored to the way it looked back in the 1800s.

Adjoining the home is the Mark Twain Museum, which contains some photographs, one of Twain's legendary white coats, and first editions of Twain's books. There also are translations of *Tom Sawyer* in more than a dozen languages, including Japanese, Hungarian, Indian, and Afrikaans. Also included are some original paintings of Tom Sawyer by Norman Rockwell. Across the street are Judge John Clemens' law office and the home of Laura Hawkins, after whom Twain modeled his Becky Thatcher. And you can't miss that white-washed fence.

Admission: $2.50 adults, $1 children 6 to 10.

Open: Summer daily 8am–6pm, spring and autumn daily 8am–5pm, winter daily 10am–4pm. **Closed:** Thanksgiving and Christmas.

HANNIBAL RIVERBOAT'S MARK TWAIN, Center Street Landing. Tel. 314/221-3222, or toll free 800/621-2322.

The Mississippi has always played an integral part in towns that sprang up beside it, and Hannibal is no exception. From May through October, you can join a one-hour cruise aboard the *Mark Twain,* built in 1964, and float past barges and the river valley while listening to a narrator describe legends, lore, and facts about the river. You'll learn, for example, that a barge can haul three times the amount a freight train can at 60% of the cost and that the Mississippi has an average depth of only 11 feet. In the evening are dinner cruises featuring prime rib on Friday and Saturday and baked chicken the rest of the week, along with live music and dancing.

Admission: One-hour cruise $6 adults, $3 children; dinner cruise Fri and Sat, $22.95, Sun–Thurs $17.95.

Open: Cruises in May daily 1:30pm and Fri and Sat 7pm; June, July, and Aug daily 11am, 1:30pm, 4pm, and 7pm; Sept daily 1:30 and 6:30pm, Sat 4pm; Oct daily 1:30pm and 4pm, and Fri and Sat 6:30pm.

MARK TWAIN CAVE, Missouri Route 79. Tel. 314/221-1656.

One mile south of Hannibal, this cave, discovered in 1819, was the one Sam Clemens played in as a young boy. Twain later used it in *Tom Sawyer* and *Huckleberry Finn* as the cave containing buried treasure, where Tom and Becky Thatcher were lost and where Injun Joe met his demise. In 1886 it became the first Missouri cave to be opened to the public, and six miles of passageways have been mapped. One-hour guided tours, departing every 15 minutes, cover less than a mile through the cave along smooth walkways carved ages ago by an underground stream. These tours are fun and informative and supply many anecdotes about Tom Sawyer and Huck Finn. Jesse James reportedly hid out here, too, and even wrote his name in the cave wall with a pencil.

Admission: $6 adults, $5 senior citizens 65 and older, $3 children ages 5 to 12.

Open: Apr–May and Sept–Oct 9am–6pm, June–Aug 8am–8pm, Nov–Mar 9am–4pm. The last tour departs one hour before closing. **Closed:** Thanksgiving and Christmas.

ROCKCLIFFE MANSION, 1000 Bird St. Tel. 314/221-4140.

Mark Twain gave a speech from this mansion's staircase during his last visit to Hannibal in 1902, and as many as 300 guests were able to hear it. This huge mansion was built by lumber magnate John Cruikshank around the turn of the century and served as his home until his death in 1924. The 30-room house was decorated, not in Victorian style, but in art nouveau style, and it was equipped with all the modern conveniences of the day, including electric lights in all the closets that turned on automatically when the doors were opened. Everything is elaborately decorated, from the miniature copy of the Waldorf-Astoria's Turkish ballroom in New York to the dining-room wallpaper imported from Paris at $134 a roll. Forty-five-minute tours of the home are given throughout the day.

Admission: $3.50 adults, $1 children 6 to 11.

Open: Mar–Nov 9:30am–5pm (last tour); Dec–Feb 11:30am–3:30pm. **Closed:** Thanksgiving, Christmas, and New Year's Day.

WHERE TO STAY

FIFTH STREET MANSION, 213 S. 5th St., Hannibal, MO 63401. Tel. 314/221-0445. 7 rms, all with bath. A/C

$ Rates: (including breakfast, afternoon tea, and wine): $55–$75 double; two-bedroom suite $70 for two adults and two children, $80 for four adults; extra person $10. AE, DISC, MC, V.

This bed-and-breakfast, built in 1858 and listed on the National Register of Historic Places, is located in the heart of Hannibal. Built in Italianate style by a former Hannibal mayor, it has a huge Tiffany window on the first landing of the front staircase, 8 fireplaces, and a total of 21 rooms. Seven rooms are available for guests, each different from the others. On the top floor is a two-room suite that's perfect for families.

GARTH WOODSIDE MANSION, R. R. 1, Hannibal, MO 63401. Tel. 314/221-2789. 8 rms, all with bath. A/C

$ Rates (including breakfast): $58–$80 double; extra person $15. Situated on 39 rolling acres south of Hannibal, this bed-and-breakfast was built in 1871 as the summer residence of John and Helen Garth. Most of its Victorian furnishings are original to the mansion, including the gaslights and even the Victorian bed where Mark Twain is reputed to have slept while visiting the Garths. An elegant breakfast is served in the formal dining hall, and Victorian nightshirts are provided. In the summer, you'll want to sit on the wraparound veranda to enjoy the peaceful view; in winter you'll wish to warm yourself at the open fireplace. All in all, this is a perfect place for experiencing Mark Twain's Hannibal—but note that children under 12 are not accepted.

HOLIDAY INN, U.S. 61 at Market St., Hannibal, MO 63401. Tel. 314/221-6610, or toll free 800/325-0777. 238 rms, 3 suites. A/C TEL TV
$ Rates: $60 single; $65–$75 double; suite $93. Extra person $7. Children 19 and under stay free in parents' room. Weekend and special packages available. AE, CB, DC, DISC, MC, V.

Like Holidomes across the nation, this Holiday Inn is a favorite with families because it offers so much for kids to do. The rooms are similar to others in this chain and face either the Holidome or the outside. Its lounge features live music Monday through Saturday evening.

    Services: Laundry service.

    Facilities: One restaurant, lounge, indoor swimming pool, sauna, whirlpool, game room, putting greens, outdoor tennis courts, jogging track, pool table, Ping-Pong tables, convenience store, gift shop, hair salon.

WHERE TO DINE

MARK TWAIN DINETTE AND FAMILY RESTAURANT, 3rd and Hill Sts., Tel. 221-5511.
    Cuisine: AMERICAN
$ Prices: $2.50–$7.50. AE, DISC, MC.
    Open: Sun–Thurs 6am–10pm, Sat and Fri 6am–11pm.

Located a stone's throw from Mark Twain's Boyhood Home, this is the epitome of a small-town family restaurant, with informal and friendly service, artificial plants and flowers, and even a drive-in service out back. Locally owned and operated since 1942, it offers biscuits and gravy, pancakes, and eggs for breakfast; lunch and dinner include burgers, sandwiches, chili, grilled chicken, steak, pork chops, halibut, and catfish from the Mississippi River. There are a salad bar and a children's menu.

MISSOURI TERRITORY RESTAURANT & LOUNGE, 600 Broadway. Tel. 248-1440.
    Cuisine: AMERICAN
$ Prices: Lunch $4.25–$6; dinner $5.50–$18. AE, MC, V.
    Open: Tues–Sat 11am–2pm and 5–10pm, Sun 11am–2pm and 5–8pm.

This restaurant occupies the first floor of what was once a federal courthouse, an impressive limestone building dating from 1888. Its luncheon specials include a variety of sandwiches, although diners are welcome to order from the dinner menu, which includes everything from more sandwiches to chicken, fish, seafood, prime rib, and steaks. There's a lounge downstairs.

DINNER THEATERS

MOLLY BROWN DINNER THEATER, 200 N. Main St. Tel. 221-8940.

Cuisine: AMERICAN **Reservations:** Required for evening show.

$ **Prices:** Lunch show $7.95 adults, $3.95 children; evening show $14.95 adults, $7.95 children, plus tax. MC, V.

Open: Memorial Day to Labor Day daily—lunch show noon–2pm, evening show 6:30–9:15pm.

Mark Twain isn't Hannibal's only famous personality. The Unsinkable Molly Brown was born here in 1867, leaving at the age of 17 in search of a rich husband in Leadville, Colorado. This dinner theater features a musical revue honoring both citizens, with performances provided by professionals who also serve the food. Lunch includes an open-face barbecued beef sandwich, while dinner gives you a choice of roast sirloin, baked lemon-pepper catfish, and barbecue beef sandwich. Fun for the entire family.

MARK TWAIN OUTDOOR THEATRE, Route 3, New London. Tel. 221-2945.

Cuisine: AMERICAN **Reservations:** Recommended.

$ **Prices:** Show and dinner $15 adults, $8 children; show only $8 adults, $4 children.

Open: Daily May–Sept, buffet from 4pm; show starts at 8:30pm.

Located four miles south of Hannibal on Highway 61, this outdoor theater presents a two-hour show reflecting the life and times of Mark Twain, with scenes from *Tom Sawyer* and *Huckleberry Finn.* The stage is separated from the audience by a body of water, complete with a 50-foot replica of a Mississippi riverboat. Before the show, you can eat all you want at a buffet, after which it's just a short walk to the stage. You also can watch the show without eating dinner.

2. SPRINGFIELD, ILLINOIS

In 1837 a young Abraham Lincoln moved to Springfield, Illinois, where he practiced law, married Mary Todd, and eventually had four sons. Almost a quarter of a century later he was elected 16th president of the United States and departed for his new office, never to return alive again.

But Springfield has never forgotten its favorite son, and Lincoln is buried here with his family. Today Springfield draws many visitors to its Lincoln Home, which presents lively tours that breathe life into the times of one of our most loved presidents. For children, the Lincoln Home is a tangible connection to Lincoln, making him much more real than the pages of a history book could. Not far from Springfield is New Salem, a reconstructed village where Lincoln lived, worked, and studied law before moving to Springfield. If you're an architecture buff, you'll want to hightail it to the Dana-Thomas House, designed by Frank Lloyd Wright and recently completely restored.

ORIENTATION

The capital of Illinois with a population of about 100,000, Springfield is located at the intersection of Interstates 55 and 72, about 102 miles from

St. Louis, 195 miles from Chicago, and 311 miles from Kansas City.

For information and brochures about Springfield, contact the **Springfield Convention and Visitors Bureau,** 109 N. 7th St. (tel. 217/789-2360, or toll free 800/545-7300)—open Monday through Friday from 8am to 5pm. More convenient, perhaps, is the Visitor Information booth at the **Lincoln Home Visitor Center,** 426 S. 7th St. (tel. 789-2357)—open daily from 8:30am to 5pm—which is where visitors pick up tickets to tour the Lincoln Home.

WHAT TO SEE AND DO

LINCOLN HOME VISITOR CENTER, 426 S. 7th St. Tel. 789-2357.

This should be the first stop on your sightseeing itinerary, because it's here that you can pick up free tickets to tour the Lincoln Home, which are for a specific time and are issued on a first-come, first-served basis. The center contains an exhibit on Springfield during Lincoln's time and presents two 20-minute films throughout the day, *Mr. Lincoln's Springfield* and *At Home with Mr. Lincoln.* There's also a bookstore with books on Lincoln as well as a Visitor Information booth with brochures on sights in Springfield. The Lincoln Home Visitor Center and the Lincoln Home are located on the Lincoln Home National Historic Site, a four-block area administered by the National Park Service. In addition to the Lincoln Home, 12 neighboring homes dating from the 1800s have been preserved (many are now used as office space).

Admission: Free.

Open: Daily 8:30am–5pm. **Closed:** Thanksgiving, Christmas, New Year's Day.

LINCOLN HOME, 8th and Jackson Sts. Tel. 492-4150.

The only house Abraham Lincoln ever owned, this served as the Lincoln family home for 17 years, and it was here that three of Lincoln's four sons were born and one died. A modest wooden home built in 1839 and later enlarged by the Lincolns, who added the entire second floor, it has been restored as authentically as possible, right down to its wallpaper, carpets, and curtains. Furnished with original Lincoln belongings and reproductions of period pieces, the home reflects the taste of Mary Lincoln, who came from a prominent Kentucky banking family. The conducted tour presents a lively account of the life and times of Lincoln and his family.

Admission: Free. (Obtain tickets at the nearby Visitor Center.)

Open: Daily 8:30am–5pm. **Closed:** Thanksgiving, Christmas, New Year's Day.

LINCOLN TOMB HISTORIC SITE, Oak Ridge Cemetery, entrance at 1500 N. Monument Ave. or N. Walnut St. Tel. 782-2717.

Lincoln was buried here in 1865, in a tomb that was built with public contributions. His wife, Mary, and three of their sons also are buried here. The site contains a number of Lincoln and Civil War sculptures, but most well known is the bust of Lincoln that guards the entrance to the tomb—generations of visitors have rubbed the nose in the belief that it will bring them luck, giving the nose a shining glow.

Admission: Free.

Open: Daily 9am–5pm. **Closed:** Thanksgiving, Christmas, New Year's Day.

OLD STATE CAPITOL, Downtown Mall. Tel. 785-7961.

Only a five-minute walk from Lincoln's Home, this handsome building served as the state capitol from 1839 to 1876; it contains the Illinois Supreme Court and a law library. Considered a perfect example of Greek Revival architecture, the capitol has been completely reconstructed, refurnished, and restored to how it looked during Lincoln's legislative years. Many of the objects now on display relate to famous people who used the building, including Stephen A. Douglas, Lincoln, and Ulysses S. Grant. On the ground floor is a handwritten copy of Lincoln's *Gettysburg Address*, the third of five surviving manuscripts. Tours of the building are conducted. Of special note are tours on Friday and Saturday (except in May), in which costumed interpreters portray historical characters of the times. In addition, in summer on Friday and Saturday evening, there are candlelit, costumed interpretive tours (call 785-9363 to reserve your seat).

Admission: Free.

Open: Daily 9am–5pm (last tour 4:30pm). Costume tours Fri and Sat 10am–noon and 1–4pm (except May); mid-June–mid-Aug 7:30pm.

DANA-THOMAS HOUSE, 301 E. Lawrence Ave. Tel. 782-6776.

Designed by Frank Lloyd Wright and built in 1902, this is considered the best-preserved and most complete of Wright's early Prairie houses. It was constructed for Springfield socialite Susan Lawrence Dana, who entertained regularly, welcomed guests from all over the world, married three times, and ended up being declared incompetent by the courts and admitted to a local hospital a few years before she died. At any rate, what makes this house especially remarkable is that it contains more than 100 pieces of original Wright-designed furniture made specifically for the house, as well as 250 examples of art-glass doors and windows and about 200 original light fixtures. Tours of the home take approximately one hour.

Admission: Free.

Open: Daily 9am–5pm (last tour 4pm). **Closed:** Thanksgiving, Christmas, New Year's Day.

NEW SALEM STATE HISTORIC SITE, Petersburg, IL. Tel. 632-7953.

Located about a half-hour's drive northwest of Springfield on Route 97, New Salem is a reconstruction of a village that once existed here. Twenty-three log cabins have been authentically reproduced on the sites mentioned in interviews that were conducted in the 1880s of people who had lived here. Its heyday was in the 1830s, with a population of 125 recorded in 1832 (the same as Chicago at the time). Lincoln lived here from 1831 to 1837, working as a laborer, store clerk, merchant, county surveyor, postmaster, and captain of the local militia. This is also where he studied law on his own and was elected to the state legislature. In 1840 the town was abandoned.

The village contains a cooper shop (the only original building, more than 150 years old); a blacksmith's shop; a tavern; a carding mill; a saw and grist mill; stores; homes; and even gardens with corn, herbs, and other crops that were cultivated in the 1830s. From April through November, interpreters in period costume are on hand to describe the buildings and the various trades conducted there.

While here, you may wish to board the *Talisman River Boat,* a replica of an 1830s steamboat, for a one-hour trip on the Sangamon River (board near the grist mill). In addition, *The Great American People Show* is an outdoor dramatic portrayal of the life of Lincoln, including his struggle for the presidency and his years in office. For ticket reservations, call 217/632-7755.

Admission: Free to New Salem; *Talisman River Boat* $1.50 adults, $1 children ages 4 to 12; *The Great American People Show* $7.50 adults, $6 students and senior citizens; $21 family rate.

Open: New Salem summer daily 9am–5pm, winter daily 8am–4pm. **Closed:** Thanksgiving, Christmas, New Year's Day. *Talisman River Boat* May–Aug daily 9am–4pm, Sept–Oct weekends only 9am–4pm. *The Great American People Show* mid-June–mid-Aug Tues–Sun 8pm.

GEORGE COLIN FOLK ART, Route 97, Salisbury, IL. Tel. 217/626-1204.

As you travel on Route 97 between Springfield and New Salem, you'll pass an ordinary house made extraordinary by a profusion of colorful art in the yard. That's the home of George Colin, well known in these parts for his folk art, which takes whimsical shape mainly as benches, chairs, tables, and sculpture painted in bright colors. There are watermelon chairs, peacock tables, strawberry benches, Lincoln statues, and much more. In his studio/barn in the back, George also draws five chalk pictures a day, which he sells in his Chicago gallery. If George is busy, his wife, Winnie, will happily show people around.

Open: Whenever the Colins are at home.

WHERE TO STAY

RAMADA RENAISSANCE HOTEL, 701 E. Adams St., Springfield, IL 62701. Tel. 217/544-8800, or toll free 800/228-9898. 316 rms. A/C MINIBAR TEL TV

$ Rates: $94–$105 single; $111–$121 double; Executive Club floor $130 single, $145 double. Extra person $15. Children under 18 stay free in parents' room. Weekend and senior-citizen discounts available. AE, DC, MC, V.

This is Springfield's top hotel, a tall brick building located downtown. Each room is comfortably appointed, outfitted with either a king-size bed or two double beds as well as minibar and cable TV with remote control and pay movies. If you feel like pampering yourself, stay at one of the Executive Club Level rooms on the top two floors, where the rooms are larger and have the added benefits of free sparkling water, terrycloth robes, hairdryers, telephones in the bathrooms, and free continental breakfast and afternoon hors d'oeuvres served in the private lounge.

Dining/Entertainment: Floreale, decorated with handblown chandeliers from Italy, is the hotel's signature restaurant, serving steaks and seafood. Lindsey's, more casual, serves breakfast, lunch, and dinner and is open on Sunday, when most downtown restaurants are closed. Glove Tavern is the hotel's bar, which serves lunch on weekdays.

Services: Babysitting service, laundry and valet service, room service to 2am, complimentary airport transportation.

Facilities: Indoor swimming pool, whirlpool, health club, game room.

HOLIDAY INN EAST, 3100 S. Dirksen Parkway, Springfield, IL 62703. Tel. 217/529-7171, or toll free 800/ HOLIDAY. 340 rms, 45 suites. A/C TEL TV

$ Rates: $65–$75 single; $74–$85 double. Extra person $8. Children under 18 stay free in parents' room. Corporate, family, and special packages available. AE, CB, DC, MC, V.

Located off I-55, about a 15-minute drive from Lincoln's Home, this is a great place for families. Its Holidome is about the size of a football field, with a lap pool, a snack bar, and a score of other diversions. The rooms were furnished by local decorators rather than by a designer from the Holiday Inn chain, giving them a more personal flavor in color schemes of light maroon and jungle green. As though its facilities weren't enough, the hotel will even rent you a VCR along with two videos for $5.

Facilities: Coffee shop, dining room, snack bar, lounge (with nightly entertainment), gift shop (with souvenirs of Springfield), indoor and outdoor pools, exercise room, whirlpool, sauna, shuffleboard, playground, game arcade, Ping-Pong table, pool tables, putting green, outdoor tennis court, coin-operated laundry.

CORINNE'S BED AND BREAKFAST, 1001 S. 6th St., Springfield, IL 62703. Tel. 217/527-1400. 5 rms, 3 with bath. A/C (TEL and TV available)

$ Rates (including buffet breakfast): High season single or double $65 without bath, $75 with bath, $85 suite; low season $60, $65, and $75, respectively. MC, V.

Built in 1883 by a prominent grocer and banker, this Queen Anne home is in the center of town, about five blocks from Lincoln's Home. It has been beautifully decorated—with a cheerful and sunny breakfast room, a comfortable communal living room with a TV and fireplace, and guest rooms that show the feminine touch of its owners. Women traveling alone will especially appreciate the homey and friendly atmosphere here. Highly recommended.

WHERE TO DINE

You can't be in Springfield long before you hear about its famous Horseshoe, a local specialty since anyone can remember: basically an open-face sandwich that originally featured ham and a cheese sauce and was served on a metal plate (the anvil) with french fries (representing the nails). Now there are many various kinds of Horseshoes, including turkey and hamburger; because the portions are massive, smaller Ponyshoes also are available.

If you're in downtown Springfield on a Sunday, when everything is closed, head for the Ramada Renaissance Hotel, where you'll find Lindsey's serving food daily from 6:30am to 11pm (see "Where to Stay," above).

MALDANER'S, 222 S. 6th St. Tel. 522-4313.

Cuisine: AMERICAN/CONTINENTAL

$ Prices: Lunch $3.25–$6; dinner downstairs $3.70–$12; entrees upstairs $15–$22. AE, DC, MC, V.

Open: Downstairs Mon–Fri 11am–9pm; upstairs Tues–Thurs 6–10pm, Fri and Sat 6–11pm.

Maldaner's has been a familiar name to the natives of Springfield ever since it first opened in 1884. Originally owned by a baker, confectioner, and caterer, it moved into its present building in 1896 and still boasts a pressed-tin ceiling and wainscot walls. The informal downstairs serves soups, salads, and sandwiches, including Horse-shoes and Ponyshoes; its dinner menu changes often but includes an interesting variety of choices—from perhaps a vegetable stir-fry to blackened catfish; Thai chicken cakes; or fettucini with chicken, artichokes, and pesto. The more formal upstairs dining hall, open only for dinner, also offers innovative selections, featuring perhaps grilled duck with apricot marmalade, sautéed veal with polenta and tomato ragout, and beef Wellington.

NORB ANDY'S, 518 E. Capitol. Tel. 523-7777.

   Cuisine: AMERICAN
$ Prices: Lunch $3–$6; dinner $3–$12. AE, CB, DC, MC, V.
   Open: Mon–Thurs 11am–10pm, Fri and Sat 11am–11pm, Sun (no food served) 7–11pm.

Norb Andy's is a well-known tavern, popular in part because of its convenient location halfway between Lincoln's Home and the new state capitol. There's been a tavern here since the 1930s (operating as a speakeasy during Prohibition), and its specialty is the Horseshoe (nine different kinds). Norb Andy's also serves sandwiches and burgers for lunch and steaks and seafood for dinner. It doesn't serve food on Sunday, but it's open for live jazz, for which there's no cover charge. There's also jazz most Wednesday through Saturday evenings.

CAPITOL TELETRACK, Chatham Square Center, 1766 Wabash Ave. Tel. 546-2111.

   Cuisine: AMERICAN
$ Prices: Appetizers $4–$7.50; entrees $7.50–$16. AE, MC, V.
   Open: Tues–Sun noon–midnight.

If you like to wager on horses, you probably won't be able to stay away from this off-track wagering facility, with its 16 betting windows. Offering closed-circuit TV monitors that broadcast races from Fairmount Park and Chicago-area tracks, Capitol Teletrack is located on the west end of town in a shopping center. You must be at least 21 to enter, and no admission is charged. The Secretariat Dining Room is the facility's formal dining room, offering personal TV monitors and entrees ranging from prime rib and filet mignon to broiled swordfish, chicken, and spaghetti. If that's too formal, you can order sandwiches and snacks in the lounge area.

GEORGE WARBURTONS, South Shore Drive, Petersburg. Tel. 632-7878.

   Cuisine: AMERICAN **Reservation:** Necessary on weekends.
$ Prices: Lunch $4–$8.50; dinner $4–$11. MC, V.
   Open: Sun, Tues–Thurs 11am–9pm, Fri and Sat 11am–10pm.

This is the best place to eat if you're visiting New Salem State Historic Site. To reach it, drive through the public parking lot and camp-ground at New Salem and then take a right (or ask directions at New Salem). Open only since 1989, George Warburtons is a pleasant and casual family restaurant with an outdoor patio and a separate bar that's designed to resemble a library. It's owned by a man-and-wife team—she's a nutritionist, he's a pork producer. Naturally, pork is the specialty here, but there also are sandwiches (including the Horseshoe); for dinner there are also steaks, seafood, and chicken.

PART TWO

KANSAS CITY

CHAPTER 12

GETTING TO KNOW KANSAS CITY

1. ORIENTATION
2. GETTING AROUND
• FAST FACTS:
   KANSAS CITY

Approximately 250 miles due west of St. Louis, Kansas City is a sprawling metropolis with approximately 1.5 million people living in the greater metropolitan area. Famous for its steaks, barbecue, jazz, and rich frontier history, Kansas City claims to have more boulevards than Paris and more fountains than any city outside Rome. As the starting point for the Santa Fe, Oregon, and California trails, Kansas City also claims that it, rather than St. Louis, served as true gateway to the West. But, alas, St. Louis thought of the claim first.

1. ORIENTATION

Located mostly on the southern shore of the Missouri River, Kansas City straddles the boundaries of the states of Missouri and Kansas, with the main part of the city—despite its name—on the Missouri side.

ARRIVING

BY PLANE

The **Kansas City International Airport** (KCI) (tel. 816/243-5237) is conveniently located about 25 minutes northwest of downtown, just off Interstate 29. It's been rated one of the most congestion-free, user-friendly airports in the nation, due in part to its architectural configuration. Three C-shaped terminals allow drivers to drive virtually to their gate, with never more than a 75-foot walk from aircraft to curbside. An interterminal red bus makes continuous rounds to all three terminals.

GETTING INTO TOWN   The easiest way to get to your hotel from the airport is of course by **taxi,** which averages about $25 for the trip downtown and takes about 25 minutes. Fares can vary widely, however, because each company is free to set its own rates. Up to five people can ride for a shared single share.

More economical is to take the **KCI Airport Express,** which delivers passengers to major hotels downtown, Crown Center, Country Club Plaza, and Johnson County. It departs Kansas City International Airport from Terminal C, Gate 63, which you can reach from the other two gates via the inter-terminal red bus. One-way fares

WHAT THINGS COST IN KANSAS CITY — U.S. $

Taxi from airport to downtown Kansas City	$25.00
Bus from downtown to Country Club Plaza	.85
Local telephone call	.25
Double at Ritz-Carlton (expensive)	145.00 to 190.00
Double at Days Hotel (moderate)	70.00
Double at Travelodge (budget)	40.00
Lunch for one at Metropolis (moderate)	11.00
Lunch for one at Arthur Bryant's (budget)	5.00
Dinner for one, without wine, at The American Restaurant (expensive)	40.00
Dinner for one, without wine, at Stephenson's Apple Farm (moderate)	25.00
Dinner for one, without wine, at Mario's (budget)	5.00
Pint of beer	2.00
Coca-Cola	1.00
Cup of coffee	.75
Roll of ASA 100 Kodacolor film, 36 exposures	5.50
Admission to Nelson-Atkins Museum of Art	3.00
Movie ticket	5.00
Ticket to StarLight Theater	4.00 to 25.00

range from $9 to $14, depending on the destination, and hours of operation from the airport are about 6am to 11pm daily. Among the many hotels served by the KCI Airport Express are the Hilton Plaza, Marriott Plaza, Westin Crown Center, Hyatt Regency, Allis Plaza, Americana Hotel, Ritz-Carlton, Embassy Suites, and Raphael. For more information, call 816/243-5950.

The cheapest way to get from the airport to downtown is via the public **Metro Bus no. 29,** which departs from bus shelters on Bonn Circle (the circle drive that serves all three terminals). However, buses depart only five times per day Monday through Friday, and the exact fare of 75¢ is required. For more information, call Metro Bus at 816/221-0660.

BY TRAIN

If you're arriving in Kansas City via train, most likely you'll arrive at the **Amtrak** depot at 2200 Main St. (tel. 816/421-3622 or 421-4725). From there taxis are available to take to your final destination.

Kansas City
St. Louis ★

MISSOURI

Amtrak Depot **6**
Bus Terminal **7**
City of Independence
  Tourism Department **9**
Convention & Visitors Bureau
  of Greater Kansas City **4**
Country Club Plaza **13**
Crown Center **8**
Downtown **5**
Garment District **3**
Independence, Missouri **10**
Kansas City
  International Airport **1**
Kansas Visitor
  Information Center **2**
Mission Hills **14**
Missouri Tourist
  Information Center **12**
Overland Park **16**
Overland Park Convention
  and Visitors Bureau **15**
Westport **11**

KANSAS CITY AREA

BY BUS

Kansas City is served by three intercity bus lines: **Greyhound/ Trailways, Jefferson,** and **TNM&O** (Texas, New Mexico, and Oklahoma). All use the same bus terminal, located at 11th Street and Troost (tel. 816/698-0080).

BY CAR

If you're arriving in Kansas City by car, try to avoid rush hour, when I-70 and I-35 are particularly congested. Once in the city, you shouldn't have any problems driving or parking. Parking at most hotels and Country Club Plaza is free.

TOURIST INFORMATION

There are several visitor information centers ready to serve you in Kansas City. If you're driving into Kansas City from St. Louis on I-70, your first stop should be the **Missouri Tourist Information Center** (tel. 816/861-8800), which overlooks the Royals stadium on the eastern end of town, off I-70 at the Blue Ridge Cutoff exit (Exit 9). In addition to information on Kansas City, it has information on other destinations in Missouri. Hours are daily from 8am to 6pm (closing an hour earlier on game days); closed on Sunday in December, January, and February.

Kansas City's main tourist office is the **Convention and Visitors Bureau of Greater Kansas City,** located downtown in the City Center Square Building, Suite 2550, 1100 Main St. (tel. 816/ 221-5242)—open Monday through Friday from 8:30am to 5pm. It distributes free brochures, maps, and other information.

Other tourist offices serving specific sections of greater Kansas City include the **City of Independence Tourism Department,** 111 East Maple, Independence MO (tel. 816/836-7111); **Overland Park Convention and Visitors Bureau,** 10975 Benson Dr., Suite 360, Building 12, Overland Park, KS (tel. 913/491-0123); and **Kansas City, Kansas, Tourism,** 636 Minnesota, KS (tel. 913/ 321-5800).

Incidentally, if you're driving west from Kansas City on I-70 to destinations in Kansas, you'll want to stop off at the **Kansas Visitor Information Center,** located off I-70 about six miles into Kansas (exit 415)—open daily in summer from 7:30am to 7:30pm and daily in winter from 9am to 5pm; closed Easter, Thanksgiving, Christmas, New Year's Day.

For a weekly recording of festivals, activities, theatrical plays, and special events in the Kansas City metropolitan area, call the **Visitor Information Phone** at 816/474-9600. For information on where to hear jazz at Kansas City's various jazz clubs, call the **Jazz Hotline** at 816/931-2888. The **Concert Line and Ticket Information** number is 816/931-3330.

CITY LAYOUT

Many newcomers are surprised to learn that the bulk of Kansas City, along with most of its attractions, is not in Kansas but in Missouri. Both the Missouri River and State Line Road serve as the state border that severs the city in half, but the division is largely an administrative one only. For Kansas Citians, the entire metropolitan area is their city and playground, regardless of whether it's Johnson County in Kansas or Country Club Plaza in Missouri. Even a telephone call made throughout most of the city is a local call that does not require use of an area code, even if it's across the state line. A call placed from Independence, Missouri, to Overland Park, Kansas, for example, is a local call. The city covers seven counties.

Downtown Kansas City is located in Missouri, approximately in the center of the greater metropolitan area. Although Kansas City's history is intertwined with the winding ribbon of the Missouri River, the city turned its back on the river more than a century ago when the railroads arrived. Downtown Kansas City is therefore about 12 blocks south of the Missouri River, and it's here that you'll find its convention center, office buildings, shops, and a handful of hotels. In the past decade, the downtown has experienced a renaissance, because many of its historic buildings have been renovated and city planners are wooing people back from the suburbs into the inner city.

Most of Kansas City's major attractions, restaurants, and nightlife are located south of downtown. Crown Center, a huge complex containing two luxury hotels, scores of shops, restaurants, entertainment facilities, and the Hallmark Visitors Center, is approximately 15 blocks due south. A 10-minute drive farther south are Westport, with its many bars and clubs; Country Club Plaza, the nation's oldest shopping center; and the renowned Nelson-Atkins Museum—all of which are in an area referred to by the locals as Midtown. On the eastern edge of the greater Kansas City is Independence, Missouri, hometown of Harry S. Truman and destination for a number of historic sites. On the other end of town, at its southwest corner, is Johnson County in Kansas, which contains Overland Park and Mission Hills, two of the city's most affluent neighborhoods.

MAIN ARTERIES AND STREETS

Although the majority of Kansas City's streets are arranged on a grid, many of its boulevards and avenues seem to wind without rhyme or reason, leading apparently to nowhere. Even though I grew up near Kansas City, I'm embarrassed to admit that I still don't know my way around, although I do usually end up where I want to be simply by heading in the right direction. Luckily, there are several landmark streets that are good standbys for orientation. In addition, Midwestern drivers are very forgiving.

In every city I always have a favorite street, and in Kansas City it's Main Street. From the heart of downtown, it runs straight south, changing character as it passes through different parts of town. Main Street leads to several of the city's most popular destinations, including Crown Center, Westport, and Country Club Plaza. Bisecting Main Street (that is, streets that run east and west) are the numbered streets, beginning with 12th and 13th in the heart of downtown. Crown Center is near 24th and Main, Westport is just to the west of 40th and Main, and the Plaza is near 47th and Main.

The easiest way to get around is to take advantage of the various highways that cut through the city. I-70 is useful if you're traveling from downtown to Independence or the Royals stadium; I-35 travels straight through the city from its northeast corner to its southwest end; and I-435 forms a loop around the core of Kansas City.

KANSAS CITY AREA

Missouri

Kansas

Downtown

Barney Allis Plaza **7**
Bartle Convention Center **6**
Chamber of Commerce **1**
City Center Square **4**
City Hall **3**
Crown Center **10**
Greyhound Terminal **5**
Kansas City Visitors &
 Convention Bureau **4**
Kemper Arena **9**
The Stockyards **8**
Union Bus Terminal **2**

FINDING AN ADDRESS

As previously mentioned, much of Kansas City is composed of a grid, with numbered streets paralleling the Missouri River and therefore running east and west. The lowest-numbered streets are those closest to the Missouri River in the north, and they increase chronologically as they go south. The heart of downtown is between 9th and 14th streets; Crown Center is on 24th Street; Country Club Plaza spreads around 47th Street. Main Street serves as the dividing line for addresses designating east or west. Thus, 220 W. 43rd Street is located 43 blocks south of the Missouri River and two blocks west of Main Street.

Block numbers for north/south streets correspond to the numbered cross streets. For example, 7427 Main lies between 74th and 75th streets.

Incidentally, here in the Midwest people tend to give directions using north, south, east, and west designations. Even at home, they talk of the "east bedroom" or "the shelf against the west wall."

IMPRESSIONS

Who in Europe, or in America for that matter, knows that Kansas City is one of the loveliest cities on earth?
—ANDRÉ MAUROIS, 1946

NEIGHBORHOODS IN BRIEF

There are so many neighborhoods and communities in Kansas City that I could write an entire guide book on them alone. For the sake of space, I have selected only those where visitors are likely to find themselves.

DOWNTOWN AND THE GARMENT DISTRICT One hundred years ago, the Garment District was the hub of Kansas City's financial and commercial center. It's named after the many garment industries once housed here, industries that in the mid-1940s ranked second only to New York's in size and stature. The Garment District lies immediately north of downtown's new commercial center, around 8th and Central. A cultural and financial desert just a decade ago, the Garment District has been undergoing a renaissance, with many of its older buildings being restored as offices and loft apartments.

CROWN CENTER Crown Center is not a neighborhood, although it's big enough to encompass one; rather, it's a sprawling complex containing two luxury hotels, an indoor shopping center, restaurants, theaters, cinemas, and Hallmark Cards. In fact, the whole complex is owned by Hallmark Cards and is sort of a city within a city. Cater-cornered from Crown Center is Union Station, which unfortunately has not been renovated like the one in St. Louis and has stood empty for years, the center of controversy over what should be done with it and who should pay for the renovation.

WESTPORT Established in 1833 as an outpost for wagon trains departing on the Santa Fe Trail, Westport pre-dates Kansas City, which has grown up around it. It contains the two oldest buildings in the city, both on the corner of Westport and Pennsylvania Avenue (one of them is Kelly's, a well-known tavern). Today Westport is one of the hottest night spots in Kansas City, with scores of bars and clubs offering live music as well as shops and boutiques. Its heart is Westport Road, Broadway, and Pennsylvania, located to the west of Main between 39th and 44th streets. Country Club Plaza is just a few blocks farther south.

COUNTRY CLUB PLAZA This was the nation's first shopping center. Built in 1922 by J. C. Nichols, it was constructed in a Spanish architectural style (Seville, Spain, is Kansas City's sister city)—with red-roofed buildings; sparkling fountains; dozens of statues; and fourteen blocks of shops, department stores, apartments, restaurants, and bars. Horse-drawn carriages clatter down the streets, and at Christmas the Plaza erupts into an extravaganza of 49 miles of

Christmas lights that outline the buildings, a tradition started in 1926. The Plaza is located just west of Main, at 47th Street and Ward Parkway.

INDEPENDENCE With approximately 112,000 residents, Independence is an independent city, although where Kansas City starts and Independence begins is hard to say as you're driving along the highway. Founded more than 160 years ago and playing a vital role in the development of the Oregon, Californian, and Santa Fe trails, it was the hometown of Harry S. Truman and today contains the Truman Home and the Truman Library and Museum. In addition, the Mormon Visitors Center, several historic mansions, and the new National Frontier Trails Center are in Independence.

OVERLAND PARK Located in Johnson County in Kansas, Overland Park is the city's fastest-growing community, with a population of 110,000, most of them around 40 years old. It contains two major shopping malls, Corporate Woods (a region of corporate buildings and headquarters), and a number of hotels and restaurants. Easy access to I-435 and I35 make it a convenient place to stay.

MAPS

The Convention and Visitors Bureau of Greater Kansas City distributes a free map of the city, which includes both an outline of the entire city and a more detailed map of the downtown area. It's adequate for most purposes, but if you wish to explore the backroads of Kansas City, you might wish to purchase one of many city maps available. The American Automobile Association, for example, has a map of Kansas City with a street index.

2. GETTING AROUND

Because Kansas City is so spread out, most people rely on their own cars to get them where they want to go. There is, however, public transportation available. Of most interest to visitors is the Trolley.

PUBLIC TRANSPORTATION

BY TROLLEY

The easiest way to travel between downtown, Crown Center, Westport, and Country Club Plaza is by the **Trolley.** Painted bright red and green, these wheeled vehicles make a continuous circuit, with stops at the Town Pavilion and Barney Allis Plaza downtown, the Garment District, Crown Center, the Hyatt Regency Hotel, Westport, the Nelson-Atkins Museum, and the Plaza. On Saturday from May through October, the Trolley also travels to the City Market near the riverfront.

The fare is $3 per person (exact fare only), which allows you to get on and off the Trolley three times during the day at no additional cost. Children five and under are free; Sunday and Monday, children under 12 can ride free when accompanied by an adult. Tickets are available from the driver or in advance at Crown Center Customer Service, the Town Pavilion Information Desk, or The Plaza Merchants Association near the corner of Wornall Road and 47th Street on the Plaza.

Hours of operation during summer months are Monday through Thursday from 10am to 10pm, Friday and Saturday from 10am to midnight, and Sunday from noon to 6pm. During March, April, May, and September through December, hours are Monday through Saturday from 10am to 10pm and Sunday from noon to 6pm. During January and February, the Trolley operates only on weekends, from 10am to 10pm on Saturday and from noon to 6pm on Sunday. For more information, call 221-3399.

BY BUS

The **Metro** is Kansas City's public bus system, serving all counties except Johnson County, Kansas (which has its own bus system). There are 43 routes, most in a north/south direction, and buses are identified with both a number and a name. The base fare is 75¢ in exact change, with an additional 10¢ charged for each zone line crossed. If you're boarding a bus heading toward downtown, you'll pay the full fare upon boarding. If you're traveling away from downtown, pay only the 75¢ base fare upon boarding, then pay additional zone charges when you exit. If you're confused, ask the bus driver how much you owe. In any case, make sure you have exact change because the electric fare boxes will take dollar bills, but they will not give change. Free transfers are available on request when you pay the base fare, enabling you to travel to any bus going any direction, if you re-board within an hour.

The primary problem, obviously, is finding the bus that you need. Bus no. 47 Roanoke is useful for travel between downtown (leaving from 10th and Main) and Country Club Plaza (Nichols Road and Jefferson). Bus no. 24 Independence makes runs from downtown (8th and Grand) and Independence. Bus no. 29 KCI Airport is useful for trips between downtown and the airport. To find out which bus you should take and where to board, call the **Metro** at 221-0660 Monday through Friday from 6am to 6pm. In addition, there are racks with brochures of the various routes available at City Hall, 12th and Oak downtown, as well as at a number of other locations.

Johnson County maintains its own bus system, with service to downtown, Crown Center, Country Club Plaza, Oak Park Mall, and other locations. For more information, call the **Johnson County Transit** at 541-8450.

BY TAXI

All taxis in Kansas City are on a deregulated meter system, allowing each company to set its own rates. Thus, fares can vary widely. The cab's basic fare must be posted on the outside of the car, and when cabs are lined up, you are not required to take the first. You are not allowed to hail a cab from the street, but there are taxi stands on the street and at hotels. Up to five persons can ride for a shared single fare.

There are more than 30 taxicab companies listed in the Kansas City *Yellow Pages*. Both **Yellow Cab** (tel. 471-5000) and **American Cab Service** (tel. 421-5555) charge $1.30 for the first tenth of a mile, plus $1 for each extra mile. The fare from downtown to the airport runs about $25.

BY CAR

Kansas City is easy to navigate, especially if you stick to the main roads and highways, have a good map, and avoid rush-hour traffic. Unless otherwise posted, you can turn right on a red light in both Kansas and Missouri. Parking downtown is either at a parking garage, on a pay parking lot, or at a meter. Crown Center also has a parking lot, but the first three hours are free if you get validation from a merchant. There is no charge for parking at Country Club Plaza.

If you need to rent a car, **Avis** has an office both at the airport (tel. 243-5760) and in Johnson County at 9301 Metcalf (tel. 383-3374). **Budget** (tel. 262-9090) has five locations in Kansas City, including the airport and downtown. Other car-rental companies with locations at the airport include **Dollar** (tel. 243-5600), **Hertz** (tel. 243-5765), **National** (tel. 243-5770), and **Thrifty** (tel. 464-5670).

FAST FACTS KANSAS CITY

This section is designed to make your stay in St. Louis as problem-free as possible by answering any questions that you may have before and during your stay. Remember, too, that the concierge at your hotel is an invaluable source of information, as is the **Convention and Visitors Bureau of Greater Kansas City** (tel. 816/221-5242).

American Express American Express Travel Services is located at Country Club Place, 114 West 47 St. (tel. 816/531-9114).

Area Code The telephone area code for the Missouri side of Kansas City is 816; on the Kansas side it's 913. Note, however, that for local calls in most parts of Kansas City, you can dial without using the area code, even if you're calling a number across the state line.

Airport The Kansas City International Airport (KCI) is located about a 25-minute drive northwest of downtown. Refer to the "Orientation" section at the beginning of this chapter for more information.

Auto Rentals See the preceding section, "Getting Around," for information on car-rental agencies.

Babysitters Most of Kansas City's major hotels provide babysitting service or can contact a babysitter should the need arise.

Buses and Trolleys For information on Kansas City's public transportation system, refer to the preceding section, "Getting Around."

Business Hours Office hours are generally Monday through Friday from 9am to 5pm, while most banks are open Monday through Friday from about 8am to 4 or 4:30pm. Shops are open longer, especially those in malls. Crown Center, for example, is open Monday through Wednesday and Saturday from 10am to 6pm, Thursday and Friday from 10am to 9pm, and Sunday from noon to 5pm. The Town Pavilion downtown is open Monday through Saturday from 10am to 6pm.

Car Rentals See "Auto Rentals," above.

Climate See the "When to Go" section in Chapter 2.

Currency Exchange For a discussion of U.S. currency and where to change foreign currencies into dollars, see Fast Facts in Chapter 3.

Dentists and Doctors Some of the expensive hotels offer the services of an in-house doctor or a doctor on call. Otherwise, check the *Yellow Pages* for a list of area doctors. An alternative is to call the **Metropolitan Medical Society of Greater Kansas City** (tel. 816/531-8432), which maintains a list of about 1,500 area physicians. If you need a dentist, contact the **Greater Kansas City Dental Society** (tel. 816/333-5454).

Drugstores There is no 24-hour drugstore in Kansas City. If you need medical attention in the middle of the night, your best bet is the **Trinity Lutheran Hospital,** 3030 Baltimore (tel. 816/751-3000), located three blocks south of Crown Center.

Emergencies As throughout the United States, the number to call in an emergency is 911 for police, fire, and ambulance. Also see "Dentists and Doctors" and "Hospitals" in this section.

Eyeglasses If you lose your eyeglasses and need a quick replacement, Lenscrafters offers custom-crafted eyeglasses in approximately one hour, with approximately 3,000 brands to choose from. Convenient locations include Bannister Mall, 5600 Bannister Rd., Kansas City (tel. 816/763-4930) and Oak Park Mall, 95th and Quivera, Overland Park (tel. 913/492-7713).

Gay and Lesbian Hotline If you need to talk to someone while in Kansas City, Gaytalk is available evenings only at 816/931-4470. During the day, you can obtain information on a variety of activities by contacting Alternate News, a gay and lesbian publication, by calling 816/531-1339.

Hairdressers/Barbers If your hotel does not have a barber shop or beauty salon, the concierge may be able to direct you to one to suit your style. Otherwise, refer to the *Yellow Pages*.

Holidays For a list of U.S. national holidays, see Fast Facts in Chapter 3. For information on Kansas City's special annual events, see the "When to Go" section in Chapter 2.

Hospitals If you need to go to a hospital in an emergency, the ambulance will deliver you to the one best suited for your situation. There are more than 25 hospitals in the Kansas City area. Some of the more centrally located include **Trinity Lutheran Hospital,** 3030 Baltimore (tel. 816/751-3000), which specializes in cardiology, diabetes, lung disease, and oncology; the **University of Kansas Medical Center,** 39th and Rainbow (tel. 913/588-5000), which has a burn center, a neonatal intensive care unit, and a cancer treatment center; and **Children's Mercy Hospital,** 24th St. at Gillham (tel. 816/234-3000), which has a poison center, a level-1 trauma center, and specialty pediatric services.

Information Locations of Kansas City tourist offices are given in the "Orientation" section at the beginning of this chapter.

Laundry/Dry Cleaning All of the expensive and most of the medium-priced hotels offer laundry and/or dry-cleaning service. Some of the budget-priced ones offer coin-operated laundry machines. If yours does not, ask the staff where the most convenient laundry facility is.

Liquor Laws The legal drinking age in both Kansas and Missouri is 21. In Kansas City, Missouri, bars in the "convention trade zones" may serve liquor daily until 3am. On Sunday, however, liquor is available in only restaurants and hotels. The remainder of Kansas City on the Missouri side follows these same guidelines, except that bars close at 1:30am. On the Kansas side, liquor by the drink is served in licensed restaurants and clubs daily from 9am to 2am.

Lost Property   There is no central lost-property office. If you lose something, call the nearest police station to report the loss.

Luggage Storage   If you need to store luggage in Kansas City and the hotel you are staying in cannot do so, your best bet is one of the lockers at the Greyhound Bus Station, 11th Street and Troost (tel. 816/698-0080). There's a 30-day limit, and the cost of a locker is $1 for the first day and $3 for each succeeding day.

Mail   The main post office of Kansas City is located at 315 Pershing (tel. 816/374-9180 or 374-9283), near Crown Center in Midtown. It's open Monday through Friday from 8am to 6:30am and Saturday from 8am to 12:30pm. Vending machines selling stamps are accessible 24 hours.

Maps   The Convention and Visitors Bureau of Greater Kansas City distributes a free map of the downtown area and city vicinity.

Newspapers/Magazines   Most hotels sell newspapers, including Kansas City's own *Kansas City Star*. If yours does not, ask your hotel concierge where the nearest newsstand is.

Photographic Needs   If you need film or camera equipment, ask your hotel concierge where the nearest photo shop is. Otherwise, there's **One-Hour Picture Perfect** in Crown Center, 2450 Grand Ave. (tel. 816/221-6000), which offers 60-minute film processing and film. It's open Monday through Wednesday and Saturday from 10am to 6pm, Thursday and Friday from 10am to 9pm, and Sunday from noon to 5pm.

Police   The emergency number for police throughout the United States is 911.

Post Office   See "Mail," above.

Religious Services   The Saturday edition of the *Kansas City Star* carries a religious section, with listings of churches according to denomination, their location, times of services, and pastor.

Restrooms   The best places to search for a public restroom are hotels and restaurants.

Safety   Whenever you're traveling in an unfamiliar city or country, stay alert. Be aware of your immediate surroundings. Wear a money belt and keep a close eye on your possessions. Never carry large amounts of cash and leave your expensive jewelry at home. Be particularly careful with cameras, purses, and wallets—all favorite targets of thieves and pickpockets.

Kansas City's crime rate is lower than that in many other major U.S. cities, but everyone should exercise caution, especially at night. Keep your car locked at all times and do not wander from nightlife districts at night. You are perfectly safe walking around Country Club Plaza and Westport at night, especially if there are two or more of you.

Shoe Repair   You can have your shoes repaired while you wait at **Shoe Pro** in Crown Center, 2450 Grand Ave. (tel. 816/842-0870), in Midtown. It's open Monday through Wednesday and Saturday from 10am to 6pm, Thursday and Friday from 10am to 9pm, and Sunday from noon to 5pm.

Taxes   The sales tax for Kansas City, Missouri, is 6.475%, which includes both state and local taxes and which is added to the price of all goods and food. The tax on all hotels throughout most of

Kansas City, Missouri, is 11.975%; for those near the airport, it's 11.725%.

On the Kansas side, a tax of 5.75%, which includes both state and local taxes, is added to the price of all goods and food. If you're staying in a hotel on the Kansas side, a hotel tax of 9.75% will be added to the price of your room.

Taxis   Refer to the preceding section, "Getting Around," for information on taxis and their fares.

Telephone   A local telephone call costs 25¢. Be sure to ask at your hotel whether a surcharge is added to calls made from your room, since sometimes these surcharges can be pretty stiff. If you need local directory assistance, dial 1-411. For local numbers when calling from a pay phone, dial 411.

Television and Radio   Kansas City's major networks are NBC on channel 4, CBS on channel 5, and ABC on channel 9. Tune to channel 19 for PBS.

As for radio stations, tune to KCUR for National Public Radio (FM 89.3); KFKF for country music (FM 94); KXTR for classical music (FM 96.5); for oldies and easy listening (FM 98.9); and KCFX for classic rock and roll (FM 101.1).

Time Zone   Kansas City follows Central Standard Time. If it's noon in Kansas City, it's 1pm in New York and 10am in Los Angeles.

Tipping   As elsewhere in the United States, serving people should be tipped 15% to 20%, and bartenders should get at least 10%. Bellhops should receive 50¢ for each piece of luggage, cab drivers expect a tip of 15% of the fare, and chambermaids should be left $1 per night of stay.

Transit Information   For information on Kansas City's bus system, the Metro, dial 816/221-0660.

Weather   For the time and temperature, call 816/844-4444. Weather information and the forecast can be obtained by dialing 816/531-4444.

CHAPTER 13

KANSAS CITY ACCOMMODATIONS

1. DOWNTOWN
2. CROWN CENTER
3. COUNTRY CLUB PLAZA
4. WESTPORT & MIDTOWN
5. OVERLAND PARK
6. NEAR TRUMAN SPORTS COMPLEX
7. KANSAS CITY, KANSAS
8. NEAR KANSAS CITY INTERNATIONAL AIRPORT
9. CAMPING

Kansas City offers a wide choice in accommodations—from historic hotels to bed-and-breakfasts, from glittering high-rises to nationwide chains. The hotels recommended in this chapter are divided according to location, but no matter where you choose to stay, you're never very far from the city's many attractions.

The rates quoted below are the standard rack rates, but keep in mind that you can often receive a discounted rate but only if you ask. Many hotels offer weekend rates that are as much as 50% off the regular weekday rate, with no extra charge for two or three extra persons in a room. There are also corporate rates available to business travelers; special packages are available at different times of the year, ranging from pre-Christmas packages to summer specials that include tickets to the theater or attractions. I'm convinced that most people end up paying less than the rack rate, so be sure to request the lowest special rate when making your reservation. Keep in mind that in addition to the rates given, a hotel tax will be added to your bill. For most of Kansas City, Missouri, it's 11.975%; for hotels near KCI Airport it's 11.725%. On the Kansas side, the tax averages about 9.75%.

When choosing a hotel, keep in mind that some offer in their rates a continental breakfast that consists of rolls, coffee, and perhaps juice and fruit. A few even offer complimentary cocktails during evening happy hours. Most hotels in Kansas City offer free parking.

The hotels are divided according to location and then further subdivided according to price. (Unless otherwise noted, all provide private baths.) The expensive hotels charge more than $100 per night for two persons; the moderate hotels offer rooms for two persons for $50 to $100; and the budget rooms are those that cost less than $50 for two. Generally speaking, the expensive hotels are those found in such choice locations as downtown, Crown Center, and Country Club Plaza. If you're on a budget, try one of the hotels in Kansas City, Kansas, or in other outlying areas. You might also consider staying in a campground.

1. DOWNTOWN

All these hotels are located in the heart of the city, near Kansas City's convention center and just off I-70 and I-35.

EXPENSIVE

ALLIS PLAZA HOTEL, 200 W. 12 St., Kansas City, MO 64105. Tel. 816/421-6800, or toll free 800/548-4782. 550 rms, 23 suites. A/C MINIBAR TEL TV

$ Rates: $105 single; $115 double; $145 Corporate Club executive floor; from $190 suite. Extra person $15. Children under 18 stay free in parents' room. Weekend rates and summer discounts available. AE, CB, DC, DISC, MC, V. Parking: Free.

Located across from Barney Allis Plaza and Bartle Hall convention center, this is *the* favorite hotel of the convention trade. A modern and rather unspectacular 22-story high-rise, the Allis Plaza makes up for its plain outward appearance with a lavishly appointed and spacious lobby, complete with a plant-filled atrium and an artificial waterfall dominating one entire wall. Facilities include everything you'd expect from a first-rate hotel: from a health club on the 22nd floor to a concierge desk that will help obtain tickets for everything from a Royals game to the theater.

Rooms are large, and each comes with a stocked refrigerator, two telephones, a TV with radio and full cable, and a bathroom equipped with a clothesline and a bathroom scale. Full-length bay windows provide a great view of the city—request a room facing Barney Allis Plaza. If you feel like pampering yourself, the Corporate Club executive level, located on the 20th and 21st floors, offers complimentary breakfast, and happy-hour cocktails and hors d'oeuvres, and its own lounge with a concierge.

Dining/Entertainment: The hotel's one restaurant serves steaks and a variety of meals in a relaxed setting. Afterward, you can enjoy a drink and listen to music at the 12th Street Bar.

Services: Room service to midnight, free morning newspaper.

Facilities: Indoor swimming pool, sauna, exercise room ($5 extra), outdoor tennis courts, gift shop, newsstand, florist shop.

MODERATE

DAYS HOTEL, 1215 Wyandotte, Kansas City, MO 64105. Tel. 816/471-1333, or toll free 800/325-2525. 176 rms, 13 suites. A/C TEL TV

$ Rates (including buffet breakfast): $64 single; $70 double; suites from $85. Extra person $5. Children under 10 stay free in parents' room. Weekend, corporate, and special rates available. AE, CB, DC, DISC, MC, V. Parking: Free.

This is a small older hotel with character, located across from Barney Allis Plaza square. It was built in 1926 and still has such charming features as an old-fashioned letter drop beside the elevator that delivers letters to the ground floor and a small lobby with its original fixtures. What's more, Days offers lots of complimentary extras, from buffet breakfasts to cocktails. Rooms are comfortable, and those with the best view are on the top floor overlooking the square. If you like historic, European-style hotels, you'll like this place. Highly recommended.

Services: Complimentary two-hour cocktail Mon–Sat 5–7pm, free local calls, complimentary coffee.

Facilities: One restaurant specializing in barbecue, laundry facilities, use of nearby health club.

HISTORIC SUITES, 612 Central, Kansas City, MO 64105. Tel. 816/842-6544, or toll free 800/733-0612. 101 suites. A/C TEL TV

$ Rates (including buffet breakfast): $88 studio; $93 one-bedroom suite; $105 queen; $115 two-bedroom suite. Rollaway bed $10. Weekend and corporate rates available; discounts for longer stays. AE, CB, DC, DISC, MC, V. Parking: Free.

I wish I could move in here permanently. Not only are all the suites huge, with tall ceilings and lots of windows, but also they're beautifully appointed—with separate living, dining, and sleeping areas. What's more, every suite has a fully stocked kitchen, with everything from a microwave oven, a dishwasher, a toaster, and a coffee machine down to a carrot peeler. The hotel's welcome pack includes complimentary coffee, tea, sugar, cream, and popcorn for the first night of your stay. And, as though that weren't enough, the staff will do your grocery shopping for free (you pay for the goods, of course), and the maid will clean all your dishes in the morning. My kind of place.

Suites, ranging from studios that are much larger than regular hotel rooms to two-bedroom suites, are located in two restored brick buildings in the Garment District, both dating from the 1890s and listed on the National Historic Register. Most of the guests here are

---

Ⓕ FROMMER'S SMART TRAVELER —HOTELS

VALUE-CONSCIOUS TRAVELERS SHOULD TAKE ADVANTAGE OF THE FOLLOWING:

1. Weekend discounts of up to 50% available at most expensive and moderately priced hotels in Kansas City.
2. Corporate rates usually offered to the business traveler may also be available to vacationers who present business cards.
3. Winter discounts available at some inexpensive hotels.
4. Less expensive hotels that often are located outside the downtown area.
5. Breakfasts included in the price of your hotel room.
6. Campgrounds and youth hostels at rock-bottom prices.

QUESTIONS TO ASK IF YOU'RE ON A BUDGET

1. Does the room rate include breakfast? Is breakfast served buffet-style, allowing you to eat all you want?
2. Is there a charge for parking? (Parking is usually free at hotels in Kansas City.)
3. Is there a surcharge for phone calls made from your room? (Some hotels offer free phone calls.)
4. Are discounts available? (Weekend rates can sometimes be less than those offered during the week.)

Allis Plaza Hotel **5**
Days Hotel **6**
Historic Suites **2**
Hotel Savoy **3**
Howard Johnson **1**
Hyatt Regency
  Crown Center **7**
Radisson Suite Hotel
  Kansas City **4**
Westin Crown Center **8**

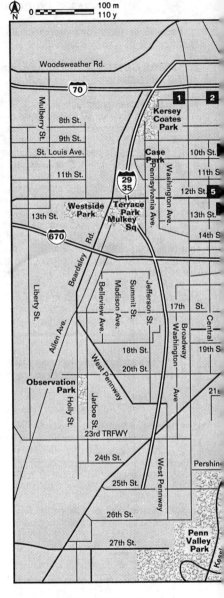

business travelers, some of whom stay for months. It's easy to see why.

Services: Free transportation to downtown businesses, same-day laundry and dry cleaning, free daily newspaper, free grocery shopping.

Facilities: Laundry facilities, outdoor pool, whirlpool, sauna.

HOTEL SAVOY, 9th and Central, Kansas City, MO 64105. **Tel. 816/842-3575.** 20 rms and suites. A/C TEL TV

DOWNTOWN KANSAS CITY ACCOMMODATIONS

$ Rates (including breakfast): $65 single or double; from $88 suites. AE, CB, DC, DISC, MC, V. Parking: Free.

Hooray, the Savoy lives! After years of neglect as a seedy and flea-bitten flophouse, the Savoy is now undergoing an ambitious and complete renovation, with the date of completion slated for 1992. That will bring to 110 the total number of rooms and suites, which offer modern conveniences without sacrificing historic quaintness. After all, this hotel, built in 1888, has the distinction of being the longest continuously run hotel west of the Mississippi with the same name. Both Teddy Roosevelt and Harry Truman ate at its renowned restaurant, and Houdini suffered the embarrassment of getting locked in a telephone booth from which he couldn't escape. Rooms have tall ceilings; some have brass beds; and bathroom fixtures include claw-foot tubs and old-fashioned sinks. Breakfast is a luxurious affair with crisp white tablecloths, a maître d' decked out in black tuxedo and bow tie, and choices ranging from smoked salmon with caviar to veal chop.

Services: Complimentary Baily Irish Cream, free Kona coffee, free morning newspaper.

Facilities: Famous Savoy Grill and Restaurant.

HOWARD JOHNSON, 610 Washington, Kansas City, MO 64105. Tel. 816/421-1800, or toll free 800/654-2000. 180 rms, 5 suites. A/C TEL TV

$ Rates: $55 single; $65 double; from $85 suite. Extra person $8. Children under 18 stay free in parents' room. Corporate rates available. AE, CB, DC, DISC, MC, V. Parking: Free.

The advantage to staying in this hotel is that it's located right on I-70 (the Broadway exit), making it easy to find if you're arriving late at night. An older hotel, it offers pleasant and clean rooms. Rooms facing north have large sliding-glass doors that open onto balconies overlooking I-70 and the river beyond, but they tend to be noisy with traffic. Ask for a room on a higher floor. Rooms facing south have a view of the Quality Hill residential area and do not have balconies.

Services: Room service to 10pm, one-day laundry and dry-cleaning service.

Facilities: One restaurant, one lounge, outdoor swimming pool, game room, laundry facilities, gift shop.

RADISSON SUITE HOTEL KANSAS CITY, 12th at Baltimore, Kansas City, MO 64105. Tel. 816/221-7000, toll free 800/333-3333. 214 rms and suites. A/C MINIBAR TEL TV

$ Rates (including breakfast): $85–$97 single; $97–$109 double; suites $109 single, $119 double. Extra person $12. Children under 18 stay free in parents' room. Weekend and corporate rates available. AE, CB, DC, DISC, ER, MC, V. Parking: Free.

This is another historic downtown hotel, built in 1930 and exalting in the art deco style. Recently renovated, the Radisson still has its original woodwork, marble, lighting, and fixtures—including an 11-foot-tall gilded statue called "Mother of the Stars," who stands on tiptoe on the crest of a wave overlooking the lobby. The hotel, a registered National Historic Landmark, stands on the site where Harry S. Truman once had a gentlemen's haberdashery. Geared toward corporate travelers, rooms offer TVs with remote controls and in-house pay movies, alarm clocks with radios, bathrobes, king- or queen-size beds, separate vanity areas with makeup mirrors, large working desks, and two telephones each. Complimentary breakfasts are cooked to order.

Services: Complimentary cocktail hour, free morning newspaper, free coffee delivered to room, free valet parking.

Facilities: Restaurant serving steaks and prime rib, sports bar and café, business center, 24-hour health club.

ⓕFROMMER'S COOL FOR KIDS
HOTELS

Hilton Plaza Inns (see pp. 170, 181) There are two Hilton Plaza Inns in Kansas City, both offering the V.I.K. (Very Important Kids) program, with a special children's menu, a free chocolate sundae, and games and toys available for check-out.

---

2. CROWN CENTER

Crown Center is a city within a city, complete with two hotels, restaurants, shops, and nightlife entertainment. Both these hotels are subsidiaries of Hallmark Cards, Inc.

EXPENSIVE

HYATT REGENCY CROWN CENTER, 2345 McGee St., Kansas City, MO 64108. Tel. 816/421-1234, or toll free 800/233-1234. Telex 434022. 689 rms, 42 suites. A/C MINIBAR TEL TV

$ Rates: $145 single; $180 double; $20 extra for Regency Club executive floor; from $215 suite. Extra person $15. Children under 18 stay free in parents' room. Weekend rates available. AE, CB, DC, DISC, MC, V. Parking: $8.

Linked to Crown Center via an enclosed skywalk, the Hyatt Regency is known for its excellent service and personal touches. Soaring 42 stories, the hotel has a spacious and dramatic lobby, patterned after the 115-year-old Galleria in Milan, Italy, and featuring a five-story atrium with skylights, plants, and a bubbling fountain.

Rooms are generously large, with original artwork and fresh plants giving them a homey and comfortable atmosphere. The top two floors are reserved for the Regency Club, which features its own lounge, full-time concierge service, free continental breakfast, and free happy-hour appetizers, as well as such extra touches as terrycloth robes, shoe-shine machines, hairdryers, and complimentary mineral water and candies.

Dining/Entertainment: The Peppercorn Duck Club is one of Kansas City's best restaurants, known for its steaks and seafood. Skies is a revolving restaurant high above the city; The Terrace is a casual, bright, and spacious restaurant open throughout the day.

Services: 24-hour room service, same-day laundry and dry cleaning.

Facilities: Outdoor swimming pool, tennis courts, sauna, whirlpool, exercise room, gift shop.

WESTIN CROWN CENTER, One Pershing Rd., Kansas City, MO 64108. Tel. 816/474-4400, or toll free 800/228-3000. 676 rms, 49 suites. A/C MINIBAR TEL TV

$ Rates: $145 single; $180 double; Executive Club floor $20 extra; from $260 suite. Extra person $30. Children under 18 stay free in parents' room. Weekend, corporate, and other rates available. AE, CB, DC, DISC, MC, V. Parking: $8.

Located right in Crown Center, the Westin Crown Center is one of Kansas City's premier hotels, and this will be evident to you as soon as you walk into the lobby. The hotel was built into the side of a limestone cliff, which was retained and utilized in the construction of the hotel—it was turned into a dramatic five-story indoor waterfall and rock garden. Service is excellent, from the front desk to the room service to the restaurants. But what appeals to most of its guests is that they can walk out of the hotel and right into shops, theaters, restaurants, and the attractions of Crown Center.

All rooms are luxuriously appointed, complete with remote-control TVs, minibars, and glass-sliding doors that open onto small balconies. Guests can receive messages either by written note or by voice mail over the telephone. On the 17th floor is the Executive Club floor, where guests are treated to such extra services as complimentary continental breakfasts; free soft drinks and snacks throughout the day; complimentary evening cocktails; free morning newspapers; and hairdryers, makeup mirrors, and mini-TVs in the bathrooms.

Dining/Entertainment: Benton's is one of Kansas City's best steak houses, made even better by the fact that it offers a rooftop view of the city. Trader Vic's serves a variety of international dishes in a tropical setting; the Brasserie offers American and continental dishes in a relaxed, bistrolike atmosphere.

Services: 24-hour room service, valet laundry service, limousine service.

Facilities: Year-round heated outdoor swimming pool, two tennis courts, health club, sauna, steam room, jogging track, putting green, games court, shuffleboard, live theater.

3. COUNTRY CLUB PLAZA

Although the Plaza is considered a part of Midtown, I consider it important enough to warrant its own heading. Keep in mind that because of the Plaza's choice location, hotels on or near it tend to be expensive. For more moderately priced hotels not far away, refer to the following section on hotels in Westport and the rest of Midtown.

EXPENSIVE

HILTON PLAZA INN, 1 East 45th St., Kansas City, MO 64111. Tel. 816/753-7400, or toll free 800/525-6321. Fax 816/753-4777. 230 rms, 10 suites. A/C MINIBAR TEL TV

$ Rates: $90 single; $105 double; from $190 suite. Extra person $12. Children under 18 stay free in parents' room. Weekend and corporate rates available. AE, CB, DC, DISC, ER, MC, V. Parking: Free valet parking.

Located on the corner of Main and 45th streets, about a five-minute walk from the Plaza, this is one of the more economical hotels in the immediate vicinity. The Hilton Plaza is built around a heated outdoor swimming pool, and in summer it offers a V.I.K. (Very Important Kids) program, with free chocolate sundae dessert and free use of games, books, and toys. Across the street from the hotel is a popular mile track with workout stations along the way.

Each room is equipped with a minibar; a TV with remote control and pay movies; a clothesline in the bathroom; and such amenities as a sewing kit, mouthwash, and shoe polish. Some rooms facing toward the outside have a view of the Plaza, while some of those facing toward the inner courtyard have sliding doors that open onto the pool.

Dining/Entertainment: Café Kona Kai specializes in Polynesian specialties, along with lamb, veal, and Kansas City steaks. M. J.'s Piano Lounge offers live piano music six nights a week.

Services: Courtesy shuttle to Westport and Plaza, valet laundry services, babysitting, free coffee mornings in the lobby, room service to 11pm.

Facilities: Heated outdoor swimming pool, cardiovascular workout center, beauty shop, barber shop, gift shop.

MARRIOTT PLAZA HOTEL, 4445 Main St., Kansas City, MO 64111. Tel. 816/531-3000, or toll free 800/228-9290. 278 rms, 18 suites. A/C TEL TV

$ Rates: $140 single; $160 double; $180 Concierge Executive floor; from $490 suite. Extra person free. Weekend, corporate, and other discounts available. AE, CB, DC, DISC, ER, MC, V. Parking: Free.

Located right beside the Hilton Plaza Inn, the Marriott is more luxuriously appointed than the Hilton, with correspondingly higher prices. The small marble lobby is elegantly simple; the guest rooms each offer cable TV with remote control and pay movies and two telephones. There are three no-smoking floors, and the 19th Concierge floor includes a complimentary continental breakfast and evening hors d'oeuvres in its prices.

Dining/Entertainment: Curios Restaurant offers a wide variety of cuisines, and presents a lunch buffet of different national cuisine daily, ranging from Asian to Italian. After dinner you can retire to the Plaza Bar, which has live entertainment and a dance floor.

Services: Room service to 11pm, complimentary morning newspaper, laundry service.

Facilities: Health club with complete Nautilus circuit, whirlpool, indoor swimming pool, sunning deck, gift shop.

THE RAPHAEL, 325 Ward Parkway, Kansas City, MO 64112. Tel. 816/756-3800, or toll free 800/821-5343. 51 rms, 72 suites. A/C MINIBAR TEL TV

$ Rates (including continental breakfast): $94–$105 single; $111–$122 double; $112–$116 single suite, $127–$131 double suite. Extra person $15. Children under 18 stay free in parents' room. Weekend, corporate, and other rates available. AE, CB, DC, MC, V. Parking: Free.

Located across the street from the Plaza, the Raphael occupies a beautiful brick building that was built in 1927 to house apartments and was converted into a hotel in 1975. Fashioned after the small and elegant hotels of Europe, it is a delightful place to stay if you prefer intimacy rather than convention crowds.

Rooms are large, each equipped with either a queen- or king-size bed, a sofa bed, a TV with remote control, and a stocked minibar. Some rooms have a view of the Plaza at no extra charge; suites, on the other hand, are charged according to whether they have a view of the Plaza. The lobby was recently renovated—maybe next they'll get around to the rooms, which, although adequate, could do with a bit of spiffing up.

Dining/Entertainment: The Raphael is a romantic restaurant just off the lobby, offering international cuisine and a cocktail bar.

Services: 24-hour room service, same-day laundry service, complimentary breakfast delivered to room, free morning newspaper.

THE RITZ-CARLTON (formerly Alameda Plaza), 401 Ward Parkway, Kansas City, MO 64112. Tel. 816/756-1500, or toll free 800/241-3333. 352 rms, 21 suites. A/C MINIBAR TEL TV

$ Rates: $145–$190 single or double; $225 Club Executive floor; from $275 suite. Extra person $20. Children under 17 stay free in parents' room. Weekend and other packages available. AE, CB, DC, DISC, ER, MC, V. Parking: Free.

The Ritz-Carlton gets my vote as the ritziest hotel in town. It opened in 1990 in what was formerly the Alameda Plaza, which is where Ronald Reagan stayed during the 1976 Republican convention. Located across the street from Country Club Plaza and offering great views, it follows the Ritz tradition with 18th- and 19th-century antiques and artwork throughout, elaborate floral arrangements, imported carpets, and crystal chandeliers. Its lobby is one of understated elegance, with a low ceiling, a marble floor, chandeliers, and mahogany walls. The service is as good as it gets anywhere, and the facilities and extra guest amenities leave nothing to be desired. This is the place to be if you wish to be pampered.

Rooms are traditionally furnished in antique reproductions, with such luxuries as imported Italian marble bathrooms, hairdryers, plush terrycloth robes, room safes, bathroom scales, and three telephones each. The more expensive rooms have balconies. For unbridled indulgence, stay on the Ritz-Carlton Club floors (floors 10 and 11), with private access, a concierge staff, and a private lounge. Guests here are treated to six food presentations a day, from a complimentary continental breakfast to afternoon tea with pastries and evening cocktails and hors d'oeuvres. Highly recommended.

Dining/Entertainment: The Grill is the hotel's signature restaurant, offering elegant dining with a view of the Plaza and American cuisine ranging from steaks to seafood. The Café offers more casual dining, including outdoor tables on a terrace with a view of the pool and Plaza, with a menu that serves light and hearty fare along with fitness cuisine. The Lounge serves an afternoon tea as well as cocktails throughout the afternoon and evening.

Services: 24-hour room service, limousine service, complimentary morning newspaper, babysitting.

Facilities: Fitness exercise room, heated outdoor swimming pool, sauna, car-rental agency, gift boutique and sundry shop.

4. WESTPORT & MIDTOWN

Westport is Kansas City's nightlife hot spot, with plenty of bars and restaurants. The hotels listed here are excellent choices, but note that the selections listed above on the Plaza are only minutes away.

EXPENSIVE

EMBASSY SUITES HOTEL, 220 W. 43rd St., Kansas City, MO 64111. Tel. 816/756-1720, or toll free 800/EMBASSY. 266 suites. A/C TEL TV

$ Rates (including buffet breakfast): $140 single; $160 double. Extra person $20. Children under 18 stay free in parents' room. Weekend, corporate, and senior-citizen rates available. AE, CB, DC, DISC, MC, V. Parking: Free.

In keeping with the Spanish architecture of the nearby Plaza, this Embassy Suites features a dramatic inner courtyard that soars 12 stories, embellished with plants ringing each floor and topped with a skylight. A fountain bubbles in the middle of the stone-floored courtyard. The hotel is located just off J. C. Nichols Parkway, less than two blocks from Westport and four blocks from the Plaza. Complimentary breakfasts here are buffet style, along with cooked-to-order dishes; the swimming pool is two-tiered, the tiers connected by a waterfall.

As with all hotels in this chain, the rooms are two-room suites, each complete with a kitchenette stocked with stove, refrigerator, coffee maker, and coffee. Cooking utensils are available on request. There are two TVs, one in the living room and one in the bedroom, with pay movies. A good choice for longer stays, it's a very popular hotel with business travelers. All suites open onto walkways that ring the inner atrium as well as onto tiny balconies on the outside of the building (not, perhaps, for the acrophobic). No-smoking suites are available.

Dining/Entertainment: The Plaza Grill serves everything from sandwiches and pasta to steaks and chicken. There's also a lounge featuring live piano music on weekends and a dance floor.

Services: Complimentary two-hour evening cocktail service.

Facilities: Indoor swimming pool, whirlpool, sauna, steam room, game room, pool tables, gift shop.

MODERATE

HOTELS

COMFORT INN, 801 Westport Rd., Kansas City, MO 64111. Tel. 816/931-1000, or toll free 800/228-5150. 109 rms. A/C TEL TV

$ Rates (including continental breakfast): $57–$64 single; $64–$72 double. Extra person $7. Children under 18 stay free in parents' room. Weekend and corporate rates available. AE, CB, DC, DISC, ER, MC, V. Parking: Free.

This is a good choice in inexpensive lodging just a few minutes' walk from the nighttime action of Westport. Rooms are large and pleasant enough, with hints of the Southwest in their

Kansas City
St. Louis ★

MISSOURI

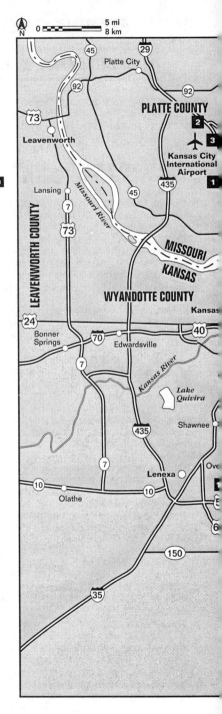

Smithville

Smithville Lake

92

169

435

291

69

Kearney

92

69

Excelsior Springs

Mosby

Prathersville

CLAY COUNTY

Liberty

Gladstone

35

291

Missouri River

71

North Kansas City

Buckner

24

Downtown Airport

KANSAS CITY

24

Independence

4

435

JACKSON COUNTY

7 8

16 15

5 6

70

9

Lake Tapawingo

40

Roeland Park

13

10

40

11

14

40

Mission Hills

Raytown

470

Blue Springs

Prairie Village

Leawood

Unity Village

Lake Jacomo

Lake Lotawana

KANSAS

MISSOURI

470

50

Longview Lake

Blue River

71

Lee's Summit

50

Grandview

Greenwood

150

Richards-Gebaur Airport

150

Raymore

Pleasant Hill

Belton

291

71

Airport

earth-tone pastels and artwork featuring Native Americans. A variety of rooms are available, including those with king-size beds or two double beds; no-smoking rooms and handicapped-accessible rooms also are available. Breakfast here consists of coffee, juice, and pastries.

Services: Complimentary snacks and sodas Tues–Thurs from 4:30–6:30pm, valet laundry service.

Facilities: Exercise room.

THE QUARTERAGE HOTEL WESTPORT, 560 Westport Rd., Kansas City, MO 64111. Tel. 816/931-0001, or toll free 800/942-4233. 116 rms, 7 suites. A/C TEL TV

$ Rates (including continental breakfast): $82 single; $99 double; from $115 suite. Extra person $15. Children under 18 stay free in parents' room. Weekend and corporate rates available. AE, CB, DC, DISC, MC, V. Parking: Free.

You can't get closer to Westport than this handsome brick hotel. Comfortable, spotless, and relatively new, it's tastefully decorated throughout and offers the basics plus a few extras. Each room features cable TV with remote control, full-length mirrors, a clock radio, two phones, and a desk.

Services: Complimentary cocktails 5–7pm, free local calls, laundry service.

Facilities: Exercise room, sauna, whirlpool.

MODERATELY PRICED BED-AND-BREAKFASTS

Both bed-and-breakfasts listed here are on the edge of Hyde Park in Midtown, about a seven-minute ride from both the Plaza and the Crown Center.

DOANLEIGH WALLAGH, 217 E. 37th St., Kansas City, MO 64111. Tel. 816/753-2667. 12 rms, all with bath. TEL TV

$ Rates (including breakfast): $60–$110 double. Extra adult or child $10. AE, MC, V. Monthly rates available. Parking: Free.

This is a turn-of-the-century mansion furnished with antiques and decorative objects culled from travels and local treasures, including furniture and silver from the old Muehlbach Hotel, which served as a landmark in downtown Kansas City for many years. The Doanleigh is owned by friendly Carolyn and Edward Litchfield, who bring their personal touches and flair to their home. Carolyn, a former home-economics teacher, places fresh cookies in guest rooms every day; breakfasts include such dishes as French toast with a honey glaze, Russian pancakes, omelets, and eggs benedict. Rooms are located in two houses located next door to one another and come in a variety of styles and prices. The Hyde Park Master Suite, for example, is the most expensive, complete with a four-poster queen bed and a working fireplace. The Westport Room and the Benton Room have porches. Communal facilities include living rooms in both houses, an enclosed brick patio, and a grand piano. There's also a kitchen available for long-term stays. Children are accepted only by prior arrangement.

MILFORD HOUSE, 3605 Gillham Rd., Kansas City, MO 64111. Tel. 816/753-1269. 6 rms, 2 with bath. A/C

$ Rates (including breakfast): $75 double. Extra adult or child $15. AE, MC, V. Parking: On the street.

Just across the park from the bed-and-breakfast above, this accommodation is a red-painted brick home, a combination of Queen Anne and Dutch colonial styles. Built in 1889 and opening as a bed-and-breakfast a century later, Milford House is owned by Ian and Pat Mills. Pat hails from Mississippi, while Ian was born and raised in the original Milford House in England. Guest rooms here are named after English royalty. Robes are provided for rooms with shared bathrooms, and in the living room is a piano (Margaret Truman's music teacher is rumored to have lived here). Note the three-story circular wooden staircase and the 70-square-foot stained-glass window in the living room, modeled after a Tiffany landscape. Only children older than 12 are accepted.

BUDGET

TRAVELODGE, 3240 Broadway, Kansas City, MO 64111. Tel. 816/531-9250, or toll free 800/255-3050. 52 rms, all with bath. A/C TEL TV

$ Rates: $35 single; $40–$45 double. Extra person $4. AE, CB, DC, DISC, MC, V. Parking: Free.

Centrally located only a five-minute drive from downtown or the Plaza, this is an older three-story hotel that is slowly receiving a much needed facelift, which should be completed by the time you read this. Rooms come with the basics, plus a courtesy coffee maker and free coffee. There's also a game room. Although there's no restaurant in the hotel, there's an International House of Pancakes next door.

5. OVERLAND PARK

MODERATE

Both these hotels are located near the intersection of I-435 and Highway 169 (Metcalf Avenue), on the southern end of Kansas City in Overland Park, Kansas. I-35 and the Corporate Woods development park are close by, and downtown Kansas City is 10 miles north.

BEST WESTERN OVERLAND PARK INN, 7200 W. 107th St., Overland Park, KS 66212. Tel. 913/648-7858, or toll free 800/528-1234. 80 rms. A/C TEL TV

$ Rates (including continental breakfast): $48 single; $55 double. Extra person $6. Children 12 and under stay free in parents' room. Weekend, corporate, senior-citizen, and other discounts available. AE, DC, MC, V. Parking: Free.

This hotel offers what you'd expect from a Best Western, which is why many people stay here. Rooms are clean and comfortable, each offering a cable TV with remote control and a clockradio; no-smoking rooms are available.

Services: Complimentary newspaper.

Facilities: One restaurant and lounge, outdoor swimming pool, laundry.

COURTYARD BY MARRIOTT, 11301 Metcalf Ave., Overland Park, KS 66212. Tel. 913/339-9900, or toll free

800/321-2211. Fax 913/339-6091. 137 rms, 12 suites. A/C TEL TV

$ Rates: $79 single; $89 double; suite from $94 single, $104 double. Extra person free. Weekend rates and discounts for longer stays available. AE, DC, MC, V. Parking: Free.

The Courtyard was designed with the business traveler in mind—from its large desks to such facilities as an exercise room for working off stress and a whirlpool for relaxation. Opened in 1989 on the edge of town, away from the mainstream of traffic, this hotel is built around an inner courtyard that contains an expanse of green and a terrace. Rooms each come with a cable TV with remote control and pay movies, a clockradio, a sofa, a sink separated from the bathroom, and in-room coffee service. Some rooms face the inner courtyard and come with balconies but not higher rates.

Services: Complimentary coffee (tea or decaffeinated coffee available on request).

Facilities: One restaurant and lounge, laundry indoor swimming pool, sunning terrace, whirlpool, exercise room.

6. NEAR TRUMAN SPORTS COMPLEX

Both these hotels are located on I-70 at the Blue Ridge Cutoff exit, approximately a 12-minute drive east of downtown Kansas City. The Truman Sports Complex is across the highway, making this area a convenient place to stay if you're here mainly to watch the Royals or the Chiefs. In addition, Worlds of Fun and attractions in Independence are close by. This is also a convenient place to stay if you're arriving from St. Louis and don't want the hassle of driving farther into town.

EXPENSIVE

ADAM'S MARK, 9103 E. 39th, Kansas City, MO 64133. Tel. 816/737-0200, or toll free 800/231-5858. 365 rms, 9 suites. A/C TEL TV

$ Rates: $95–$115 single; $115–$135 double; from $135 suite. Extra person $16. Children under 18 stay free in parents' room. Weekend, corporate, and other rates available. AE, CB, DC, DISC, MC, V. Parking: Free.

This hotel caters largely to group and convention travelers, many of whom want to take advantage of the Royals and Chiefs stadiums across the street. On game days, the hotel even offers a free shuttle bus to the Sports Complex. A sister hotel to the landmark Adam's Mark in downtown St. Louis, this has dependably good service and a wide range of facilities.

Rooms are pleasant and clean, with either queen-size or king-size beds or two double beds. Rooms on the 15th floor have higher ceilings and tend to be quieter than those closer to the highway. The best views are those of the stadiums or downtown Kansas City.

Dining/Entertainment: Remington's, the hotel's premier restaurant, serves steaks and seafood in the tradition of the American West. The Pantry is a casual dining room open for breakfast through dinner. The Players Lounge has a big-screen TV before which you can drink and watch sports; Quincy's is the hottest night spot around, offering live entertainment and dancing as well as happy-hour drinks and buffets.

Services: Complimentary shuttle to Truman Sports Complex, valet laundry service, room service to 11pm.

Facilities: Indoor and outdoor swimming pools, sauna, whirl-pool, exercise room, tennis courts, gift shop.

MODERATE

DRURY INN, 3830 Blue Ridge Cutoff, Kansas City, MO 64133. Tel. 816/923-3000, or toll free 800/325-8300. 133 rms. A/C TEL TV

$ Rates (including continental breakfast): $50 single; $60 double. Extra person $6. Children under 19 stay free in parents' room. Senior-citizen discount. AE, CB, DC, DISC, MC, V. Parking: Free.

Drury Inn is a St. Louis–based hotel chain that offers clean and comfortable accommodations at remarkably low prices. Half the rooms here are no-smoking, and all offer cable TVs with remote control and pay movies. Drury Inn is located across the street from the Adam's Mark hotel.

Services: Free local phone calls.

Facilities: Outdoor swimming pool, Denny's restaurant (adjacent).

7. KANSAS CITY, KANSAS

Kansas City, Kansas, is less than a five-minute drive west of downtown Kansas City, on the other side of the Missouri and Kansas rivers. Thus, the two hotels listed here are good choices if you wish to stay close to downtown but don't want to pay downtown prices. To reach them, take I-70 west from downtown to the Minnesota Avenue exit.

MODERATE

RIVERVIEW INN, 424 Minnesota Ave., Kansas City, KS 66101. Tel. 913/342-6919, or toll free 800/542-2983. 201 rms. A/C TEL TV

$ Rates: $53–$57 single; $60–$63 double. Extra person $5; rollaway bed $7. Children under 18 stay free in parents' room. Weekend and other packages available. AE, CB, DC, DISC, MC, V. Parking: Free.

Formerly a Holiday Inn, this eight-story hotel offers simple accommodations, plus a few added extras. Rooms are clean and comfortable, and the best views are those afforded by the higher floors with a Southern exposure, from which you can see the river and the downtown skyline.

Services: Complimentary happy-hour hors d'oeuvres and special drink prices Mon–Fri, free local calls, room service to 9pm.

Facilities: One restaurant, one lounge, outdoor swimming pool.

BUDGET

GATEWAY GARDENS INN, 425 Minnesota Ave., Kansas City, KS 66101. Tel. 913/621-3085. 208 rms. A/C TEL TV
$ Rates: $39.95 single or double. Extra person $5. Children under 18 stay free in parents' room. AE, DC, D, MC, V. Parking: Free.
Located across the street from the Riverview Inn (above), Gateway Gardens Inn is an older hotel with inexpensive rooms. If all you want is a place to lay down your head at night, this is a good choice. Rooms are simply decorated with just the basics of TVs, phones, and self-controlled air conditioning and heating. The next year should see most rooms outfitted with new carpets, drapes, bedspreads, and a fresh coat of paint. When making a reservation, ask for a renovated room.

---

8. NEAR KANSAS CITY INTERNATIONAL AIRPORT

All these hotels are located near the Kansas City International Airport north of downtown, off I-29.

EXPENSIVE

KANSAS CITY AIRPORT MARRIOTT, 775 Brasilia, Kansas City, MO 64153. Tel. 816/464-2200, or toll free 800/228-9290. Fax 816/464-5613. 382 rms. A/C TEL TV
$ Rates: $145 single or double; Concierge Executive floor $152 single, $162 double. Extra person $10. Children under 18 stay free in parents' room. Weekend and corporate rates and extended-stay discounts available. AE, CB, DC, DISC, E, MC, V. Parking: Free.
Its location beside an artificial lake right next to the airport assures this hotel one of the highest occupancy rates in town. The Airport Marriott is the closest hotel to the airport, and it offers such conveniences as a free shuttle bus to the terminals and a park-and-fly policy that allows hotel guests to keep their cars in the hotel parking lot for up to two weeks free.
    Rooms, decorated on an Asian theme, each offer remote-control cable TV with pay movies; the TV also doubles as a screen for calling up hotel bills and messages. Large windows feature double panes to shut out the noise of overhead planes, and the best view is that of the lake.
    Dining/Entertainment: The King's Wharf serves American food throughout the day, with tables overlooking the lake. Cocktails are served in the Windjammer Lounge.
    Services: Free shuttle to airport, free newspaper, laundry service, room service to 11pm.

Facilities: Indoor swimming pool, exercise room, sauna, whirl-pool, gift shop.

MODERATE

AIRPORT HILTON PLAZA INN, I-29 and N. W. 112th St., Kansas City, MO 64195. Tel. 816/891-8900, or toll free 800/525-6322. 348 rms. A/C TEL TV

$ Rates: $82–$105 single; $92–$118 double. Extra person $10. Children under 18 stay free in parents' room. Weekend and corporate rates available. AE, CB, DC, DISC, ER, MC, V. Parking: Free.

Located off I-29 (take Exit 12), about a five-minute drive from the airport, this 11-story hotel is slowly undergoing a much-needed restoration. Since the prices are the same, request a south-facing room that has already been renovated, from which you have a view of downtown far in the distance. There are two no-smoking floors; room windows can be opened; and the hotel attracts business, group, and convention clientele.

Services: Free shuttle to the airport, free coffee, same-day dry cleaning, room service to 11pm.

Facilities: Two restaurants, two lounges, indoor and outdoor swimming pools, whirlpool, sauna, tennis courts, exercise room, business center, laundry, game room, gift shop.

BUDGET

MOTEL 6, 8230 N.W. Prairie View Rd., Kansas City, MO 64152. Tel. 816/741-6400. 86 rms. A/C TEL TV

$ Rates: $29.95 single; $35.95 double. Extra person $6. Children under 18 stay free in parent's room. AE, CB, DC, DISC, MC, V. Parking: Free.

⑤ Known for inexpensive lodging, Motel 6 is a nationwide chain that offers the basics of a room and a few added extras. This one has an outdoor pool and soda-vending machines. Rooms, equipped with showers instead of tubs, have TVs with free in-house movies; local telephone calls are free. Guests can park near their rooms, and there are both no-smoking and handicapped-accessible rooms. Ask for a room as far away from I-29 as you can get, to cut down on traffic noise. Motel 6 is located off I-29 at the Barry Road exit (Exit 8), approximately four miles from the airport.

9. CAMPING

KOA KAMPGROUNDS, P.O. Box 191, Oak Grove, MO 64075. Tel. 816/625-7515. 77 trailer sites, 23 tent sites.

$ Rates: $14–$19 for two people. Extra person $2; $1 for children ages 5–17. MC, V. **Season:** Mar–Oct.

This KOA is located 16 miles east of Kansas City, just off I-70 at the Oak Grove exit (Exit 28). Facilities include a store, showers, a laundry, a snack bar, ice and firewood, mini-golf, video games, a swimming pool, and a playground.

TRAILSIDE CAMPERS' INN, Grain Valley, MO 64029. Tel. 816/229-CAMP. 83 trailer sites, 20 tent sites.
$ Rates: $14–$16 for two people. Extra person $1.50. MC, V.
Season: Year round.

This eight-acre campground is located 20 minutes east of downtown Kansas City, off I-70 at the Grain Valley exit (Exit 24). Facilities here include showers, a swimming pool, a laundry, a store, a playground, and a game room.

CHAPTER 14

KANSAS CITY DINING

1. **DOWNTOWN**
2. **CROWN CENTER**
3. **COUNTRY CLUB PLAZA**
4. **WESTPORT & MIDTOWN**
5. **OVERLAND PARK**
6. **SOUTH KANSAS CITY & MARTIN CITY**
7. **INDEPENDENCE & EAST KANSAS CITY**
8. **SPECIALTY DINING**

Kansas City is justifiably famous for its steaks and barbecue. This is the place to come if you're hungering for a 25-ounce steak or wish to dine at a different barbecue restaurant every night for two months solid. Kansas Citians love to argue about which barbecue restaurant is the best, each convinced that his or her favorite is it. But the fact that the city supports more than 60 barbecue restaurants is testimony to the fact that "best" often signifies just a difference in tastes. There are probably more different types of barbecue sauces in Kansas City than anywhere else in the world—ranging from the gritty, cayenne-flavored sauce of Arthur Bryant's to the hot and tangy sauce of Gates & Sons.

Kansas City barbecue is always slow-smoked over wood, usually hickory, and it includes barbecued pork, ribs, brisket, ham, sausage, and chicken. Once the food of Kansas City's poor black population with a tradition that stretches back to the 1920s, barbecue is still served in simple and no-nonsense establishments, with the most popular dish consisting of brisket piled high on white bread and slathered with thick sauce, accompanied by a mountain of fries. This is roll-up-your-sleeves cuisine, and if by chance you become addicted, most restaurants sell bottles of their sauce that you can take home.

But Kansas City is more than beef and barbecue. Italian, French, Greek, Asian, Mexican, Cajun, and other ethnic restaurants have found an enthusiastic welcome in Kansas City, as have restaurants dishing out hearty portions of American food, both traditional and new American.

The restaurants below have been divided according to location and then further subdivided by price. Expensive restaurants are those where dinners will cost you more than $25 per person, excluding wine, drinks, and tip. Moderately priced restaurants will range from $15 to $25 for a meal, while inexpensive restaurants offer meals that will cost from $7 to $15. At budget restaurants, you can dine for less than $7. Keep in mind, however, that many restaurants offer a cheaper menu and daily specials during lunch hours. Thus, you can splurge for lunch at a restaurant that may be way out of your price range for dinner.

Remember that a 6.475% tax will be added on to restaurant bills in Kansas City, Missouri; on the Kansas side the tax averages about 5.75%. Tips should average about 15%, rising to 20% at the better restaurants or for special service.

1. DOWNTOWN

Restaurants listed here range from those located in the heart of downtown to those near the City Market, the Stockyards, and other locations within a few minutes' drive to the south and east of downtown.

EXPENSIVE

SAVOY GRILL, 9th and Central. Tel. 842-3890.
   Cuisine: AMERICAN **Reservations:** Recommended.
$ **Prices:** Lunch $4.75–$16; dinner entrees $12.50–$26; fixed-price dinners $27–$38. AE, CB, DC, DISC, MC, V.
   Open: Mon–Thurs 11am–11pm, Fri and Sat 11am–midnight; Sun 4–10pm.

The Savoy Grill opened in 1903 and has been a Kansas City landmark ever since. It's a restaurant in the old tradition— with turn-of-the-century stained-glass windows; high-backed booths; wainscoting; wall murals with scenes of the Santa Fe Trail; white tablecloths; and gallant, efficient service. There's no other place in town that better conveys what Kansas City was like during its cowtown heyday, when West was best and the nearby stockyards were at their zenith.

The food is unabashedly straightforward and traditional American cuisine, featuring seafood and steaks. There are about two dozen selections of fish and seafood, including a mixed crab plate, lobster, broiled salmon, walleye pike, channel catfish, and frog legs. Other entrees include baked lobster pie, chateaubriand, veal marsala, and T-bone steak. Lunch ranges from sandwiches to heartier entrees, such as red snapper, crabmeat crêpes, and braised lamb with artichokes and lemon.

MODERATE

FITZPATRICK'S SALOON AND CAFÉ, 931 Broadway. Tel. 474-1468.
   Cuisine: AMERICAN **Reservations:** Recommended for lunch.
$ **Prices:** Lunch $5.50–$7.50; dinner entrees $9–$18. AE, MC, V.
   Open: Lunch Mon–Fri 11am–2:30pm; dinner Mon–Sat 5–10:30pm.

Opened as a saloon in 1911 by James E. Fitzpatrick and operating as such until Prohibition closed its doors, Fitzpatrick's still retains many of its original architectural features—including its tile floor, molded-tin ceiling, plaster molding, and copper facade. A colorful mural adorning one wall pays tribute to famous people who once lived in

Kansas City: Count Basie, Thomas Hart Benton, George Caleb Bingham, Walt Disney, Ernest Hemingway, Charlie Parker, and Frederic Remington, and others. The lunch menu includes the buffalo burger, black angus prime rib sandwich, pasta specials, and a fish of the day; dinner includes selections of beef, seafood, pork tenderloin, chicken, pork ribs, and daily specials. On Tuesday and Thursday evening there's live jazz.

HEREFORD HOUSE, 20th and Main. Tel. 842-1080.
Cuisine: STEAKS **Reservations:** None.
$ Prices: Lunch $4.95–$13; dinner entrees $9–$27. AE, DC, MC, V.
Open: Mon–Thurs 11am–10pm, Fri 11am–10:30pm, Sat 4–10:30pm, Sun 4–9pm.

This Kansas City steak house, decorated with pictures of the old West and the days of the cattle drives, has been serving cuts of prime beef since 1957. A happy hour featuring specials on drinks and appetizers is offered Monday through Friday from 3 to 6pm. Lunch includes everything from more than a half-dozen varieties of burgers to chicken, seafood, sandwiches and steaks. Dinner is heavy on steaks, lobster, fish, and shrimp, with the specialty of the house a 12-ounce filet mignon. All dinners include salad, baked potato or french fries, and bread.

 FROMMER'S SMART TRAVELER —RESTAURANTS

VALUE-CONSCIOUS DINERS SHOULD TAKE ADVANTAGE OF THE FOLLOWING:

1. Lunch menus offering entrees at cheaper prices than those on dinner menus; save money by eating a big meal at noon.
2. Daily specials offered by many restaurants, which are not on the regular menus and may offer a main course and side dish at a good price.
3. Fixed-price meals, each of which includes an appetizer or soup, a main course, and a dessert, at prices much cheaper than ordering à la carte.
4. Inexpensive entrees, such as chicken or pasta, offered by some of the more expensive restaurants, where even budget travelers can dine in style by choosing carefully.
5. Kansas City's steaks and barbecue, hearty portions at inexpensive prices.
6. Food offered by many pubs, bars, and taverns, usually hearty portions at bargain prices.

QUESTIONS TO ASK IF YOU'RE ON A BUDGET

1. Does the entree come with a side dish such as a vegetable or potato? (If so, it may be all you want to order, unless you have a voracious appetite.)
2. Is there a special of the day or a fixed-price meal not listed on the regular menu?

Acapulco 🔶17
The American Restaurant 🔶16
Arthur Bryant's 🔶10
Benton's Steak and
  Chop House 🔶13
City Seen, Town Pavilion 🔶8
Fitzpatrick's Sallon and Café 🔶6
Garozzo's 🔶2
Golden Ox 🔶18
Hereford House 🔶12
Italian Gardens 🔶7
Jennie's 🔶4
Kabuki 🔶15
Manny's 🔶11
Margarita's 🔶16
Milano 🔶15
Peppercorn Duck Club 🔶14
Ponak's 🔶15A
Savoy Grill 🔶3
Town Pavillion Food Court 🔶8
Trader Vic's 🔶13
Walt Bodine's 🔶9
Winslow's Smoke House 🔶1

INEXPENSIVE

CITY SEEN, Town Pavilion, 1111 Main. Tel. 472-8833.
   Cuisine: AMERICAN/INTERNATIONAL **Reservations:** Not
   necessary.
$ Prices: $5.75–$17. AE, MC, V.
   Open: Mon–Thurs 11am–2:30pm and 5–9pm, Fri and Sat
   11am–11pm.
One of the few restaurants in the heart of downtown, this is the only

one in Town Pavilion shopping center that remains open past 6pm. Its food is fun and creative, including international recipes with a liberal use of spices and seasonings. You might wish to start with oysters served with a ginger-saffron glaze; Vietnamese spring rolls; or chicken breast strips rolled in bread crumbs and shredded coconut, fried, and served with a honey-mustard sauce. The list of sandwiches includes such tempting combinations as charbroiled chicken breast with Cajun seasoning, cheese, and barbecue sauce; and Ozark ham served with Jarlsberg cheese and tomato chutney on foccacia bread. Entrees include baby-back ribs, calamari steak, lamb chops, and steak—all also available by the half order for diners with smaller appetites.

GAROZZO'S, 526 Harrison. Tel. 221-2455.

Cuisine: ITALIAN **Reservations:** Recommended on weekends.

$ Prices: Lunch $4.30–$9.60; dinner pasta entrees $7–$15, meat courses $9.25–$20. AE, MC, V.

Open: Mon–Thurs 11am–10pm, Fri 11am–11pm, Sat 5–11pm.

"Fine Italian Cuisine at Family Prices" is the motto of this newcomer to the Italian food scene in Kansas City. Located north of I-70 and east of the City Market, Garozzo's is a casual establishment in the heart of the city's old Italian district, which now includes new waves of Asian immigrants. Specialties include a lightly breaded veal sautéed in butter, lemon, fresh mushrooms, capers, and black olives; and beef medallions breaded and charbroiled, then topped with melted cheese and served in a sauce of white wine, butter, lemon, and fresh mushrooms. More than a dozen pastas dishes are available, including such popular choices as fettuccine served in a spicy tomato sauce with shrimp, calamari, clams, and fresh mussels; ziti in cream sauce with fresh broccoli and mushrooms; and rigatoni with tomato sauce, cream sauce, peas, mushrooms, and prosciutto.

GOLDEN OX, 1600 Genessee. Tel. 842-2866.

Cuisine: STEAKS

$ Prices: Lunch $3–$8 for sandwiches, $5.50–$18 for steaks; dinner entrees $7–$17. AE, CB, DC, DISC, M, V.

Open: Mon–Fri 11:30am–10pm, Sat 4:30–10:30pm, Sun 4–9pm.

The Golden Ox opened in 1950, primarily to satisfy the hearty appetites of ranchers bringing their livestock to the stockyards next door. Now the stockyards are a ghost of their former glory, but the Golden Ox continues to draw crowds, with beef aged and cut on the premises. Prime rib and steaks broiled over a hickory charcoal flame are the specialties—all served with a choice of baked potato or french fries, garlic toast, and salad. The dining hall has maintained its 1950s look, with wood paneling on the walls and shining busts of golden ox heads everywhere. To reach the restaurant from downtown, take 12th Street west or I-35 south to the Kemper-Genessee exit.

ITALIAN GARDENS, 1110 Baltimore. Tel. 221-9311.

Cuisine: ITALIAN **Reservations:** None needed. Free valet parking after 5pm.

$ Prices: Lunch $4.70–$12, fixed-priced lunch $4.90; dinner pasta courses $6.50–$12.50, meat courses $8–$13. AE, CB, DC, MC, V.

Open: Mon–Thurs 11am–10pm, Fri and Sat 11am–11pm.

This popular restaurant has been in continual operation since 1925. An informal family restaurant with red-and-white checked tablecloths and a children's menu, Italian Gardens specializes in homemade pizza, lasagne, ravioli, chicken, and veal dishes and features daily lunch specials. Don't pass up the cheesecake. Adjoining the restaurant is the Ciao Lounge.

JENNIE'S, 511 Cherry St. Tel. 421-3366.
Cuisine: ITALIAN
$ Prices: Lunch $4.50–$7; dinner pasta courses $7–$11, meat courses $9.50–$15. AE, DC, MC, V.
Open: Mon–Thurs 11am–9pm, Fri 11am–10pm, Sat noon–10pm, Sun noon–8pm.

This is another long-standing Italian restaurant, open since 1938 and now managed by Jennie's grandson. Specializing in Sicilian food, it caters to two distinct crowds—bringing in downtown white-collar workers during lunch and serving as a blue-collar family establishment for dinner. Adjoining the restaurant is a bar, a watering hole for people who live and work in the area. Most foods are made from scratch, and Jennie's was probably the first establishment in town to serve pizza. It excels in red sauces, with lasagne and cheese ravioli its most popular dishes. Dinner entrees include veal, steak, chicken parmigiana, and eggplant parmigiana. Jennie's is located in the old Italian district, north of I-70 and east of the City Market.

BUDGET

ACAPULCO, 310 Admiral Blvd. Tel. 471-8989.
Cuisine: MEXICAN
$ Prices: $3.50–$10. AE, MC, V.
Open: Mon–Thurs 11am–9pm, Fri and Sat 11am–10pm.

This simple restaurant, near 7th and McGee, has been serving authentic Mexican fare for more than 35 years, long before the Mexican-food craze swept the country. There are no corners cut in the preparation of Acapulco's food, from its fried nachos to its refried beans, and its margaritas are made individually. The menu, the same for lunch and dinner, includes burritos; tacos; enchiladas; tostadas; and platters that come with an entree, Spanish rice, beans, and a salad. Because orders are completed in a flash, Acapulco is a popular spot for lunch.

ARTHUR BRYANT'S, 1727 Brooklyn. Tel. 231-1123.
Cuisine: BARBECUE
$ Prices: $5–$7. No credit cards accepted.
Open: Mon–Thurs 10am–9:30pm, Fri and Sat 10am–10pm, Sun 11am–8pm.

This, the granddaddy of barbecue restaurants in Kansas City, was once rated by food critic Calvin Trillin as the "single, best restaurant in the world." Former presidents Harry Truman and Jimmy Carter made a point of dining here on visits to Kansas City, as did Emperor Haile Selassie of Ethiopia back in 1937. But you'd never guess at Arthur Bryant's fame by looking at the place, a simple two-story brick building located a few minute's drive east of downtown in what is a predominately black neighborhood. Hungry customers from throughout the city are willing to stand in line for the privilege of ordering from the counter of this no-frills establishment. This is the place to pig out without reservation. Sandwiches are the specialty, piled sky high with beef, pork, ham, sausage, or chicken, best ordered with side dishes of french fries or baked beans. There are also ribs. Arthur died in 1982, and even though his successors have cleaned up the place a bit (customers used to be able to skid across the floor on a layer of grease and french fries), little has changed—many Kansas Citians consider this the best barbecue place in town. Arthur Bryant's sauce, gritty and made with a secret recipe that includes cayenne, paprika, vinegar, and celery, is for sale at the restaurant. Highly recommended.

MANNY'S, 207 Southwest Blvd. Tel. 474-7696.

Cuisine: MEXICAN
$ Prices: $3–$10. AE, MC, V.
Open: Mon–Thurs 11am–10pm, Fri and Sat 11am–11pm.

This is a large, popular Mexican restaurant, located between downtown and Crown Center, where Southwest Boulevard, 20th Street and Central Street all converge. Manny's strives for authenticity in its homemade tamales, as well as in its preparation of tacos, chile rellenos, enchiladas, fajitas, and burritos. Burgers and a children's plate also are available; a house specialty is its margaritas, available by the pitcher or the glass.

MARGARITA'S, 2829 Southwest Blvd. Tel. 931-4849.

Cuisine: MEXICAN **Reservations:** None taken.
$ Prices: Fixed-price meals $6–$8. AE, MC, V.
Open: Mon–Thurs 11am–10pm, Fri and Sat 11am–11:30pm, Sun noon–10pm.

"Always a party scene" is how one employee described this popular Mexican restaurant, one of the many Mexican establishments that stretch along Southwest Boulevard beside the railroad tracks, about a five-minute drive southwest of downtown. Margarita's is so crowded that customers expect to belly up to the bar while waiting for a table, drinking some of the 40 gallons of margaritas that are mixed and sold each day. The food, prepared by Mexican cooks, includes a dozen selections of complete meals along with some à la carte items. The most popular platter is the Margarita's Special, which features a flour tortilla stuffed with pork, beef, beans, cheese, and onions and topped with chili con queso and served with rice. There's an outdoor patio.

PONAK'S, 2856 Southwest Blvd. Tel. 753-0775.

Cuisine: MEXICAN
$ Prices: Fixed-price meals $5–$7.50. AE, MC, V.
Open: Mon–Thurs 11am–10:30pm, Fri and Sat 11am–11:30pm, Sun noon–9pm.

When this restaurant opened in 1978 in the Hispanic part of town, none of the cooks spoke English. Today the original recipes are faithfully followed in the restaurant's open kitchen, but now all the cooks speak English. All the meat is cut and ground on the premises, and the chili rellenos and tamales are homemade. Ponak's is the place to dine if you want menundo (a soup made with tripe and hominy in a clear broth—considered a good cure for a hangover) or chicken mole. Another popular item is the guacamole platter, which features one burrito, one tostada, one enchilada with avocado dip, Spanish rice, and beans. Almost 50 different brands of beer are available.

TOWN PAVILION FOOD COURT, 3rd Floor, 1111 Main St. Tel. 472-9600.

Cuisine: INTERNATIONAL
$ Prices: $1.50–$6.50. No credit cards accepted.
Open: Mon–Sat 10am–6pm.

Town Pavilion is a downtown mall with more than 40 shops and restaurants. On the third floor is its Food Court, a bright and cheerful place with skylights and a pleasant dining area separate from the various food counters, giving it a restaurant atmosphere. Burgers, hot dogs, barbecue, pizza, tacos, salads, sandwiches, and Chinese and Greek specialties are available.

WINSLOW'S SMOKEHOUSE, 20 E. 5th St. Tel. 471-RIBS.
Cuisine: BARBECUE
$ Prices: $3–$13. No credit cards accepted.
Open: Daily 10am–10pm.

This family-owned and operated restaurant, serving barbecue at the City Market for more than 20 years, is famous for its ribs and spicy smoked chicken wings. It uses certified black Angus beef, slow-cooked over green hickory, and its sauce is made with fresh produce along with blackstrap molasses. Also on the menu of this informal eatery are sandwiches and smoked sausage. A good place for lunch if you're visiting City Market, located north of I-70.

2. CROWN CENTER

In addition to the restaurants listed here, be sure to check the "Specialty Dining" section at the end of this chapter for hotel restaurants and restaurants with a view, including Benton's and The Peppercorn Duck Club.

EXPENSIVE

THE AMERICAN RESTAURANT, Crown Center, 200 E. 25th St. Tel. 471-8050.
Cuisine: AMERICAN **Reservations:** Recommended on weekends. Free valet parking.
$ Prices: Appetizers $10.50–$13; entrees $22–$30. AE, MC, V.
Open: Mon–Thurs 6–10pm, Fri and Sat 6–11pm.

ⓕFROMMER'S COOL FOR KIDS
RESTAURANTS

Italian Gardens (see p. 188) This family-style restaurant, serving a variety of pasta and pizza dishes for decades, also offers a children's menu.

Winstead's (see p. 195) Show your child what a 1940s diner was all about. Hamburgers are served wrapped in tissue, sodas are made the old-fashioned way, and there's a jukebox with tunes of the 1950s and early 1960s.

Stephenson's Apple Farm (see p. 205) This has been a popular family destination for decades, for both its home cooking and its rustic, antique setting.

Tasso's (see p. 204) Children love the drama at Tasso's, a Greek restaurant that features a live band and the lively personality of Tasso himself.

✪ Gourmet American cuisine best describes the food served by this great restaurant, one of the best in Kansas City. Its dining room (with only 21 tables) is an unexpected delight, featuring a dramatic 25-foot-high ceiling and floor-to-ceiling windows that are shuttered against the daylight but opened after nightfall to reveal a view of the city. A pianist appears nightly.

The menu capitalizes on regional specialties that include such ingredients as buffalo, cracked Kansas wheat, and morels. The menu changes often but may include such main courses as roasted salmon with lemon grass and ginger, pan-roasted pheasant breast with morels, and grilled T-bone steak with onions and a tomato-horseradish salsa. There are also evening specials, and the wine list is extensive. Jackets are required for men, but ties are optional.

MODERATE

KABUKI, Crown Center, 2450 Grand Ave. Tel. 472-1717.
  Cuisine: JAPANESE **Reservations:** Recommended for lunch and weekend dinners.
  $ Prices: Lunch entrees $5.50–$9; dinner entrees $11–$21. AE, DC, MC, V.
  Open: Lunch Mon–Fri 11:30am–2pm, Sat noon–2pm; dinner Mon–Thurs 5:30–10pm, Fri and Sat 5:30–11pm, Sun 5–10pm.

This restaurant gets my vote as the best Japanese restaurant in town. Decorated in traditional style with paper screens and bamboo, it has a Japanese staff and offers a wide variety of Japanese cuisine—including tempura (deep-fried meats and vegetables), teriyaki, tonkatsu (breaded pork cutlets), sukiyaki (thinly sliced beef cooked in broth with vegetables), and sushi. There are no knife-brandishing teppanyaki chefs in sight.

INEXPENSIVE

MILANO, Crown Center, 2450 Grand Ave. Tel. 471-2003.
  Cuisine: ITALIAN
  $ Prices: Lunch entrees $6.25–$12; dinner pizza and pasta $6.50–$12, meat courses $8.50–$14. AE, MC, V.
  Open: Mon–Fri 11:30am–2:30pm and 5–10pm, Sat 11:30am–2:30pm and 5–11pm, Sun 11:30am–10pm.

This has to be one of the most pleasant dining rooms in Kansas City. Light and airy, with so many skylights and plants that eating here is like dining in a greenhouse, Milano serves Northern Italian cuisine. Pasta dishes include bow-tie pasta with four cheeses and a shrimp linguine; pizza choices range from artichoke and oven-dried tomato to Italian sausage. Main courses include shellfish risotto, sautéed veal, and broiled salmon medallions.

3. COUNTRY CLUB PLAZA

For information on the Grill at the Ritz-Carlton, check the "Specialty Dining" section at the end of this chapter.

EXPENSIVE

FEDORA CAFÉ AND BAR, 210 W. 47th St. Tel. 561-6565.
Cuisine: CONTINENTAL **Reservations:** Recommended for dinner.
$ Prices: Lunch $6.25–$10; dinner pizza and pasta courses $9.50–$14.50, meat courses $15–$24. AE, CB, DC, DISC, MC, V.
Open: Lunch Mon–Sat 11:45am–2:30pm; dinner Sun–Thurs 5:30–10pm, Fri 5:30–11pm, Sat 5–11pm; Sun brunch 10:30am–3pm.

This is a favorite choice for many Kansas Citians when they are celebrating special occasions, from birthdays to anniversaries; it is a place to see and be seen. The clientele is always smartly dressed, and the restaurant, boasting an open kitchen, has a decor that gives it a turn-of-the-century art nouveau elegance. The innovative menu, which changes once a year, offers both familiar and exotic choices. Past dishes, for example, have included Thai noodles stir-fried with shrimp and vegetables; pizza topped with garlic cream, smoked salmon, tomatoes, garlic, scallions, onion, and feta and fontina; veal sweetbreads with morels, ham, cognac, and heavy cream; and grilled quail and barbecued shrimp quesadilla. Lunch offers lighter fare, including salads, pasta, pizza, and sandwiches.

LA MEDITERRANEE, 4742 Pennsylvania. Tel. 561-2916.
Cuisine: FRENCH **Reservations:** Recommended.
$ Prices: Lunch $5.50–$10; dinner entrees $14–$25. AE, DC, MC, V.
Open: Lunch Mon–Fri 11:15am–1:45pm; dinner Mon–Sat 6–9:45pm.

French restaurants have never hit it big in Kansas City, but this intimate and elegant one has been serving what's probably the best French food in the city for more than 20 years, which means that it must be doing something right. Dining is in three cozy rooms that make the place seem more like a private home than a restaurant. Many dishes are prepared tableside.

French owner/chef Gilbert Jahier offers an extensive menu with selections of fish, seafood, veal, steak, duck, and lamb, as well as wild game in season (wild boar, pheasant, or partridge). Entrees include frog legs in a menthe sauce; sweetbreads in a lobster, shrimp, and cognac sauce; Kansas City steak with sauce béarnaise, crabmeat, and asparagus; beef Wellington; and chateaubriand with goose liver in truffle and mushroom sauce. Lunch is lighter, including salads, omelets, fish, pasta, and daily specials.

MODERATE

BRISTOL BAR AND GRILL, 4740 Jefferson. Tel. 756-0606.
Cuisine: SEAFOOD **Reservations:** Recommended, especially weekends.
$ Prices: Lunch $6.50–$12; dinner entrees $13.95–$21.95; Sun brunch $9.95. AE, CB, DC, DISC, MC, V.
Open: Lunch Mon–Fri 11am–2:30pm, Sat 11:30am–3pm; dinner Mon–Thurs 5:30–10:30pm, Fri and Sat 5–11:30pm, Sun 4:30–9:30pm; Sun brunch 10am–2pm.

Bristol Bar and Grill, first opened on the Plaza in 1980, has proved so successful that it has opened at several locations across the country. Its slightly masculine decor is reminiscent of venerable seafood restaurants in England, with a molded-tin ceiling, brass railings, stained-glass lamps, newspapers hanging from a rack, and a standup marble-top bar with a brass foot rail. Its specialty is seafood—including oysters, swordfish, lobster, Alaskan king crab legs, jumbo shrimp, sea scallops, and daily specials that usually include a dozen or so fresh fish. Particularly recommended is the shellfish cioppino, which is fresh fish, sea scallops, Maine mussels, shrimp, clams, and stone crab claw, served in a red-wine tomato-herb sauce. Steaks also are available. All entrees include a soda biscuit (deliciously flaky) and a choice of potatoes or pasta.

INEXPENSIVE

FIGLIO, 209 W. 46th St. Tel. 561-0505.
Cuisine: ITALIAN
$ Prices: Lunch $6.75–$8.50; dinner pasta and pizza $7.50–$9, meat courses $12.25–$17.50. AE, CB, DC, DISC, MC, V.
Open: Lunch Mon–Fri 11:30am–2:30pm, Sat 11:30am–3:30pm; dinner Mon–Thurs 5–10pm, Fri and Sat 5–11pm, Sun 4–10pm.

Figlio, one of Kansas City's newer Italian restaurants, offers great food at modest prices. Simply decorated with hardwood floors, pink walls, modern lighting, palm trees, and an open kitchen, it specializes in Northern Italian food. Especially recommended are the homemade pasta and the gourmet pizza, cooked in a wood-burning oven. Try the Spaghettini Napoletana (thin spaghetti with roma tomatoes, garlic, olive oil, and fresh basil); three-cheese ravioli; or Stromboli Figlio, which is a rolled pizza stuffed with prosciutto, mushrooms, and romano and mozzarella cheeses. For an entree, you might consider tender beef marinated in fresh herbs and Bardolino wine, grilled with vegetables over hardwood coals, and served on linguine. Finish your meal with homemade chocolate mousse wrapped in an espresso-and-Amaretto-soaked sponge cake.

HOULIHAN'S OLD PLACE, 4743 Pennsylvania. Tel. 561-3141.
Cuisine: AMERICAN
$ Prices: $6.25–$12. AE, CB, DC, DISC, MC, V.
Open: Sun–Thurs 11am–11pm, Fri and Sat 11am–midnight.

This was the very first Houlihan's, open for almost two decades and now part of a chain with more than 50 locations nationwide. It's a fun and informal place, popular with a professional working crowd and families (there's a children's menu). The menu is extensive—including burgers; sandwiches; quiches; salads; and an eclectic mix of entrees that range from fajitas and Cajun shrimp to barbecued ribs, teriyaki steak, chicken stir-fry, and blackened chicken quesadilla. Happy hour is Monday through Friday from 4 to 8pm, with discounts on drinks and appetizers.

ROZELLE COURT, Nelson-Atkins Museum of Art, 4525 Oak. Tel. 751-1279.
Cuisine: CONTINENTAL

$ Prices: Salads $2–$4; entrees $6. MC, V.

Open: Tues–Fri 10am–3:30pm, Sat 10am–4pm, Sun 1–4pm.

S This is one of the most unusual and beautiful places to dine in Kansas City, a light and airy Venetian courtyard with a stone floor, fountain, pillars, and a super-high ceiling topped with a skylight. The food, served cafeteria style, includes a changing selection of salads; sandwiches; soup; and entrees that may include lasagne, game hen, crabcakes, catfish, and veal stew. Since Rozelle Court is located in the Nelson-Atkins Museum of Art, east of the Plaza, you have to pay the $3 museum admission in order to eat here. Highly recommended.

BUDGET

ANNIE'S SANTA FE, 100 Ward Parkway. Tel. 753-1621.

Cuisine: MEXICAN

$ Prices: $5.75–$8. AE, CB, DC, D, MC, V.

Open: Sun–Thurs 10:30am–11pm, Fri and Sat 10:30am–midnight.

Serving an American version of Mexican food, this has long been a favorite restaurant on the Plaza. Fajitas are its most popular dish, but platters offer everything from Mexican pizza or tamales to chimichangas, enchiladas, empanadas, and tacos. An especially good deal is the lunch buffet offered Monday through Friday for $4.95. Other branches are at 5600 E. Bannister Rd. (tel. 966-1400) at Bannister Mall and 11855 W. 95th St. (tel. 492-6121) in Overland Park.

GATES & SONS Bar-B-Q, 47th & Paseo. Tel. 921-0409.

Cuisine: BARBECUE

$ Prices: $4.45–$11.99. No credit cards accepted.

Open: Mon–Sat 10am–2am, Sun 10am–midnight.

★ Gates & Sons' trademark is the manner in which employees greet customers, yelling "May I help you?" as soon as someone walks through the door. In business since 1945, it ranks alongside Arthur Bryant's as one of the best barbecue restaurants in Kansas City; it gets my vote as having the best sauce in town, particularly its hot and spicy version (available for sale in bottles). The menu includes sandwiches, ribs, sausage, chicken, and mutton. This branch, easily recognizable with its red roof, is located a few minutes' drive east of the Plaza, past Troost. Other locations include 12th and Brooklyn (tel. 483-3880) and 10440 E. 40 Highway (tel. 353-6880) in Independence.

WINSTEAD'S, 101 Brush Creek. Tel. 753-2244.

Cuisine: BURGERS

$ Prices: $1.50–$3. No credit cards accepted.

Open: Sun–Thurs 10:30am–midnight, Fri and Sat 10:30am–midnight.

★ Winstead's is a nostalgic trip back to the days of the diner, when waitresses wore pinafores and hamburgers were served in tissue. Its jukebox features music of the 1950s and early 1960s. A Kansas City tradition since 1940, Winstead's is the place to go for hamburgers or grilled-cheese sandwiches or to satisfy cravings for ice-cream sodas, milk shakes, root-beer floats, cheesecakes, and sundaes. It's located about a five-minute walk east of the Plaza. Other locations include 8817 W. 63rd (tel. 384-2224), 8333 W. 95th (tel. 383-3330), and 1428 Noland Rd. (tel. 252-9363) in Independence.

4. WESTPORT & MIDTOWN

Most of these restaurants are located either in the heart of Westport (Pennsylvania Street and Westport Road) or north of Westport on West 39th Street, near the University of Kansas Medical Center.

EXPENSIVE

CAFÉ ALLEGRO, 1815 W. 39th St. Tel. 561-3663.
   Cuisine: CONTINENTAL **Reservations:** Recommended.
$ Prices: Lunch $7.25–$10; dinner entrees $18–$27. AE, CB, DC, MC, V.
   Open: Lunch Mon–Fri 11:30am–2pm; dinner Mon–Sat 6–10pm.

A well-heeled, older crowd patronizes this cheerful restaurant, which manages to be casual, civilized, and artsy at the same time. Café Allegro features exposed-brick walls, cane chairs, flower arrangements, white tablecloths, and original artwork. The service is attentive, and the food is artfully arranged and presented.

This restaurant has one of the most extensive wine lists in Kansas City, mainly American but also page after page of French wines. Approximately 40 wines are available by the glass at any one time, but you may wish to opt for one of its 400 choices in bottles. Highly recommended food choices are the rack of lamb, marinated and charcoal-grilled over a wood fire and served with a mustard and pine-nut crust; the duck breast with caramelized sweet garlic; the veal tenderloin with thyme and lemon vinaigrette; and the peppered filet with blue cheese.

MODERATE

CAFÉ LULU, 1706 W. 39th. Tel. 931-5858.
   Cuisine: INTERNATIONAL **Reservations:** Recommended on evenings.
$ Prices: Appetizers $5.50–$7.50; entrees $8–$17. AE, MC, V.
   Open: Lunch Mon–Fri 11:30am–2:30pm; dinner Mon–Sat 5pm–midnight.

There's something joyously upbeat about this restaurant, from the bold splashes of color in its avant-garde decor to the creativity evident in its dishes. I'm not sure why, but dining here makes me want to wear the most outrageous clothing I own. The food is eclectic, mixing ingredients and concepts from all over the world; the menu changes often. Appetizers might include a duck burrito and lamb riblets with spicy peanut sauce. Other tempting dishes might include Oriental noodles with soy sauce, sesame oil, chili dressing, chicken, green onions, and peanuts; fish steamed in banana leaves; Southwestern grilled pork tenderloin; and black-bean stew and rice. There's an extensive wine list as well as a full bar.

CALIFORNOS, 4124 Pennsylvania. Tel. 531-7878.
   Cuisine: AMERICAN **Reservations:** Recommended on weekends.
$ Prices: Lunch $7–$20; dinner entrees $10–$30. AE, CB, DC, MC, V.
   Open: Lunch Mon–Sat 10am–2pm; dinner Sun–Thurs 5–10pm, Fri and Sat 5–11pm.

California-inspired cuisine is featured in this bright bistrolike restaurant in the heart of Westport. Decorated in hot pink with white tablecloths and black chairs, Californos offers both indoor and outdoor seating and live piano music every evening. For an appetizer, you might consider an artichoke-chili cheese spread or sourdough rounds topped with pesto, black olives, tomatoes, and cheese. Entrees include grilled tuna, crab strudel, king salmon, swordfish with pesto butter, and grilled chicken with homemade salsa. Steaks, lamb chops, and lobster round out the menu. Lunch features a wide selection of entree salads along with sandwiches and light entrees.

METROPOLIS, 303 Westport Rd. Tel. 753-1550.
   Cuisine: INTERNATIONAL **Reservations:** Recommended on evenings.
$ Prices: Lunch $6.50–$11; dinner pizza and pasta $10.95; entrees $8–$20. AE, DC, MC, V.
   Open: Lunch Mon–Fri 11:30am–2:30pm; dinner Mon–Thurs 5:30–10pm, Fri and Sat 5:30pm–midnight.

This is an ultramodern, chic restaurant, one small room sleekly decorated in black and teal, with black tables, a black carpet, and neon-colored placemats. Even the service staff are dressed in black. One of the two owners is always on hand to greet customers. The dishes, artfully presented, are an imaginative blend of regional American cuisine with international ingredients, including Italian and Asian. For the first course, you might select Vietnamese-style eggrolls or cioppino (Italian fishermen's stew). There are several choices of pizza and pasta; entrees include salmon stuffed with chorizo sausage and topped with caviar-and-cheese sauce; papaya flank steak; lemon chicken; and sole wrapped in phyllo, stuffed with brie, chives, and sorrel, and topped with candied ginger and safflower sauce. For dessert, try the white-chocolate flan or the chocolate-peanut butter–nut crunch.

INEXPENSIVE

ATHENA ON BROADWAY, 3535 Broadway. Tel. 756-3227.
   Cuisine: GREEK
$ Prices: Lunch $5.75–$8.50; dinner entrees $9–$15. AE, MC, V.
   Open: Lunch 11:30am–2pm; dinner Mon–Thurs 6–10pm, Fri and Sat 6–10:30pm.

You can't tell upon entering that this is a Greek restaurant—no blaring bouzouki music, no belly dancing, and no pictures of the

Acropolis. Rather, there are paintings and artwork that are for sale, fresh flowers on the tables, and even crayons at each table should you feel inclined to scribble. Athena is a casual and subdued establishment that offers great Greek food, including moussaka, souvlaki, homemade Greek sausage, grilled octopus, and baklava. There are also daily specials that range from fresh fish to grilled rack of lamb; lunch features sandwiches and lighter dishes.

JIMMY AND MARY'S, 3400 Main. Tel. 753-9397.

Cuisine: ITALIAN/STEAKS
$ Prices: Sandwiches $3.80–$7; pasta courses $5.25–$10; meat courses $8.25–$15. AE, CB, DC, DISC, MC, V.
Open: Mon–Thurs 4pm–midnight, Fri and Sat 4pm–1:30am, Sun 4–10pm.

⑤ Sizzling steaks served on hot platters have been a specialty at this family-owned and -operated restaurant ever since it opened in 1944; other specialties are lasagne, spaghetti, ravioli, and sautéed chicken liver with onions. Additional dishes include chicken broiled with garlic butter, veal parmigiana, chicken cacciatore, lobster tail, catfish, and sandwiches. There's also a children's menu. Telly Savalas, Bill Cosby, and Neil Diamond have walked through the doors to Jimmy and Mary's, which is delightfully unpretentious, right down to its fake flowers.

KIKI'S BON TON, 1515 Westport Rd. Tel. 931-9417.

Cuisine: CREOLE/CAJUN
$ Prices: Lunch $4–$7.50; dinner $5–$10. AE, DC, MC, V.
Open: Sun–Thurs 11am–10pm, Fri and Sat 11am–11pm.

★ This is a fun and funky kind of place, with stucco alligators crawling on the walls and lobsters stenciled below a pressed-tin ceiling. The walls are painted a deep bayou green; there are palm trees; and charts on the walls show various species of fish, mushrooms, and sea life. Above the bar is a collection of accordions, along with a neon sign that proclaims "Laissez les Bonton Roulez," which is exactly what happens every Wednesday at 9:30pm and Saturday at 10:30pm, when the Bon Ton Soul Accordion Band plays (reservations a must). The menu includes gumbo, soup, alligator sausage, crawfish pie, Creole crabcakes, red beans and rice, jambalaya, and Po-Boy sandwiches. There's an extensive collection of hot sauces available—if you bring in a variety not already available, you'll get a free drink in trade.

MAMA STUFFEATI'S, 3947 Main St. Tel. 931-0522.

Cuisine: ITALIAN
$ Prices: Lunch $6.50–$8; dinner entrees $8–$15. AE, DC, MC, V.
Open: Lunch Mon–Sat 11am–4pm; dinner Mon–Thurs 5–10pm, Fri and Sat 5–11:30pm, Sun 4–10pm.

An abundance of neon, glass bricks, a stone floor, brick walls, and a tall ceiling with exposed pipes announce that this is no ordinary, traditional Italian restaurant; rather, it's a trendy establishment serving Italian food with an American flair. There are almost a dozen selections of pasta, from fettuccini primavera to rigatoni and ravioli. Entrees, served with a soup or salad and breadsticks, include manicotti, veal parmigiana, lasagne, cioppino, and fresh fish of the day. If you have a thing for salt-and-pepper shakers, you've come to the right place—each table has a different, rather corny set, the kind most of us got rid of in garage sales long ago. Maybe your old set has ended up here.

BUDGET

MARIO'S, 204 Westport Rd. Tel. 531-7187 or 531-9898.
Cuisine: ITALIAN
$ Prices: Sandwiches and grinders $3.30–$3.90, entrees $3.30–$5. No credit cards accepted.
Open: Mon–Thurs 10:30am–7:30pm, Fri and Sat 10:30am–8pm.

One of the best deals in Westport, Mario's is a simple and inexpensive establishment selling grinders, sandwiches, and entrees ranging from spaghetti and lasagne to steak parmigiana. Food is available either for carry-out or for dining at one of the tables covered with red-and-white-checked tablecloths.

TORRE'S PIZZERIA, 4112 Pennsylvania. Tel. 931-0146.
Cuisine: ITALIAN
$ Prices: $2.40–$9.60. AE, MC, V.
Open: Mon–Thurs 11am–10pm, Fri and Sat 11am–1:30am, Sun 4–10pm.

The specialty here is pizza, available by the slice, in four different sizes, and as a stuffed pie. There are also sandwiches and a salad bar. Torre's is located in the heart of Westport, in a building dating from 1856.

WESTPORT FLEA MARKET BAR AND GRILL, 817 Westport Rd. Tel. 931-1986.
Cuisine: BURGERS
$ Prices: $3–$5. No credit cards accepted.
Open: Mon–Sat 9am–midnight, Sun 11am–6pm.

As its name implies, this very casual bar and grill is located in the middle of an indoor flea market (the market itself is open only on Saturday and Sunday). It's best known for its gigantic hamburgers, made with 10 ounces of ground chuck. Also on the menu are hot dogs, Polish dogs with sauerkraut, Italian sausage, chicken-breast sandwiches, soups, and salads. There are happy-hour appetizer and drink specials Monday through Friday from 3 to 7pm, when 16-ounce draws of beer go for $1.

5. OVERLAND PARK

INEXPENSIVE

BANGKOK PAVILION, Windmill Square Shopping Center, 7249 97th St. Tel. 341-3005.
Cuisine: THAI

$ Prices: Fixed-price lunches $4–$5.50; dinner entrees $6.50–$11. AE, MC, V.

Open: Lunch Mon–Sat 11:30am–2:30pm; dinner Mon–Thurs 5:30–10pm, Fri and Sat 5:30pm–10:30pm, Sun 5:30–9:30pm.

S Authentic Thai food is served in this pleasant and unpretentious restaurant located in southwest Kansas City, just north of I-435 on the corner of Metcalf Avenue and 97th Street. My favorite way to start a Thai meal is with Tome Khah Gai—chicken soup with galanga, lemon grass, and coconut milk—and an appetizer of grilled beef with mint leaves and lemon. Entrees include a wide selection of chicken, seafood, pork, beef, noodles, rice, and vegetarian dishes, including the national dish, Phad Thai noodles. Fixed-price lunches are a bargain, including soup, an appetizer, fried rice, and a choice of entrees ranging from cashew chicken or broccoli in oyster sauce to Phad Thai noodles.

K. C. MASTERPIECE BARBECUE AND GRILL, 110th and Metcalf Ave. Tel. 345-1199.

Cuisine: BARBECUE

$ Prices: Lunch $5.25–$8; dinner $5.75–$15. AE, DC, DISC, MC, V.

Open: Mon–Thurs 11am–10pm, Fri and Sat 11am–11pm, Sun 11am–9:30pm.

There are some who believe that any respectable barbecue joint must carry with it a layer of grease and a homey air of neglect. K. C. Masterpiece, located just south of I-435, defies all that. Neither greasy nor falling apart, it's in suburbia, is spotless, and is a phenomenal success, with bottles of its sauces now marketed throughout the region. K. C. Masterpiece uses hickory for slow cooking and pecan logs for grilling meats and fish. It's best known for its baby-back ribs, which are so tender that the meat practically falls off the bone, and its hickory-smoked filet of pork. Other items on the menu include beef brisket, smoked chicken, skewered shrimp, and sandwiches.

6. SOUTH KANSAS CITY & MARTIN CITY

South Kansas City refers to the southern part of Kansas City, Missouri, close to I-435. Most of these restaurants are either on or near Wornall Road, north of I-435, or in Martin City, which is about as far south in the city as you can get. Although these restaurants are a bit out of the way, they warrant the trip.

EXPENSIVE

JASPER'S, 405 W. 75th St. Tel. 363-3003.

Cuisine: ITALIAN **Reservations:** Recommended, especially on weekends.

$ Prices: Appetizers $7.50–$9.50; entrees $17.50–$30. AE, CB, DC, MC, V.

Open: Mon–Thurs 6–10pm, Fri and Sat 6–11pm.

It's easy to see why many consider this Kansas City's best restaurant. Jasper's, in operation for almost 40 years, was the first restaurant in the city to receive a four-star *Mobil Travel Guide* Award, which it has won consistently for more than a decade. The atmosphere is elegant without being too stuffy, and the service is excellent. It's a favorite destination for Kansas Citians celebrating special occasions.

Jasper's cuisine is Northern Italian, but it also offers steaks, fish, and veal. Pasta dishes include homemade ravioli stuffed with lobster and served in a pink lobster sauce, and linguine with lobster, crab, scallops, and shrimp in a tomato sauce. For an entree, you might choose baby veal stuffed with prosciutto and cheese in a piquant sauce; prime tenderloin of beef with crabmeat, white asparagus, and Barolo wine sauce; or shrimp sautéed with mushrooms, garlic, tomato, and white wine. Jackets are required for men. There's a separate bar area where you can enjoy an after- or before-dinner drink.

INEXPENSIVE

JESS & JIM'S STEAK HOUSE, 517 E. 135th St., Martin City. Tel. 942-9909.
Cuisine: STEAKS
$ Prices: Lunch $2.75–$5; dinner entrees $8.50–$25. AE, DISC, MC, V.
Open: Mon–Sat 11am–11pm, Sun noon–9pm.

A 25-ounce boneless steak is Jess & Jim's claim to fame, bringing in hungry carnivores by the droves. Even if your appetite dictates one of the smaller cuts of beef (eight types and sizes are available), you'll still want to gawk at that huge chunk of meat in the glass-enclosed display case in the front room. This is a no-nonsense eating establishment that has been in operation since 1938, the kind of place where no one takes notice of the nondescript decor and fake plants. Rather, people come here for steaks served sizzling hot, although catfish, shrimp, rainbow trout, frog's legs, pork chops and chicken also are available. Entrees come with a salad, choice of potato, and bread. Lunch offers digestible sizes of beef, a wide range of sandwiches, and daily specials.

PRINCESS GARDEN, 8906 Wornall Rd. Tel. 444-3709.
Cuisine: CHINESE
$ Prices: Lunch $4.20–$5.30, fixed-price lunches $4; dinner entrees $6.75–$22, fixed-price dinners $10–$14. AE, DC, MC, V.
Open: Lunch Mon–Sat 11:30am–2pm; dinner Mon–Thurs 5–10pm, Fri and Sat 5–11pm, Sun noon–10pm.

This pleasant restaurant, decorated with Chinese lanterns, a dragon-motif ceiling, and subdued lighting, serves authentic Mandarin and Szechuan cuisine prepared and served by a Chinese staff. Of the more than 100 items listed in the dinner menu, standouts include the Hunan beef in a hot garlic sauce, Peking duck, and Mandarin noodles. The fixed-price lunches and dinners are real bargains.

Kansas City

St. Louis ★

MISSOURI

Annie's Sante Fe 30
Athena on Broadway 3
Bangkok Pavilion 24
Bristol Bar and Grill 14
Café Allegro 2
Café Lulu 1
Californos 8
Clinton's 21
Courthouse Exchange 20
Fedora Café and Bar 13
Figlio 12
Houlihan's Old Place 16
Gates & Sons Bar-B-Q 18
Jasper's 23A
Jess & Jim's
    Steak House 27
Jimmy and Mary's 4
K.C. Masterpiece
    Barbecue and Grill 25
Kiki Bon Ton 11
La Mediterranee 15
Mama Stuffeati's 5
Mario's 6
Metropolis 7
Princess Garden 31
Rozelle Court 17
Smoke Stack 26
Stephenson's Apple
    Farm Restaurant 22
Strouds 23B
Tasso's 23
Torre's Pizzeria 9
Westport Flea Market
    Bar and Grill 10
Winsteads 19

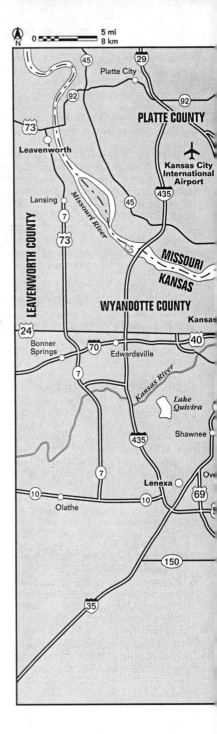

Smithville

Smithville Lake

35

92

69

92

Kearney

Excelsior Springs

169

Mosby

Prathersville

435

291

69

CLAY COUNTY

Gladstone

35

Liberty

71

291

Missouri River

North Kansas City

Buckner

Downtown Airport

24

KANSAS CITY

24

Independence

70

435

20

21

JACKSON COUNTY

4

5

1

2

6

8

7

70

22

9

10

11

40

Lake Tapawingo

40

Roeland Park

12

17

15

30

14

18

Raytown

470

Mission Hills

16

19

Prairie Village

23

23
A

Blue Springs

23
B

31

Leawood

Unity Village

Lake Jacomo

Lake Lotawana

KANSAS MISSOURI

71

470

50

Blue River

Longview Lake

Lee's Summit

50

150

Grandview

Richards-Gebaur Airport

26

150

Greenwood

27

↓

Belton

Raymore

Pleasant Hill

71

291

Airport ✈

There's another branch at 8505 College Blvd. (tel. 339-9898) in Overland Park.

SMOKE STACK, Holmes and 135th St., Martin City. Tel. 942-9141.

Cuisine: BARBECUE **Reservations:** None accepted.

$ Prices: Lunch $4.50–$8; dinner $8.50–$13. AE, MC, V.

Open: Mon–Thurs 11am–10pm, Fri 11am–10:30pm, Sat 11:30am–10:30pm, Sun 11:30am–10pm.

This place is always packed, even though it's on the edge of nowhere. A family-owned business since 1957, it is a cozy and casual restaurant, with a low wooden ceiling, wooden tables, and plants. Smoke Stack serves ribs and barbecued beef, pork, sausage, turkey, and chicken as well as Cajun chicken breast, hickory-grilled beef kabob, steaks, fresh seafood, grilled pork chops, lamb ribs, and sandwiches. All dinner entrees come with french fries, coleslaw, and toasted French bread; there's a wide selection of beers, including about 30 different kinds of imports.

STROUDS, 1015 E. 85th St. Tel. 333-2132.

Cuisine: CHICKEN

$ Prices: Sandwiches from $3.50; entrees $8.70–$15. AE, MC, V.

Open: Mon–Thurs 4–10pm, Fri 11am–11pm, Sat 2–11pm, Sun 11am–10pm.

This is a Kansas City tradition, specializing in pan-fried chicken prepared the old-fashioned way ever since its opening in 1933. Strouds is a plain and almost painfully modest establishment, a wooden building with a wooden floor and red-and-white checked tablecloths. Yet the food is so famous that it's been written up in a number of publications through the years, including *People, Esquire, The New York Times,* and *USA Today.* Strouds also offers steak, pork chops, shrimp, catfish, and sandwiches. All entrees come with a salad or soup, choice of potato, green beans, gravy, and homemade cinnamon rolls.

TASSO'S, 211 W. 75th St. Tel. 363-4776.

Cuisine: GREEK

$ Prices: Lunch $4.95; dinner entrees $8.75–$13, sandwiches $3–$4.50. AE, MC, V.

Open: Lunch Tues–Fri 11am–2:30pm, Sat noon–5pm; dinner Tues–Thurs 5pm–midnight, Fri and Sat 5pm–1am.

Fun is the catchword here, and owner Tasso is always on hand to make sure that even the most surly succumb to the merriment. The decor gives you something to smile about—fake grapes galore, kitsch everywhere, walls painted a Mykonos white and blue, and obligatory pictures on the wall (thankfully, Tasso's wife says, she didn't let him decorate their home). There's also a Greek band, and, as though that weren't enough, Tasso has been known to dance impromptu on the tables and to break dishes in hot-blooded Greek fashion, just to add drama to the occasion. The liveliest evenings are Friday and Saturday. The menu includes all the Greek favorites, from moussaka and souvlaki to pastitsio (macaroni and beef in béchamel sauce), spring lamb, gyros, and kabobs. There's a daily vegetarian special, as well as combination plates that let you sample a variety of dishes. An adjoining grocery store sells Greek specialties.

7. INDEPENDENCE & EAST KANSAS CITY

In addition to the restaurants listed here, Gates & Son's Bar-B-Que has a branch at 10440 E. 40 Highway (tel. 353-5880) and Winstead's serves its burgers at 1428 Noland Rd. (tel. 252-9363), both in Independence. For information on both, refer to Section 3 on the Country Club Plaza earlier in this chapter.

MODERATE

STEPHENSON'S APPLE FARM RESTAURANT, Hwy 40 at Lee's Summit Rd. Tel. 373-5400.

Cuisine: BARBECUE **Reservations:** Recommended.

$ **Prices:** Lunch $6–$12; dinner entrees $12–$23. AE, DISC, MC, V.

Open: Mon–Fri 11:30am–10pm, Sat 11:30am–11pm, Sun 10am–9pm; Sun brunch 10am–2pm.

What started out in 1946 as a modest restaurant begun by twin brothers on the edge of their family's fruit orchard has blossomed into one of Kansas City's best-known restaurants, popular with families and groups. The farm still produces apples, peaches, berries, and sweet cider, but the modest original restaurant has now grown into a huge barnlike structure, filled with antiques. There are a variety of dining rooms, each one different from the others but all decorated in slightly corny country style. The mock apple-orchard room, for example, features a plastic apple tree in the center and wrought-iron patio chairs. But what the heck, this is Americana kitsch at its best, and the food is great. Stephenson's specializes in hickory-smoked chicken, brisket, loin pork chop, whitefish, pork ribs, and jumbo shrimp—all slow-cooked over hickory. The enormous dinner entrees each come with baked potato with a cheese sauce, green rice casserole, hot bread and apple butter, relish, salad, and hot apple fritter. Alcoholic specialties include apple and peach daiquiris and fruit wine. Stephenson's is located about a 15-minute drive east of downtown, off I-70.

INEXPENSIVE

THE COURTHOUSE EXCHANGE, 113 W. Lexington, Independence. Tel. 252-0344.

Cuisine: AMERICAN

$ **Prices:** $3–$16. MC, V.

Open: Mon–Sat 11am–9pm.

Located across from the courthouse on Independence Square, in the heart of Independence, this is a convenient place to eat if you're visiting the many sites in the vicinity. The Courthouse Exchange is an informal, basement establishment, with exposed rafters, wooden booths, and a separate bar area that offers happy-hour specials weekdays from 5 to 7pm. The menu includes steaks, pork chops, shrimp, deep-fried catfish, grilled chicken breast, and sandwiches. There's a salad bar.

BUDGET

CLINTON'S, 100 W. Maple, Independence. Tel. 833-2625.
   Cuisine: BURGERS
$ **Prices:** $1.40–$2.50. No credit cards accepted.
   Open: Mon–Thurs 11am–5:30pm, Fri and Sat 11am–7pm, Sun 12:30–5pm.

Harry S. Truman got his first job here at Clinton Drugstore, opening the store every morning at 6:30am, cleaning, and working the fountain. After he worked there for a year, his employer asked him to dust the entire stock of bottles—and Harry decided to look for a job somewhere else. Today Clinton's is a nostalgic reminder of the soda fountains of yore, complete with a marble counter at which you can sip on sodas and eat burgers or sandwiches. It's located on Independence Square across from the courthouse, a stone's throw from the Truman Visitor's Center.

8. SPECIALTY DINING

HOTEL DINING

The restaurants listed here and under "Dining with a View" represent the best of Kansas City's hotel dining, with correspondingly high prices.

DOWNTOWN

WALT BODINE'S, Radisson Suite Hotel Kansas City, 12th at Baltimore. Tel. 221-7000.
   Cuisine: STEAK **Reservations:** Not necessary.
$ **Prices:** Lunch $5.50–$20; dinner entrees $15–$25. AE, CB, DC, DISC, MC, V.
   Open: Lunch Mon–Fri 11:30am–2pm; dinner Sun–Thurs 5–10pm, Fri and Sat 5–11pm.

Named after a longtime Kansas City broadcaster, food critic, and local personality, Walt Bodine's is located in a historic downtown hotel, complete with original 1930s lamps and woodwork and an open kitchen. The limited menu, featuring steaks, includes prime rib, Kansas City strip steak, and filet mignon. There's also a fresh fish of the day, lobster tail, and chicken. Lunch focuses on lighter meals, including a variety of salads, sandwiches, and beef.

IMPRESSIONS

Not all the best restaurants in the world are in Kansas City, just the top four or five.
   —CALVIN TRILLIN, columnist for *The New Yorker*

CROWN CENTER

PEPPERCORN DUCK CLUB, Hyatt Regency Crown Center, 2345 McGee St. Tel. 421-1234.
Cuisine: CONTINENTAL **Reservations:** Imperative on weekends.
$ **Prices:** Lunch $9.85–$14.85; dinner entrees $23–$29. AE, CB, DC, DISC, MC, V.
Open: Lunch Mon–Fri 11:30am–2pm; dinner Sun–Thurs 5:30–10pm, Fri and Sat 5:30–10:30pm; Sun brunch 10am–2pm.

The Peppercorn Duck Club is considered one of the top restaurants in the city, famous for its spit-roasted duck cooked in a rotisserie built especially for the restaurant. In the middle of the restaurant is Market Island, a buffet featuring a fantastic array of domestic and imported cheeses, terrines, pâtés and galantines, innovative salads; and the Ultra Chocolatta Bar with its fresh pastries and chocolates prepared by the house pastry chef. Diners can choose the Market Island as a main entree for both lunch and dinner, eating to their heart's content. Other lunch selections include fresh seafood, crabcakes, barbecued shrimp, spit-roasted duck, and steak; dinner offers a wider choice of seafood, beef, veal, lamb, and game entrees—including salmon, lobster, steak, rack of lamb, braised pheasant breast, and duck. Coats and ties are required for men.

TRADER VIC'S, Westin Crown Center, One Pershing Rd. Tel. 391-4444.
Cuisine: INTERNATIONAL **Reservations:** Not required.
$ **Prices:** Lunch $7.50–$15; dinner entrees $15–$25. AE, CB, DC, DISC, MC, V.
Open: Lunch Mon–Fri 11:30am–2:30pm; dinner Sun–Thurs 5–10pm, Fri and Sat 5–11pm.

Apart from the wonderful selection of international dishes, the thing I like most about Trader Vic's is that dining here is like taking a minivacation. Decorated as though it were a thatched-roof cottage on a beach in the South Seas, Trader Vic's is an escape into the world of exotic, tropical cocktails (more than 50 on the menu) and a cuisine that takes its inspiration from China, the South Seas, and Southeast Asia.

You might wish to begin your meal with a Mai Tai, a rum concoction invented by Trader Vic in the 1940s, or such favorites as the Suffering Bastard, the Navy Grog, and the Black Widow. Appetizers not to miss include the crab rangoon; the crisped prawn with lemon grass; the sliced barbecue pork; and the grilled bamboo skewers of swordfish, scallops, prawns, and chicken. Your next choice should be the Bongo Bongo, a soup of puréed oyster and spinach bisque. Entrees include a variety of meats grilled in the restaurant's special Chinese smoker oven, including ginger chicken, Indonesian lamb roast, sirloin steak, salmon, and Chinese roasted pork. Other intriguing dishes are marinated duck served with chutney and bok choy leaves, shiitake chicken, Thai-spiced sea scallops, and almond duck. There also are a variety of curry dishes, as well as seasonal dishes that may include a Hawaiian paella, swordfish with lime sauce, and medallions of veal.

DINING WITH A VIEW

CROWN CENTER

BENTON'S STEAK AND CHOP HOUSE, Westin Crown Center, One Pershing Rd. Tel. 474-4400.

Cuisine: STEAK **Reservations:** Recommended.
$ Prices: $20–$30. AE, CB, DC, DISC, MC, V.
Open: Mon–Sat 5:30–10pm; Sun brunch 10am–2:30pm.

Benton's, named after Kansas City artist Thomas Hart Benton, features his original artwork, including one oil painting and some lithographs. Located on the 20th floor of the Westin Crown Center, it affords a view of the city in a nonfussy setting of simple blond wood, brass fixtures, large windows, and plants. Benton's specializes in Kansas City steaks and chops as well as fresh seafood, all charbroiled and brought sizzling from the grill. All entrees, ranging from steak and filet mignon to prime rib, chicken, veal chops, and salmon steak, come with a bucket of shrimp, breads, a salad, a vegetable of the day, and a choice of potato or rice pilaf. Jackets are recommended, but not necessary, for men. There's an adjoining lounge, where you may also come solely for a drink.

SKIES, Hyatt Regency Crown Center, 2345 McGee St. Tel. 421-1234.

Cuisine: AMERICAN **Reservations:** Recommended on weekends.
$ Prices: Appetizers $4.50–$8; entrees $18–$25. AE, CB, DC, DISC, MC, V.
Open: Sun–Thurs 5:30–9:30pm, Fri and Sat 5:30–10:30pm.

You can't dine nearer to heaven than this 42nd-floor restaurant, which is also the only revolving restaurant in town. Skies gives a fantastic view over the entire city—and it is also a great place from which to watch those Midwest sunsets or even thunderstorms come rolling in. The limited menu opens with such appetizers as a cheese-and-beer soup, oysters, and blackened sea scallops; entrees include broiled lamb chops, king crab legs served with prime rib, mesquite-broiled veal chops, lobster tails, fresh fish, and black Angus beef. On the same floor is Skies Lounge, open from 4pm.

COUNTRY CLUB PLAZA

THE GRILL, The Ritz-Carlton, 401 Ward Parkway. Tel. 756-1500.

Cuisine: CONTINENTAL **Reservations:** Recommended, especially on weekends.
$ Prices: Lunch $10.75–$20; dinner $19–$35. AE, CB, DC, DISC, MC, V.
Open: Lunch Mon–Fri 11:30am–2pm; dinner daily 5:30–10pm; Sun brunch 10:30am–2pm.

This restaurant, located on the 12th floor of the Ritz-Carlton, has long been a favorite with Kansas Citians, especially the well-heeled older generation who come to celebrate anniversaries, birthdays, and other special occasions. The Grill is fitted with authentic English and French antiques, bronze sculptures, a crystal chandelier, and a working fireplace. It offers great views of the Plaza, which is especially impressive from Thanksgiving to New Year's, when the entire Plaza is outlined in festive lights. There's live piano music, and on the same floor is also a bar with live entertainment and a view of the Plaza.

The menu, which focuses on seafood and steaks, highlights regional specialties prepared in unusual ways. You may wish to start your meal with the Kansas City corn chowder, a steak-and-potato soup, or perhaps oysters on the half shell. Seafood selections include a 2½-pound Maine lobster; Ozark trout; and blackened Atlantic tuna, served with red onion and tomato-cilantro salsa. From the grill there's Kansas City strip steak, Colorado lamb chops, an extra-thick cut of veal chop, and a 24-ounce porterhouse steak. Other specialties include pan-fried capon breast with grilled eggplant, mozzarella, and marinara sauce; roast prime rib of beef with Yorkshire pudding and horseradish sauce; and baked, deep-dish spinach tortellini with three cheeses and prosciutto.

LIGHT, CASUAL, AND FAST FOOD

BARNEY'S CAFÉ, Barney Allis Plaza, 12th and Wyandotte (Downtown). Tel. 871-3798.
  Cuisine: BURGERS/SNACKS
$ **Prices:** $1–$4. No credit cards accepted.
  Open: Mon–Fri 11am–3pm.
This is a café located on an open-air square in the heart of downtown Kansas City, with both indoor and outdoor seating. It serves hamburgers, hot dogs, nachos, salads, ice cream, sodas, and beer, as well as a daily lunch special.

LAMAR'S DONUTS, 240 E. Linwood. Tel. 931-5166.
  Cuisine: DOUGHNUTS
$ **Prices:** 20¢–60¢. No credit cards accepted.
  Open: Mon–Sat 6am–6pm, Sun 6:30am–4pm.
Lamar's, located in a converted service station not far from 31st and Main streets, hasn't changed much since it opened in 1933. There are some Kansas Citians so hooked on these doughnuts that they cannot let a week go by without dropping in; when the place opens up at 6am there's usually a line already waiting at the door. As many as 500 people will pass through before 10am, loading up on the 30-some variety of doughnuts. Lamar's is famous for its cinnamon twist, but other varieties are German chocolate, French, apple spice, blueberry, chocolate glazed, and double chocolate. At day's end, whatever is left over is donated to the Salvation Army, soup kitchens, nursing homes, and halfway houses.

SUNDAY BRUNCH

All hotels in the expensive and moderate ranges have restaurants that serve breakfast; many of them also offer a Sunday brunch. The **Peppercorn Duck Club,** located in the Hyatt Regency Crown Center, offers Sunday brunch from 10am to 2pm, featuring a huge spread with an omelet station, prime rib, cured ham, two types of duck, three types of egg dishes, fish, fresh lunch meats, fruit, pastries, desserts, and even champagne. The all-inclusive price is $16.95 for adults and $8.95 for children.

Also at Crown Center is **Benton's Steak and Chop House,** where diners are awarded the extra treat of a panoramic view of the city. Its Sunday brunch, available from 10am to 2:30pm, features a bountiful spread of assorted fresh fruits, pastries, croissants, breads, spinach and romaine salads, cheeses, omelets, bacon, sausage, biscuits and gravy, roast beef, assorted cold meats, pasta dishes, country-style fried potatoes, fresh salmon, oysters, and caviar. It costs $14.95 for adults and $8.95 for children.

On the Plaza, the favored spot for Sunday brunch is **The Grill** at the Ritz-Carlton, served from 10:30am to 2pm. If you're lucky enough to get a window seat, you'll dine with a view of the Plaza. Costing $17.50 for adults and $8.75 for children, brunch features an appetizer table with salads, cold cuts, cheeses, smoked fish, fruits and berries, pâtés, pastries, muffins, croissants, and fruit bread. There's a different roast offered each week; the main buffet table runs the gamut from breakfast eggs and meats to lunch entrees. Of course, there's also a dessert table.

More recommendations for Sunday brunch on the Plaza include **Fedora Café and Bar,** 210 W. 47th St. (tel. 561-6565), which from 10:30am to 3pm offers a selection of breakfast entrees ranging in price from $6.95 to $12.95, including trips to a buffet laden with fruit and pastries; and **Bristol Bar and Grill,** 4740 Jefferson (tel. 756-0606), which charges $9.95 per person for its brunch from 10am to 2pm.

One of my personal favorites for Sunday brunch is the Classic Cup, which has two convenient locations. The **Classic Cup Sidewalk Café,** 301 W. 47th St. (tel. 753-1840), located on the Plaza, offers outdoor seating. One of the few places on the Plaza that is open for breakfast throughout the week, it also offers a Sunday brunch from 10am to 3pm that costs $8.95. There's another **Classic Cup** in Westport at 4130 Pennsylvania (tel. 756-0771), a great place to start the day. Its entrees, which change weekly but may range from buttermilk pancakes and chicken enchiladas to omelets and other egg dishes, each cost $7.95 and are served with a fruit dish.

LATE NIGHT/24 HOUR

LUCILLE'S, 1604 Westport Rd., (Midtown). Tel. 561-5111.
Cuisine: AMERICAN
$ Prices: $4.50–$8. AE, MC, V.
Open: Mon–Tues 6:30am–midnight, Wed–Sun 24 hours.
Lucille's is a reproduction of a 1950s diner; with its polished-chrome facade and Formica tabletops, Lucille's looks more 1950s than anything ever did back then. It's decorated with a delightful assortment of nostalgic kitsch—including Sputnik-inspired lamps, gaudy table lamps, tableside juke boxes, and other feasts for the eyes. Water is served in Mason jars. Unfortunately, the food doesn't live up to the decor, but who cares at 2am? Part of the fun in dining here is in seeing what other poor souls are wandering the streets at such an ungodly hour. Breakfasts range from omelets and eggs Florentine to Mexican-inspired dishes; lunch and dinner include burgers, a tuna melt, grilled Reuben sandwiches, and platters that include side dishes.

NICHOLS LUNCH, 39th and S. W. Trafficway, (Midtown). Tel. 561-5200.
Cuisine: AMERICAN
$ Prices: $2–$6; fixed-price dinners under $5. No credit cards accepted.

Open: Tues–Sat 24 hours. **Closed:** Mon.

Nichols has been the place to go for late-night dining ever since it opened back in 1921. It features old-fashioned home cooking, with more than 100 items on the menu and changing dinner specials that range from catfish and cod to meatloaf and macaroni and cheese. Breakfast is always available.

PICNIC FARE AND WHERE TO EAT IT

The best place to buy picnic ingredients is Country Club Plaza because it offers a variety of specialty stores clustered together. Both Volker Park and Brush Creek Park are located immediately to the east of the Plaza, within a few minutes' drive, so they are ideal places for you to spread out your picnic goodies. The best and largest park in town, however, is Swope Park, located at Meyer and Gregory boulevards; it offers picnic shelters (tel. 363-7800 for reservations), nature hiking trails, and acres of rolling hills.

THE BETTER CHEDDAR, 604 W. 48th St. Tel. 561-8204.

Open: Mon–Sat 9am–9pm, Sun 11am–6pm.

If you buy bread at La Bonne Bouchée (below), come here to buy things to put on the bread. This shop sells imported cheeses, sausage, chutney, mustard, jams, caviar, imported gourmet items, wine, and gift baskets.

THE GOURMET GROCER, 614 W. 48th St. Tel. 561-5888.

Open: Mon–Sat 7am–7pm, Sun noon–5pm.

OK, so you want to go on a picnic but want someone else to prepare the food? The Gourmet Grocer sells the ultimate in picnic food: gourmet items to go (there's even a drive-through window). Items include salads, sandwiches, soups, a dozen or more vegetarian dishes, quiches, potato dishes, and entrees. Salads range from pasta primavera to couscous and curried rice; entrees include beef Wellington, lasagna, and seafood Florentine. There also are complete box lunches, each of which includes a sandwich, a salad, a dessert, utensils, and a napkin—beginning at $6.

LA BONNE BOUCHÉE, 618 Ward Parkway. Tel. 931-5230.

Open: Mon–Fri 7am–6pm, Sat 8am–5pm, Sun 8am–2pm.

This is the place to go for freshly baked breads, rolls, croissants, boules, baguettes, cookies, tarts, cakes, and desserts. As its name implies, it features French breads and pastries, baked each day in an imported French oven.

MUEHLBACH'S WEST, 4807 Jefferson. Tel. 756-1115.

Open: Mon–Sat 8am–9pm, Sun 9am–6pm.

Grocers since 1874, Muehlbach's serves as a full-line grocery store for people living around the Plaza, carrying everything from fruits, vegetables, and meats to health food, liquor, and canned goods. Buy all your essentials here.

CHAPTER 15

WHAT TO SEE & DO IN KANSAS CITY

1. **THE TOP ATTRACTIONS**
2. **MORE ATTRACTIONS**
3. **COOL FOR KIDS**
4. **ORGANIZED TOURS**
5. **SPORTS & RECREATION**

Kansas City does not have as many major museums and renowned attractions as St. Louis has. In fact, its three biggest draws—the Royals baseball games, Worlds of Fun theme park, and Woodlands racetrack—are not attractions unique to Kansas City. However, Kansas City does offer a wide variety of things to do and see—the fine Nelson-Atkins Museum of Art, with its Henry Moore Sculpture Garden; historic forts; Country Club Plaza; cruises on the Missouri River, and so forth. There are also many small towns in Missouri and Kansas that are worth a day's or an overnight excursion.

SUGGESTED ITINERARIES

Kansas City's sights are spread throughout the metropolitan area, including Independence and Leavenworth, making it necessary to plan your itinerary geographically. Here are some suggested itineraries to help you get the most out of your visit and guide you to the most important attractions.

IF YOU HAVE ONE DAY

If you're so unfortunate as to have only one day in Kansas City, I suggest that you start downtown and slowly work your way south, using Main Street as your guide to both Crown Center and Country Club Plaza. It's best to have your own car to see Kansas City in a day, but even if you're vehicle-less, you can see most of the sights listed in this day's outing by boarding the Trolley downtown at Barney Allis Plaza on 12th Street and taking it to Crown Center, the Nelson-Atkins Museum, and the Plaza.

If you're sightseeing on Saturday, you should begin your day by rising early in the morning and heading for the City Market, located near the Missouri River, just north of downtown at 5th and Walnut streets. First erected in 1888 and now undergoing gradual restoration, the market is at its busiest on Saturday but is still worth a visit during the week. Surrounding the market is an old district of brick warehouses, which are gradually being renovated as loft apartments and offices.

DID YOU KNOW . . . ?

- More than one-third of the U.S. population resides within 600 miles of Kansas City.
- Kansas City has more miles of boulevards than Paris and more fountains than any city except Rome.
- Kansas City leads the country in underground storage space and the publishing of greeting cards.
- The Kansas City area served as the starting point for the Santa Fe, California, and Oregon trails.
- Kansas means "People of the South Wind" in the language of the Kansas tribe.
- At one time it was against the law to serve ice cream on cherry pie in Kansas.

From the market, head south across I-70 to the old Garment District, located in downtown Kansas City, around 8th and Central. Once the hub of Kansas City's financial and commercial district, it contains many fine old buildings. (See Chapter 16 for more information.)

Next head south on Main to Pershing, where you'll see the now-defunct Union Station to your right (empty for years and still the object of debate about its future) and Crown Center to your left. A city within a city, Crown Center occupies 85 acres of land and contains two hotels; offices; indoor shops and restaurants; and the Hallmark Visitors Center, where you can learn about the history of Hallmark cards and how they're made. If you're hungry for a snack or lunch, refer to Chapter 14 for restaurants in Crown Center, the Hyatt Regency, and Westin Crown Center.

From Crown Center head to the Nelson-Atkins Museum of Art, one of the most comprehensive art museums in the country. If you visit only one museum in Kansas City, this should be it. In addition to its outstanding oriental collection and outdoor Henry Moore Sculpture Garden, it has a delightful restaurant.

Finally, complete your quick tour of Kansas City at America's oldest shopping center, Country Club Plaza, renowned for its Spanish architecture, statues, fountains, shops, and restaurants. Refer to Chapters 14 and 17 for recommendations on restaurants and bars.

IF YOU HAVE TWO DAYS

Day 1 Follow the itinerary outlined above.

Day 2 Devote your energies to pursuing your own special interest, whether it's more shopping at Crown Center or the Plaza, a Royals baseball game, or a trip to Fort Osage or Fort Leavenworth. If you're sightseeing on a Wednesday or Thursday, you may want to head for the Kansas City Stockyards at 11am to see a cattle auction. One of Kansas City's newer, but immensely popular, attractions is the Woodlands racetrack, featuring horses in summer and greyhounds the rest of the year. If you have children, head for the Worlds of Fun theme park; the Green Mill Candy Factory, with its samples of peanut brittle; or the Kaleidoscope, a creative art exhibit sponsored by Hallmark Cards, Inc., in Crown Center. Missouri Town 1855 is a reconstructed 1800s Missouri town, with original homes and shops brought from other locations and reconstructed here. For evening entertainment, head for Westport, located in Midtown, just north of Country Club Plaza.

IF YOU HAVE THREE DAYS

Days 1 and 2 Follow the itinerary outlined above.

Day 3 Head for Independence, Missouri, a 15-minute drive from downtown Kansas City (take I-70 east to Noland Road, then head north, watching for the many signs). This was the hometown of Harry S. Truman, 33rd president of the United States. Your first stop should be the Truman Home Ticket and Information Center, Truman Road and Main Street, to pick up your ticket to tour the Truman Home. You'll learn more about Truman, his life in Independence, and his days in office at the Harry S. Truman Library and Museum. Other sights worth seeing in Independence include the National Frontier Trails Center, dedicated to those who traveled the Santa Fe, Oregon, and California trails; the Mormon Visitors Center, with exhibits relating Mormon history, settlement in Independence, and relocation to Salt Lake City; and Vaile Mansion and the Bingham-Waggoner Estate, two restored mansions open to the public. For evening entertainment, consider a cruise on the *America* or *Missouri River Queen*, which offer such diversions as blues, gospel, and other live music on trips along the Missouri River. Alternatives include an evening at Tiffany's Attic or the Waldo Astoria, two dinner theaters; an outdoor concert or musical at the beautiful Starlight Theatre in Swope Park; or a late-night jam session of jazz at the Mutual Musician's Foundation.

IF YOU HAVE FIVE DAYS OR MORE

Days 1 through 3 Follow the itinerary outlined above.

Day 4 It's time to head farther afield. Approximately 55 miles north of Kansas City is St. Joseph, Missouri, where the legendary Pony Express began and Jesse James met his end; both of these are commemorated with museums. Fort Scott, located in Kansas about 100 miles south of Kansas City, boasts a military fort dating from the mid-1800s and a charming downtown that has preserved its frontier heritage. Within an hour's drive west of Kansas City is Lawrence, home of several museums, the University of Kansas, and a vibrant downtown area that is fast becoming a shopping mecca.

Day 5 If you feel like taking an overnight excursion, good destinations include Excelsior Springs, Missouri, with its famous and historic Elms Resort Hotel and spa treatments; Abilene, Kansas, home of the Eisenhower Center and a number of other attractions; and Lindsborg, Kansas, a Swedish settlement that has preserved its history and heritage.

1. THE TOP ATTRACTIONS

In addition to the attractions listed here, other top Kansas City draws are the Worlds of Fun theme park (see the "Cool for Kids" section later in this chapter), and also Royals baseball games and the Woodlands racetrack (see the "Sports and Recreation" section at the end of this chapter).

NELSON-ATKINS MUSEUM OF ART, 4525 Oak St. (Midtown), Kansas City, MO. Tel. 561-4000.

Located about a 15-minute walk east of Country Club Plaza, the Nelson-Atkins Museum of Art boasts one of the most comprehensive art collections in the country. Founded in 1933 by William Rockhill Nelson, the flamboyant owner of the *Kansas City Star,* it is a massive building constructed primarily in Greek classic style. Its galleries represent all civilizations, from Sumeria in 3,000 B.C. to paintings and sculpture in modern times—including Oriental, European, Classical, African, pre-Columbian, American, and modern art.

Particularly outstanding is the museum's collection of Oriental art, including Japanese art and screens and Chinese porcelain, furniture, and sculpture. Among the works to look out for are the seated guanyin, Chinese deity of mercy and compassion, dating from about the 11th century, and pottery figures produced during the Tang dynasty (A.D. 618–906) and used in important burials. Both are located on the second floor in the Chinese Temple room.

In the museum's European collections are works representing all important schools and periods, including early Italian Renaissance and Venetian works; French paintings, furniture, and decorative arts; and Dutch, Flemish, Spanish, and English paintings. Many artists are represented: Degas, Monet, Pissarro, van Gogh, Gauguin, Paul Klee, Max Beckmann, Emil Nolde, Rembrandt, and others. Among works to watch out for are Caravaggio's *St. John the Baptist,* painted in 1604, one of only seven original works by the artist in the United States; and the *Boulevard des Capucines, Paris,* painted by Monet in 1873–74, the museum's most famous Impressionist painting.

American artists also are well represented, with works by Georgia O'Keeffe, Andrew Wyeth, George Caleb Bingham, John Singer Sargent, Raphaelle Peale, and Willem de Kooning. One of my favorite pieces is Raphaelle Peale's *Venus Rising from the Sea—A Deception (After the Bath).* The museum also has a large collection by Thomas Hart Benton, a native Kansas Citian.

On the museum's south lawn is the Henry Moore Sculpture Garden, with 12 sculptures spread on 17 acres. It is the largest collection of monumental bronze sculptures by Moore outside England. The museum also contains a fine book and gift store and a delightful restaurant called Rozelle Court, which resembles a Venetian courtyard.

Admission: Free to Henry Moore Sculpture Garden; Nelson-Atkins Museum of Art is $3 adults, $1 students and children, children 5 and under free. All permanent collections free on Saturday.

Open: Tues–Sat 10am–5pm, Sun 1–5pm. **Closed:** July 4, Thanksgiving, Christmas, New Year's Day.

COUNTRY CLUB PLAZA, 47th and Ward Parkway (Midtown), Kansas City, MO. Tel. 753-0100.

Country Club Plaza, usually referred to simply as the Plaza, opened in the early 1920s as America's first shopping center. Built in Spanish architectural style with red-tiled roofs, it's a delightful area for strolling, shopping, and dining. The wide boulevards are lined with trees, and the ornate buildings are topped with towers; throughout the Plaza are more than $1 million worth of

KANSAS CITY AREA

Missouri

Kansas

Downtown

fountains and bronze sculptures. A peculiarity of the Plaza is that there are no stoplights or stop signs, in keeping with the belief of Plaza founder J. C. Nichols that all visitors to the Plaza would behave so courteously that no such measures would be necessary. Maybe that was true back then, but experience has taught me to look both ways before venturing from the curb. Another characteristic of the

Plaza is that parking is absolutely free. Highlights include the Christmas lighting ceremony, which takes place every year on Thanksgiving evening, and the Plaza Art Fair in September.

Admission: Free.

Open: Most shops Mon–Sat 10am–6pm, Sun noon–5pm. Many open Thurs to 9pm.

CROWN CENTER, 2450 Grand Ave., Kansas City, MO. Tel. 274-8444.

Located between the Plaza and downtown, Crown Center is a huge living and working environment occupying 85 acres. Of interest to visitors are its three levels of shops, boutiques, and restaurants, as well as its outdoor ice-skating rink, the American Heartland Theatre, and the Coterie Children's Theatre. The entire complex is under the management of Hallmark Cards, Inc., the world's largest greeting-card company, which publishes cards in 20 languages. Be sure to see the Hallmark Visitors Center, with its displays chronicling more than 75 years of Hallmark history. During summer months, there are free outdoor concerts every Friday at 8pm on Crown Center Square.

Admission: Free to Crown Center and Hallmark Visitors Center.

Open: Shops Mon–Wed and Sat 10am–6pm, Thurs and Fri 10am–9pm, Sun noon–5pm. Hallmark Visitors Center Mon–Fri 9am–5pm, Sat 9:30am–4:30pm. **Closed:** Thanksgiving, Christmas, New Year's Day.

HARRY S TRUMAN HOME, 219 N. Delaware St., Independence, MO. Tel. 816/254-7199 or 254-9929.

Americans still flock to Independence to pay tribute to Harry S Truman, 33rd president of the United States, with a visit to the Truman Home. Built in 1867 by Bess Truman's grandfather, this 14-room Victorian housed four generations of her family. Modest for a president's home, it's still furnished exactly as it was when Harry and Bess Truman retired here after Truman's two terms in the White House, with the Truman's 1972 Chrysler still in the garage and Harry's hat and coat still hanging in the foyer. After Bess Truman died in 1982 at the age of 97, the home became a National Historic Site under the administration of the National Park Service. According to Bess Truman's will, only the ground floor is open to the public as long as the couple's only daughter, Margaret Truman Daniel, is still alive.

Note: Tours, which depart every 15 minutes and last slightly less than half an hour, must be booked through the Harry S Truman Ticket and Information Center, 223 N. Main St. Tickets are distributed on a first-come, first-served basis, with no advance reservations. Be sure to come here first, therefore, upon your arrival in Independence. The Center offers a 12-minute slide show on Truman, from his courtship with Bess to his grave.

Admission: $1 adults, children 16 and younger and seniors 62 and older free.

Open: Harry S Truman Ticket and Information Center daily 8:30am–5pm. Tours in summer daily 9am–4:45pm (last tour); in winter (Labor Day to Memorial Day) daily Tues–Sun 9am–4:45pm. **Closed:** Thanksgiving, Christmas, New Year's Day.

HARRY S TRUMAN LIBRARY AND MUSEUM, Hwy. 42 and Delaware St., Independence, MO. Tel. 816/833-1400.

The Harry S. Truman Library—one of eight Presidential Libraries in the United States—contains more than 14 million pages of manuscripts, books, and other historical materials relating to the former president. Of the most interest to the more than 150,000 visitors per year, however, is the adjoining museum that focuses on Truman's life and career. Serving as vice president only 82 days before being sworn in as president upon Franklin Roosevelt's death on April 12, 1945, Truman was in office during the end of World War II, went on to win a surprise victory over opponent Thomas Dewey in the 1948 presidential election, and served as president during the Korean War. All these events are faithfully chronicled in the museum's excellent displays.

Also in the museum is an exact reproduction of the Oval Office as it appeared in the 1950s, complete with a voice recording of Truman describing the items in his office. On display are many gifts that were given to the Trumans from all over the world, including a silver tea set sent by the Dalai Lama of Tibet in 1945, a carpet from Iran with 29 million hand-tied knots, and a dining set from the Philippines. In the lobby of the museum is a large mural by Thomas Hart Benton entitled *Independence and the Opening of the West*. Both Harry and Bess Truman are buried in the courtyard of the library.

Admission: $2 adults, children 15 and under free.

Open: Daily 9am–5pm. **Closed:** Thanksgiving, Christmas, New Year's Day.

2. MORE ATTRACTIONS

MUSEUMS

AGRICULTURAL HALL OF FAME AND MUSEUM OF FARM-ING, 630 N. 126th St., Bonner Springs, KS. Tel. 913/721-1075.

Kansas is a fitting place for this memorial to America's farmer, set amidst rolling hills 15 miles west of Kansas City, just off I-70. It boasts the country's largest and most varied exhibit of agricultural artifacts, as well as items relating to everyday life on the American farm. Altogether there are more than 5,000 items on display—every single one donated by individuals. Included are rustic toys, kitchenware, antique washing machines, a collection of old telephones (which had a profound influence on isolated farm life), a collection of barbed wire, a blacksmith's shop, a one-room schoolhouse, and a harness-maker's shop.

The museum's agricultural machinery collection (10 times larger than the Smithsonian's) contains thousands of engines, vehicles, machines, tools, and tillers—including a replica of the 1831 McCormick reaper, a 1903 Dart farm truck, a horse-drawn plow used by Harry S Truman as a young man, an original sodbuster plow, a 1781 Native American plow, tractors of the 1916–29 era, and threshing machines. The Hall of Fame honors individuals who helped in the advancement of agriculture, from Squanto to Eli Whitney and George Washington Carver.

Admission: $4 adults, $1.50 children ages 6 to 16.

Open: Mon–Sat 9am–5pm, Sun 1–5pm (must enter by 4pm). **Closed:** Dec–Mar.

LIBERTY MEMORIAL AND MUSEUM, Penn Valley Park,

FROMMER'S FAVORITE
KANSAS CITY EXPERIENCES

Lunch at Arthur Bryant's Once rated by *New Yorker* food critic Calvin Trillin as the "single, best restaurant in the world," Arthur Bryant's is the city's most well known barbecue restaurant and has served presidents and kings. It's a roll-your-sleeves-up kind of place, the place to pig out without reservation. Worth the wait in line as people from around the city come for that famous meat piled high on white bread and doused with Bryant's legendary sauce.

Cattle Auctions at the Stockyards Kansas City's stockyards were once alive with cattle that had been driven up the Chisholm Trail from Texas to Abilene and then brought to Kansas City by rail. The stockyards are still here—now hauntingly empty and crumbling. But on Wednesday and Thursday at 11am, part of that former glory comes alive with cattle auctions, held in the Sales Barn.

A Stroll through Country Club Plaza Country Club Plaza is the nation's oldest shopping center, a 14-block area with tree-lined streets, horse-drawn carriages, Spanish architecture, and more than $1 million worth of fountains and statues. Come for a meal, shopping, browsing, and strolling. Great also for people-watching.

City Market on Saturday For more than 100 years, the City Market has been selling fruit, vegetables, flowers, live chickens, eggs, and other produce to Kansas Citians. Now undergoing gradual renovation, the City Market is still going strong, with Saturday bringing in huge crowds that also shop for T-shirts, kitchen appliances, and other goods. Great fun.

A Day at the Races The Woodlands, one of Kansas City's newest, and most popular attractions, offers greyhound racing from mid-September to mid-May and horse racing the rest of the year.

A Royals Baseball Game The Royals bring in more visitors to Kansas City than any other attraction—and for good reason. Watching baseball is a great summertime activity, and the Royals stadium is one of the best.

An Evening at Starlight On a warm summer evening, there's no better place for an outdoor concert or musical than the Starlight Theatre. Set amid the lush greenery of Swope Park, this amphitheater features brick architecture that faintly resembles a castle, vine-covered trellises, and sometimes a full moon hovering above the stage. Very romantic.

Late-Night Jam at the Mutual Musicians Foundation This place doesn't open until after midnight, when jazz musicians who have finished their regular gigs come here to jam the rest of the night away. Don't plan on going to bed before dawn.

100 W. 26th St. (Downtown), Kansas City, MO. Tel. 221-1918.

Located on the crest of a hill near Crown Center and Union Station, this is the only military museum and archives in the United States devoted to World War I. Its towering Torch of Liberty, a familiar Kansas City landmark, rises 300 feet and contains an elevator and an observation platform affording a panoramic view of the downtown skyline. The small museum, located to the west of the tower, starts with an explanation of the causes of World War I and continues with displays relating to America's role in the Great War. Also displayed are military clothing, items the doughboy carried in his pack, gas masks, medals and decorations, posters urging enlistment, and other memorabilia. There's even a full-scale replica of a trench and underground.

Admission: Free to museum; Torch of Liberty tower $1 adults, 25¢ children 6–12.

Open: Tues–Sun 9:30am–4:30pm. **Closed:** Thanksgiving, Christmas, New Year's Day.

NATIONAL FRONTIER TRAILS CENTER, 318 W. Pacific Ave., Independence, MO. Tel. 816/254-0059.

Opened in 1990, this new museum commemorates Independence's historic role as the only location that served as the starting point for the three major westward trails: the Santa Fe, California, and Oregon trails. Housed in a former flour mill near a spring where pioneers filled their water barrels, the museum gives visitors, through letters and diary entries, a vivid description of what life was like for those who made the arduous trek westward. A young girl writes of her family's emotional parting with families and friends as they begin their voyage westward, never to return; another girl writes of her sister's death on the trail. There are passages describing the beauty of the prairies, encounters with Native Americans, death, dust, and tribulations of the five months it took to travel the 2,000-mile Oregon Trail. A 14-minute movie describes the path and purpose of the three trails.

Admission: $2 adults, $1.50 seniors, 50¢ children ages 10 to 15.

Open: Daily 9am–4:30pm. **Closed:** Veteran's Day, Thanksgiving, Christmas, New Year's Day.

TOY AND MINIATURE MUSEUM, 5235 Oak St. (Midtown), Kansas City, MO. Tel. 333-2055.

This restored 1911 mansion contains a fantastic collection of antique toys and fine, exact-to-scale miniatures, including houses, rooms, and furniture. Even if you've never given much thought to the world of toys and miniatures, you'll be captured by the spell woven by the museum's beautiful displays: You can peek inside doll houses so realistic that in a photograph they would be indistinguishable from the real thing or marvel at a violin that has been opened up to reveal a violin-maker's shop inside, complete with tiny playable violins strung with human hair. There also are antique lead figures, dolls, puppets, marionettes, and toy kitchens that prepared girls for their future.

Admission: $2.50 adults, $2 seniors, $1.75 students over 12, $1.50 children ages 5 to 12.

Open: Wed–Sat 10am–4pm, Sun 1–4pm. **Closed:** Major holidays and first two weeks of Sept.

HISTORIC FORTS, SITES, AND HOMES

FORT LEAVENWORTH AND THE FRONTIER ARMY MUSEUM, north of Leavenworth on Grant Ave. Tel. 913/684-3191 or 684-4051.

Located about 35 miles northwest of Kansas City, Missouri, and reached by taking I-70 west and then U.S. 73 north, Fort Leavenworth was established in 1827 to protect those traversing the Santa Fe Trail and later pioneers traveling the California and Oregon trails. The first fort established west of the Mississippi River, it, in contrast to many other forts in the area, is still in service. Serving as an education center for the U.S. Army, Fort Leavenworth is the home of 1,500 enlisted men, 2,500 officers, and approximately 11,000 students. The fort occupies a bluff overlooking the Missouri River and contains beautiful brick and Victorian wood homes. Custer, Eisenhower, and Patton all passed through Fort Leavenworth.

Your first stop should be the Frontier Army Museum on Reynold's Avenue. In addition to its displays portraying Fort Leavenworth's role in the opening of the West, including exhibits of uniforms, sabers, and other artifacts, it boasts one of the largest and best collections of carriages and wagons in the United States. This collection contains a Conestoga wagon, a carriage used by Abraham Lincoln, a sleigh that once belonged to General Custer, surries, stagecoaches, sleighs, and buggies. At the museum, be sure to pick up a brochure outlining a self-guided tour through Leavenworth, which takes visitors past the U.S. Disciplinary Barracks (with approximately 1,400 inmates); the National Cemetery; and the Rookery, built in 1832 and Kansas' oldest house.

Admission: Free.

Open: Fort open 24 hrs; museum Mon–Sat 10am–4pm, Sun and holidays noon–4pm. **Closed:** Easter, Thanksgiving, Christmas, New Year's Day.

FORT OSAGE, Sibley, MO. Tel. 816/881-4431.

Fort Osage was erected in 1808 as the first U.S. outpost following the Louisiana Purchase, on a site chosen by William Clark (of Lewis and Clark fame). Abandoned in 1827 after the frontier pushed westward, Fort Osage has been reconstructed on its original site, complete with hewn log barracks, a blockhouse, officers' quarters, and other buildings. Living history interpretations are featured by staff and volunteers dressed in period costumes and portraying the work and life of fort residents. To reach Fort Osage, 14 miles northeast of Independence, take Highway 24 from downtown Kansas City to Buckner, Missouri, where you should turn north onto Sibley Street and travel 3 miles to Sibley. The fort is one mile north of Sibley.

Admission: $2 adults, $1 seniors and children ages 5 to 13.

Open: Mid-Apr–mid-Nov daily 9am–5pm; mid-Nov–mid-Apr Sat and Sun 9am–5pm. **Closed:** Thanksgiving, Christmas, New Year's Day.

MISSOURI TOWN 1855, Lake Jacomo, Blue Springs, MO. Tel. 816/881-4431.

Missouri Town 1855 is a collection of original, mid-19th-century structures brought to their present site from throughout western

Missouri and arranged to resemble a typical Midwestern farming community. Occupying approximately six city blocks, the town contains more than 30 structures, including houses with barns and outbuildings, a schoolhouse, a church, a tavern, a lawyer's office, a livery stable, and slave quarters. These structures represent a variety of architectural styles prevalent from the 1820s through the 1850s— Greek Revival, Georgian, and New England-style, and so on. Staff members, dressed in 1850s attire, provide insight into the lives and work of people of the times. To reach Missouri Town 1855, take I-70 east to I-470 south, then exit at Colbern Road, turning east (left) on Colbern to Cyclone School Road, where you should turn north (left) and follow it for two miles.

Admission: $2 adults, $1 seniors and children ages 5 to 13.

Open: Mid-Apr–mid-Nov daily 9am–5pm; mid-Nov–mid-Apr Sat and Sun 9am–5pm. **Closed:** Thanksgiving, Christmas, New Year's Day.

THOMAS HART BENTON HOME, 3616 Belleview (Midtown), Kansas City, MO. Tel. 931-5722.

This two-and-a-half-story stone house, built around the turn of the century on a tree-lined residential street, was the home and studio of Kansas City's most famous contemporary artist from 1939 until his death in 1975. The house, which contains many of Benton's personal belongings, displays a handful of originals, some reproductions, and some prints and lithographs. Benton's studio in a former carriage house holds many of his tools and equipment.

Admission: $1.25 adults, 75¢ children ages 6 to 12.

Open: Summer Mon–Sat 10am–4pm, Sun noon–5pm; winter Mon–Sat 10am–4pm, Sun 11am–4pm. **Closed:** Easter, Thanksgiving, Christmas, New Year's Day.

JOHN WORNALL HOUSE, 146 W. 61st Terrace, Kansas City, MO. Tel. 444-1858.

This pre–Civil War brick home, built in 1858 in Greek Revival style, was once located on 500 acres of farmland but is now surrounded by the city. Used as a hospital for the wounded of both the Confederate and the Union armies during the Battle of Westport in 1864, it belonged to John Wornall, a well-to-do farmer. Tours of the home, offered throughout the day, impart interesting bits of information about life in the 1800s—such as the fact that women required their own style of chairs, due to the fact that they wore hooped skirts and didn't lean back and the fact that wives arose every morning two hours early just to start the coals for breakfast and then had to contend with flies, mice, and long skirts that could easily catch fire.

Admission: $2.50 adults, $1.50 seniors, 50¢ children under 12.

Open: Tues–Sat 10am–4pm, Sun 1–4pm. **Closed:** All major holidays.

BINGHAM-WAGGONER ESTATE, 313 W. Pacific Ave., Independence, MO. Tel. 816/461-3491.

Built in 1855, occupied by Missouri artist George Caleb Bingham from 1864 to 1870, and then serving as the home of the Waggoner family for nearly a century until 1976, this grand building sits on a 20-acre estate. It features a porch that wraps around the entire house, 26 rooms furnished almost entirely with belongings of the Waggoner family, 8 coal-burning fireplaces, marble washbasins throughout, mahogany imported from Africa, a walk-in ice box, and an intercom system from the kitchen to the second floor. Tours, lasting 45 minutes, are offered throughout the day. There's a large gift shop in the former carriage house.

Admission: $2.50 adults, $2 seniors 62 and older, 50¢ children ages 3 to 11.

Open: Mon–Sat 10am–4pm. **Closed:** Nov 1 to day after Thanksgiving and Jan–Mar.

VAILE MANSION, 1500 N. Liberty, Independence, MO. Tel. 816/833-0040.

This 31-room mansion, built in 1881 at a whopping cost of $150,000, is a fine example of Second Empire Victorian architecture; it once boasted a lake, arbors, fountains, and a greenhouse on its grounds. The house has had a checkered past—Sophia Vaile killed herself here with an overdose of morphine in 1883, a year after she and her husband, Harvey, moved in; following Harvey Vaile's death in 1894, the home was used successively as an inn, a private mental institute and sanatorium, and then as a nursing home. The Vaile Mansion contains furnishings of the period, as well nine marble fireplaces and some beautifully handpainted ceilings. Tours last approximately 40 minutes.

Admission: $2.50 adults, $2 seniors, 50¢ children 12 and under.

Open: Mon–Sat 10am–4pm, Sun 1–4pm. **Closed:** Nov–mid-Mar.

1859 JAIL AND MARSHAL'S HOME, 217 N. Main St., Independence, MO. Tel. 816/252-1892.

Located next to the Truman Home Ticket and Information Center, this 12-cell jail held prisoners from 1859 to 1933 and also served as the marshal's living quarters. Famous prisoners included Frank James, brother of Jesse, and William Quantrill, a Confederate guerilla. In the courtyard is an 1870 schoolhouse, relocated here in 1960.

Admission: $2 adults, $1.50 seniors 62 and older, 50¢ children 12 and under.

Open: Summer Mon–Sat 10am–5pm, Sun 1–4pm; winter Tues–Sat 10am–5pm, Sun 1–4pm. **Closed:** Jan, Thanksgiving, Christmas.

SIGHTSEEING MISCELLANY

NCAA VISITORS CENTER, 6201 College Blvd., Overland Park. Tel. 339-0000.

This new facility, opened in 1990, salutes intercollegiate athletics with photographs and videos highlighting all 21 sports and 77 championships administered by the National Collegiate Athletic Association (NCAA). The displays begin in the lobby, with a 96-foot mural outlining the history of the NCAA and depicting various aspects of college sports: the displays continue with photographic and multimedia presentations chronicling some of the great moments and significant achievements in NCAA history, from basketball and baseball to lacrosse, volleyball, gymnastics, skiing, and track and field. It's located in Overland Park just south of I-435, between Roe and Metcalf avenues, on the southern edge of Kansas City.

Admission: $2 adults, $1 students and children.
Open: Mon–Fri 10am–7pm, Sat 10am–6pm, Sun noon–5pm.
Closed: Thanksgiving, Christmas, New Year's Day.

THE STOCKYARDS, 1600 Bell, Kansas City, MO. Tel. 842-2829.

Once famous for its heads of cattle passing through, the Kansas City stockyards is now a ghost of its former self. The maze of former feeding and holding pens remain, now empty and long neglected. However, there are still twice-a-week cattle auctions held here inside a yellow building officially known as the Livestock Exchange Building but usually referred to as the Sales Barn (located directly behind the Golden Ox restaurant). To reach the stockyards from downtown, take 12th Street west or I-35 south to the Kemper-Genessee exit. It's best to arrive around 11am because the auction continues only as long are there cattle to sell.
Admission: Free.
Auctions: Summer Wed and Thurs 11am–noon; winter Wed and Thurs 11am–5pm.

KANSAS CITY BOARD OF TRADE, Third Floor, 4800 Main (Midtown), Kansas City, MO. Tel. 753-7500.

Founded in 1856, the Kansas City Board of Trade is the world's predominant marketplace for wheat and grain sorghum, as well as a trading place for soybeans, corn, and oats. A visitor's gallery on the third floor allows guests to observe futures trading in the pit, with explanations describing what's going on.
Admission: Free.
Open: Mon–Fri 8:30am–3:15pm. **Closed:** Major holidays.

MORMON VISITOR'S CENTER, 937 W. Walnut Ave., Independence, MO. Tel. 816/836-3466.

Members of the Church of Jesus Christ of Latter-Day Saints (Mormons) immigrated to Independence in 1831, along with their leader and church president, Joseph Smith. He hoped to build the city of Zion, a community based on righteous living and unselfish cooperation. Persecution, however, drove the Mormons onward to Utah by the end of the decade, but before they left Smith designated land in Independence as site for a temple. This visitor's center describes the history of the Mormons and the concepts of their faith through displays, a slide show, and free 20-minute guided tours.
Admission: Free.
Open: Daily 9am–9pm. **Closed:** Christmas.

RLDS AUDITORIUM, 1001 W. Walnut Ave., Independence, MO. Tel. 816/833-1000.

Built in the 1920s next to the Mormon Visitor's Center above, this huge auditorium serves as world headquarters of the Reorganized Church of Jesus Christ of Latter-Day Saints. Occupying a section of the temple lot designated by Joseph Smith, it contains the 110-rank Aeolian Skinner organ, one of the largest church organs in the country with 6,500 pipes. Twenty-minute tours of the auditorium are given throughout the day; try to schedule a visit during an organ recital.
Admission: Free.
Open: Tours Mon–Sat 9am–noon and 1–5pm, Sun and hols

1–5pm. Organ recitals: Summer daily 3pm; winter Sun 3pm. **Closed:** Christmas, New Year's Day.

3. COOL FOR KIDS

WORLDS OF FUN, I-435, Exit 54, Kansas City, MO. Tel. 454-4444.

This 230-acre family entertainment park is one of Kansas City's top attractions, drawing more than 1.3 million visitors per year. It's based on Jules Verne's *Around the World in Eighty Days* and is divided into five areas—the Orient, Scandinavia, Europa, Africa, and Americana—throughout which are more than 140 rides, stages featuring live entertainment and shows, arcades, food outlets, and other attractions. Its leading rides are the Timber Wolf, a 4,230-foot wooden roller coaster that includes a 95-foot drop, and the Orient Express, a steel-track roller coaster with two interlocking loops. Other popular rides include the Fury of the Nile, Viking Voyager, and Python Plunge—all water rides. Families with small children should head for Pandemonium, with more than a dozen rides and attractions, including a carousel, playground, and small Ferris wheel. Worlds of Fun is located in the northeastern part of Kansas City, north of the Missouri River off I-435.

Admission (includes all rides and attractions): $18.95 adults, $14.95 seniors 60 and over and children ages 4 to 11. Combination ticket to Worlds of Fun and Oceans of Fun: $24.95 adults and children.

Open: Apr, May, Sept, and Oct Sat and Sun from 10am; June, July, and Aug daily from 10am. Telephone for closing times, which vary widely. **Closed:** Labor Day.

OCEANS OF FUN, I-435, Exit 54, Kansas City, MO. Tel. 459-WAVE.

Located beside Worlds of Fun, this is the Midwest's largest tropically themed water park, featuring 60 acres of water slides, lakes, and pools. It offers more than 35 water-related attractions, including a million-gallon wave pool designed for body surfing and rafting, and Caribbean Cooler, 800 feet of gently rushing water in a tropical setting through which you can swim or float. Be sure to bring your swimsuit.

Admission: $13.95 adults, $11.95 seniors 60 or over and children ages 4 to 11. Combination ticket with Worlds of Fun, $24.95 adults and children.

Open: Daily Memorial Day weekend to Labor Day weekend, from 10am. Telephone for closing times, which vary.

KALEIDOSCOPE, Crown Center, 25th and McGee, Kansas City, MO. Tel. 274-8300 for information, 274-8301 for reservations.

Sponsored by Hallmark Cards, Inc., Kaleidoscope is a creative art exhibit that encourages children to touch, participate in, and create their own works of art. Only children ages 5 to 11 are allowed to join the 1½-hour sessions, which begin with a journey through the Discovery Room and end in the Art Studio, where children are allowed to create their own art. Parents are not allowed to enter Kaleidoscope but can watch the activities through one-way mirrors.

Admission: Free, with tickets issued 30 minutes before each session.

Open: Summer (mid-June to late Aug) Mon–Fri 10:30am, 12:30pm, 1:30pm, 2:30pm, Sat 11am, 1:30pm, 3pm. Winter Mon–Fri 9 or 9:30am, 10:30am, 1pm, Sat 9:30am, 11am, 1:30am, 3pm. Since winter is reserved mainly for school groups, telephone beforehand to confirm the schedule and make a reservation.

THE COTERIE CHILDREN'S THEATRE, Crown Center, 25th and Grand Ave., Kansas City, MO. Tel. 474-6552.

This professional theater company stages seven productions per year—primarily for children and their families—from classics of children's literature to original material. Past shows have included George Orwell's *Animal Farm;* a musical adaptation of Hans Christian Andersen's *The Ugly Duckling;* and *Pooh,* adapted from the stories of A. A. Milne.

Admission: $5 children and adults.

Performances: Tues–Fri 10am, sometimes also 1pm; Sat and Sun usually 2pm. **Closed:** Jan and between performances.

GREEN MILL CANDY FACTORY, 2020 Washington (Downtown), Kansas City, MO. Tel. 421-7600, or toll free 800/369-2462.

This candy factory, in operation since 1914, produces peanut brittle, peanut clusters, and cream candies. It offers four tours daily, which last about 45 minutes and include a film presentation and a look at the production of peanut brittle and chocolate. Each tour participant receives free confections fresh off the assembly belt, plus a box of peanut brittle. There's also a factory outlet here should you feel tempted.

Admission: $1.50 per person.

Tours: Mon–Fri 10am, 11am, 1pm, 2pm.

---

4. ORGANIZED TOURS

BOAT CRUISES

One of the most relaxing ways to enjoy the Kansas City skyline is on a cruise along the Missouri River, either on the *Missouri River Queen* or the *America.* Both boats are moored in Kansas City, Kansas, off I-70 at the Fairfield Industrial District exit. They travel from the Kansas River onto the Missouri River, with views of the skyline and rural countryside.

The **Missouri River Queen** is a replica of a 19th-century paddlewheeler, an ornate triple-decked boat. In operation from March through October, it offers a variety of cruise options—including a one-hour sightseeing cruise that departs daily at 2pm through the summer months and on Saturday and Sunday at 2pm during March, April, May, September, and October; it costs $5.75 for adults, $5 for seniors 60 and older, and $2.75 for children 12 and under. There's also a 2½-hour dinner cruise with a buffet of prime rib and live entertainment, offered Friday and Saturday only during March and April and Tuesday through Sunday evening from May through October; it costs $24.95 per person on Saturday evening; the rest of the week it's $22.50 for adults, $20.25 for seniors, and $11.25 for children. Other options include a two-hour Moonlight Entertainment Cruise offered Friday and Saturday at 9pm; a popular two-hour Gospel Entertainment Cruise offered every Monday at 7pm from May through September, which includes a fried-chicken buffet and live gospel entertainment; and a two-hour Sunday brunch at 11:30am from April through October.

The **America,** a modern luxury liner, offers a wide variety of options throughout the year, including a two-hour lunch cruise that departs daily at noon and costs $15.95 for adults, $14.50 for seniors, and $8 for children ages 3 to 12. A 2½-hour dinner cruise, departing every night except Monday, offers dinner with live entertainment; the cost is $31.95 per person on Friday and Saturday night; the rest of the week it's $29.95 for adults, $27 for seniors, and $15 for children. On Friday and Saturday there's a Moonlight Cruise departing at 10pm, and on Monday at 7:30pm there's a Blues Cruise, featuring a live blues band.

For more information on these cruises, prices, and reservations, call 281-5300 in Kansas City, or toll free 800/373-0027.

BUS TOURS

With the help of this guide, you should be able to see all of Kansas City's major sights on your own. However, for orientation purposes you may wish to join a tour upon your arrival and then return later to explore at leisure. The **Gray Line** offers a two-hour Kansas City tour, which departs daily at 10am and costs $10 per person. This tour takes in the sights of downtown, Westport, Country Club Plaza, and other areas. The **Truman Country Tour,** which lasts three hours beginning at 1pm and costs $15 per person, tours Independence's main attractions, including Truman Library. For more information, call Gray Line at 913/268-5252.

5. SPORTS & RECREATION

SPECTATOR SPORTS
BASEBALL

The Kansas City Royals, 1985 World Champions, provide the best in American League baseball action from April to October, with more than 80 home games each year. The **Harry S. Truman Sports Complex,** on I-70 on the eastern edge of the city, is home of both the Royals Stadium, and the Kansas City Chiefs (football) Arrowhead Stadium. Ticket prices range from $4 for general admission to $11 for box seats. For ticket information, call 816/921-8000. You can also charge tickets to your credit card by calling 921-4400 in Kansas City, or toll free outside Kansas City at 800/422-1969. You can order tickets by mail at Kansas City Royals, Ticket Office, P.O. Box 419969, Kansas City, MO 64141-6969.

FOOTBALL/SOCCER

The Kansas City Chiefs, champions of the 1970 Super Bowl, play at **Arrowhead Stadium** in the Truman Sports Complex from August to December, with approximately 10 home games each season. Ticket prices start at $10 for children 12 and under and seniors, $20 for adults. The Arrowhead ticket office is open Monday through Friday from 8:30am to 5pm; you can charge tickets to your credit card by calling 924-3333 or 931-3330. Outside Kansas City, call toll free at 800/877-1214.

The Kansas City Comets, of the Indoor Soccer League, play their games October through April at **Kemper Arena,** located near downtown in the stockyards district. Tickets, in the $8 to $12 range, usually are available the day of the game at Kemper Arena. For more information, call 421-7770.

HORSE AND GREYHOUND RACING

Although open only since 1989, the Woodlands is already among the top-three attractions in Kansas City, with both horse- and dog-racing arenas. The Woodlands is located in Kansas City, Kansas, on I-435 two miles north of its intersection with I-70. For information on both horse and greyhound racing, call 299-9797.

The horse-racing season is from the end of May to September and features both thoroughbred and quarter horses on a one-mile track. Races are held Thursday through Monday at 1:30pm, with prices ranging from $2 for general admission to $7 for the club house. Parking is $2. Patrons are invited to view the action from the infield of the track, where they can spread a blanket and have a picnic.

Greyhound racing, held from mid-September to mid-May on a quarter-mile track, takes place at 1:30pm on Wednesday, Friday, Saturday, and Sunday and at 7:30pm on Monday, Wednesday, Thursday, Friday, and Saturday. Prices here range from $1 for general admission to $5 for the club house, plus $1 for parking.

RECREATION

Swope Park, with 1,769 acres of greenery and facilities, is one of the largest city parks in the nation. Located in Kansas City, Missouri, at Gregory and Meyer boulevards, it offers a number of recreational facilities, including two 18-hole public golf courses, a swimming pool, two fishing lakes, boating areas, bicycle paths, two tennis courts, picnic tables, and shelters. The **Blue River Golf Course** (tel. 523-5830) charges green fees of $9.50 on weekdays and $10.50 on weekends; the **Swope Memorial Golf Course** (tel. 523-9081) charges $10.50 on weekdays and $12.50 on weekends and holidays. The **Swope Park Pool** on Lewis Road and Riverside Drive, open every day except Monday, charges a $1.50 admission.

Other recreational diversions are almost limitless. For more information on recreation in Kansas City, contact Kansas City's tourist office or consult the *Yellow Pages*.

CHAPTER 16

STROLLING AROUND KANSAS CITY

1. DOWNTOWN
2. COUNTRY CLUB PLAZA

Because Kansas City's sights and attractions are spread throughout the city, the town doesn't lend itself to many sightseeing strolls. Two exceptions are the downtown area and Country Club Plaza, both unique mainly for their architectural styles.

WALKING TOUR 1 — Downtown

Start: City Hall, 12th and Oak.

Finish: Town Pavilion, 11th and Main.

Time: Allow approximately 2 hours, not including stops.

Best Times: Weekdays, when buildings and restaurants are open.

Worst Times: Saturday and Sunday, when some buildings and most shops are closed.

This stroll introduces you to some of Kansas City's most significant architectural treasures, from grand brick buildings dating from the 1880s to the city's wealth of art deco treasures.

FROM CITY HALL, 12TH AND OAK, TO THE SAVOY, 9TH AND CENTRAL

1. **City Hall,** completed in 1937, is a 30-story building on the corner of 12th and Oak. it's built in typical art deco style, with a cluster of stepbacks near the top of the building, emphasized by light-colored verticals and darkened window spandrels. On the top floor is an observation deck, which you can reach by taking the elevator to the 28th floor and then the stairs to the 30th. Open free to the public Monday through Friday from 8am to 5pm, it affords a clear view of the city.

   From City Hall, walk west two blocks on 12th Street, taking

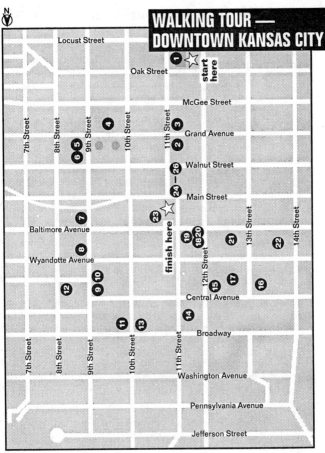

Locust Street

Oak Street

start here

McGee Street

Grand Avenue

Walnut Street

Main Street

finish here

Baltimore Avenue

Wyandotte Avenue

Central Avenue

Broadway

Washington Avenue

Pennsylvania Avenue

Jefferson Street

7th Street
8th Street
9th Street
10th Street
11th Street
12th Street
13th Street
14th Street

1. City Hall
2. Professional Building
3. Bryant Building
4. Federal Reserve Bank
5. Scarritt Building
6. Scarritt Arcade
7. New York Life Building
8. New England Building
9. Savoy Hotel and Grill
10. Savoy Grill
11. Fitzpatrick's Saloon and Cafe
12. Murphy's
13. Coates House
14. Folly Theater
15. Barney Allis Plaza
16. Municipal Auditorium
17. Barney's Cafe
18. Hitter's
19. Italian Gardens
20. Radisson Suite Hotel
21. Midland Theater
22. Kansas City Power and Light Building
23. City Center Square
24-26. Town Pavilion, food court, City Seen

a right onto Grand Avenue. At the corner of Grand and 11th is the:
2. **Professional Building,** which was one of a half-dozen major office buildings under construction in downtown Kansas City when the Depression hit. Across the street, at 1101 Grand, is the:
3. **Bryant Building,** one of the city's best examples of art deco with a Beaux Arts tower. Take a peak at its ornate lobby.
   Continue walking north on Grand to the:

4. **Federal Reserve Bank,** 925 Grand Ave., one of only 12 Federal Reserve banks in the country. Built in 1921 and renovated in the mid 1980s, this beautiful neo-classical building contains a Visitor's Center on its mezzanine, with displays that explain the function of the Federal Reserve system and the history of money and banking. It's open free to the public Monday through Friday from 8am to 5pm. After touring the Visitor's Center, be sure to stop by the Information Counter in the lobby and ask for a free souvenir—a bag of shredded money.

Just a stone's throw from the Federal Reserve Bank is one of my favorite buildings in the city, the:

5. **Scarritt Building,** located on the northwest corner of 9th and Grand. Constructed in 1906, it was one of the city's first modern skyscrapers and shows strong influences from the Chicago-style of architecture, particularly in its terra-cotta embellishments and its vertical thrust. Walk through the lobby, head downstairs through the corridor, and you'll find yourself in the wonderful:

6. **Scarritt Arcade** (located behind the Scarritt Building), with its four-story atrium and skylight. Beautifully constructed, it's a sight to behold.

Exit Scarritt Arcade onto 9th Street and head west, where immediately on your right will be the:

7. **New York Life Building,** 20 W. 9th St., an impressive and massive brownstone. At the time of its completion in the late 1880s, it was the largest and most distinguished building in the city and is still considered by many to be the most significant historic building downtown. Currently undergoing renovations that will transform its interior into luxury apartments, it is guarded by an imposing Augustus Saint-Gaudens bronze eagle perched above its entryway. Nearby is another building of the same period, the:

8. **New England Building,** 112 W. 9th St., designed by a Boston firm and noted for its projecting corner window and the seals of the five New England states carved below its first set of windows. Just a minute's walk farther west on 9th street is the:

9. **Savoy Hotel and Grill,** 9th and Central. It was built at the turn of the century, with a restaurant that claims to be the city's oldest continuous restaurant and still highly recommended for its atmosphere, steaks, and seafood. Note the stylistic lead windows, a rare example of art nouveau in the United States. The Savoy building, a sorely rundown flophouse just a few years ago, is now being restored and offers rooms with turn-of-the-century charm.

REFUELING STOPS You can't go wrong dining at the **10. Savoy Grill,** 9th and Central, one of Kansas City's most famous historic restaurants. Almost as old is **11. Fitzpatrick's Saloon and Café,** 931 Broadway, which opened in 1911, serves moderately priced American food, and still boasts a molded-tin ceiling, plaster molding, and bright copper facade. For less formal dining or simply for a drink, head for **12. Murphy's,** located in a renovated brick building in the Garment District at 323 W. 8th St. It serves burgers, salads, and sandwiches and offers 18 beers on tap.

FROM THE SAVOY AT 9TH AND CENTRAL TO BARNEY ALLIS PLAZA, 12TH AND WYANDOTTE From the Savoy, walk one block south on Central, turn right onto 10th, and walk one more block to the corner of 10th and Broadway. Here you'll see the beautifully restored:

13. **Coates House,** completed in 1891 and once the most lavishly appointed hotel in the city (Presidents Grover Cleveland and Benjamin Harrison stayed here). Empty for years, now housing apartments, it is the crowning restoration achievement of surrounding Quality Hill. Once one of the wealthiest residential districts after the Civil War, Quality Hill suffered almost a century of decline and neglect before vigorous redevelopment began in the 1980s, changing more than 45 historic structures into residences and mixed-use commercial space.

    From Coates House, walk two blocks south on Broadway, turning left onto 12th Street. At the end of the block on your left, at 300 W. 12th St., is the:

14. **Folly Theater,** built in 1900 and now Kansas City's only turn-of-the-century theater still in existence. Used for burlesque revues before shutting down in 1973, it has been lovingly restored and now features all types of entertainment, including concerts and theater.

    Just cater-cornered from the Folly is:

15. **Barney Allis Plaza,** a large open square bounded by Kansas City's convention center. That monumental structure on the southern edge of the plaza is the:

16. **Municipal Auditorium,** completed in 1934 in art deco style and a venue for concerts, theater, and exhibitions.

REFUELING STOPS If the weather's fine, a great place for a snack is: **17. Barney's Café,** located on Barney Allis Plaza and offering open-air seating where you can sip a beer and munch on nachos. Much more uptown is: **18. Hitter's,** located on the corner of 12th and Baltimore, an ultramodern sports bar with TV screens and happy-hour specials from 4:30 to 7pm. If you're ravenous, head for: **19. Italian Gardens,** 1110 Baltimore, in operation since 1925 and specializing in homemade pizza, lasagne, and daily specials at low prices.

FROM BARNEY ALLIS PLAZA TO TOWN PAVILION, 11TH AND MAIN From Barney Allis Plaza, head east on 12th Street, where on the corner of 12th and Baltimore you'll find the:

20. **Radisson Suite Hotel.** Built in 1930 and exalting in the art deco style, it boasts a great statue in the lobby above the entryway, an 11-foot-tall gilded statue called "Mother of Stars," standing on tiptoe on the crest of a wave.

    Take a right onto Baltimore, and to your right will soon be the:

21. **Midland Theater,** 1221 Baltimore, built in the 1920s as the grandest movie theater the city had ever seen. Ornate and opulent in Renaissance Revival style, it serves as a center for the performing arts.

    Less than two blocks farther south, at 14th and Baltimore, is my most favorite building (I do have several favorites), the:

22. **Kansas City Power and Light Building,** probably the best example of art deco in town. Completed in 1931, it soars to a height of about 480 feet and for many years was the tallest building in Missouri. Its upper six stories feature a lighting system that changes colors at night, which always fascinated me as a child.

Backtrack north on Baltimore to 11th street, where you should take a right and walk one block east to Main. Here, at 1100 Main, is:

23. **City Center Square,** where on the 25th floor you'll find offices of the Convention and Visitors Bureau of Greater Kansas City. Stop here for brochures and information on the city if you haven't already done so.

Across the street, at 1111 Main, is:

24. **Town Pavilion,** a new building that nevertheless incorporates art deco concepts to make it compatible with the older buildings around it. It houses a number of shops and food outlets as well as a museum with changing exhibits.

FINAL REFUELING STOPS On the third floor of Town Pavilion is a **25. Food Court,** a bright and cheerful dining hall with various counters serving everything from barbecue and burgers to tacos and Chinese food. For more formal dining, **26. City Seen,** located on the ground floor of Town Pavilion, offers international cuisine, steaks, and sandwiches.

WALKING TOUR 2 — Country Club Plaza

Start: J. C. Nichols Memorial Fountain, 47th St. and J. C. Nichols Parkway.

Finish: Swansons, 47th and Wyandotte.

Time: Allow approximately one hour, not including stops.

Best Times: Monday through Saturday, when all stores are open.

Worst Time: Sunday morning, when shops are closed.

Located just five miles south of downtown, Country Club Plaza was developed in 1922 and is the oldest shopping center in the country. This 14-block area is modeled after Seville, Spain (Kansas City's sister city), with pastel-colored buildings topped by tiled roofs and ornate towers. Most people come here to shop in its more than 150 stores and boutiques or to eat at one of its two dozen restaurants, with nothing more than a quick glance at the 30-some statues and fountains that grace the Plaza's tree-lined streets, many imported from Europe with a total value of more than $1 million. This walk will direct you to the Plaza's highlights.

FROM J. C. NICHOLS MEMORIAL FOUNTAIN AT 47TH AND J. C. NICHOLS PARKWAY TO SEVILLE SQUARE, PENNSYLVANIA AND NICHOLS ROAD On the corner of 47th Street and J. C. Nichols Parkway is:

1. **Mill Creek Park,** dominated by a massive fountain of thrashing horses and heroic horsemen. Dedicated to the developer of the Plaza, this fountain was sculpted in Paris in 1910 by Henri Greber. From the fountain, walk west on 47th Street, crossing J. C. Nichols Parkway. To your left is:

2. **Giralda Tower,** an exact replica of Giralda Tower in Seville, except that this one is only two-thirds the original's size. Of the 14 towers on the Plaza, this is the tallest, and it sounds carillon bells throughout the day.

   Continue walking west on 47th Street to Central, where on the corner to your left you'll see:

3. **Function Junction,** a favorite Kansas City outlet for practical and functional items for the kitchen and home. Behind it is a small clothing shop:

4. **Asiatica,** a women's clothing store that shows Asian designer influence. One block farther west is:

5. **Sharper Image,** 333 W. 47th St., the yuppie's store for extravagant playthings.

   At the intersection of 47th and Broadway is another statue of note:

6. **Sleeping Child,** sculpted in 1963 by the Romanelli Studios in Florence and made of Carrara marble. Also at this intersection is:

7. **Dillard's,** a dependable and popular department store.

   Head south on Broadway one block to Nichols Road, where you should take a right. This is the heart of the Plaza, with its tree-lined streets and horse-drawn carriages available for hire. At the corner of Nichols Road and Pennsylvania is:

8. **Saks Fifth Avenue,** one of the Plaza's most upmarket stores, as well as:

9. **Seville Square,** with its many indoor shops. Across the street are a number of smaller boutiques, including Crabtree and Evelyn, Gucci, and The Gap. And next to Seville Square is McDonald's, in front of which is a statue of a boy eating—you guessed it—a hamburger.

REFUELING STOPS If you're looking for a fun place for a drink, in the basement of Seville Square is the **10. Longbranch Saloon,** known for its food specials, drinks and "Kansas City's Meanest Waitresses." Nearby, at 4743 Pennsylvania, is the original **11. Houlihan's Old Place,** which opened almost two decades ago and now has branches across the country. Cater-cornered from Houlihan's is **12. Parkway 600 Grill,** a place to be seen for Kansas City's upwardly mobile. More important, it offers outdoor seating and is one of the few places serving alcohol in the morning. For serious dining, head for the **13. Bristol Bar and Grill,** 4740 Jefferson, great for seafood, or **14. La Mediterranee,** a posh restaurant serving Kansas City's best French cuisine.

FROM SEVILLE SQUARE, PENNSYLVANIA AND NICHOLS, TO SWANSONS, 47TH AND WYANDOTTE Backtrack one block east on Nichols Road, where on Broadway you'll find the:

15. **Mermaid Pool,** the Plaza's oldest work of art. Made of Carrara marble and dating from about 1680, the mermaids

guard a pool inlaid with ceramic tile. Throw in some coins—they go to Children's Mercy Hospital.

Back on Nichols, continue heading east one block, where on the corner of Nichols and Central you'll see the statue of:

16. Boy and Frog, one of the more bizarre statues on the Plaza. Take a look at it and decide for yourself what's going on. It was purchased in 1928 and is an original by Raffaello Romanelli of Florence, whose father, Pasquale, founded the Romanelli Studios in 1860. Cater-cornered from the statue is:

17. Halls, another department store. Across Wyandotte Street is:

18. Swanson's, a chic apparel store.

FINAL REFUELING STOPS Quench your thirst at local watering hole **19. Fred P. Ott's,** 4770 J. C. Nichols Parkway, which has a small patio. Next door is **20. Annie's Santa Fe,** great for margaritas and Mexican food. **21. Fedora Café and Bar,** 210 W. 47th St., offers upscale dining with an innovative menu. **22. Figlio,** 209 W. 46th St., serves great Italian food at modest prices in a modern setting.

CHAPTER 17

KANSAS CITY SHOPPING

1. SHOPPING AREAS
2. ANTIQUES & ART

In the days of wagon caravans heading west along the Santa Fe, California, and Oregon trails, Independence and Westport served as important trading and outfitting centers. Those days have long gone, and Kansas City has never regained a reputation as a shopper's paradise. Nevertheless, it does offer a unique shopping experience—Country Club Plaza, the nation's oldest shopping center. In addition, there are malls and antiques shops offering hours of exploration.

---

1. SHOPPING AREAS

DOWNTOWN AND ELSEWHERE

City Market, sandwiched between the Missouri River and I-70, just north of downtown, has been the scene of a colorful and brisk Saturday business ever since its covered stalls were first erected in 1888. Although a few vendors are on hand Monday through Friday from about 9am to 3pm to sell produce and flowers, the busiest day of the week is Saturday, when a great multitude of vendors, shoppers, and browsers converge on the scene to make it one of the liveliest places in the city.

One of the great things about City Market is that it is just that—a city market that draws a wide mix of people, blue-collar and white-collar workers, young and old, and various ethnic backgrounds. Second- and third-generation families sell fruit, vegetables, flowers, plants, live chickens, and eggs, while entrepreneurial newcomers hawk T-shirts, kitchen appliances, and odds and ends (nothing used is allowed to be sold at the market). Fast food is available, from hot dogs to barbecue, as well as soft drinks. The Saturday market begins at about 5am and continues to about 3pm. On Saturday, the Trolley includes City Market on its circuit.

COUNTRY CLUB PLAZA

Located just five miles south of downtown, Country Club Plaza is the nation's oldest shopping center, dating from 1922. It's a 14-block, 55-acre shopping district modeled after Seville, Spain, complete with pastel-colored buildings topped with red-tiled roofs and towers, tree-lined boulevards, horse-drawn carriages, and more than $1 million worth of fountains and statues. To reach the Plaza from downtown, take Main Street south to 47th Street, where you should turn right.

The main draws of Country Club Plaza are its shops, department stores, and boutiques, which number more than 150 and offer a wide variety of goods and services. Department stores include Dillard's on the corner of 47th Street and Broadway; Saks Fifth Avenue on the corner of Pennsylvania and Nichols Road; and Halls at Nichols Road and Central. Seville Square, Nichols Road and Pennsylvania, is a shopping center with approximately 40 boutiques.

Clothing stores on the Plaza include Asiatica with its Asian-influenced designs for women, Ann Taylor, Banana Republic, Benetton, Brooks Brothers, The Gap, Jaeger International, Laura Ashley, Outrigger, Overland Outfitters, Plaza Pendleton, Polo/Ralph Lauren, Swanson's, N. Valentino, and Woolf Brothers.

Shops and boutiques offering specialty items include Gucci, with its many accessories; Bennett Schneider, a bookstore; Crabtree and Evelyn, with its soaps, sachets, and other products; Sharper Image, with its gadgets, accessories, and playthings; Function Junction, with household items and kitchenware; and Tivol, Inc., a family-owned jewelry store.

Parking throughout the Plaza is free, and most shops are open Monday through Saturday from 10am to 6pm and Thursday to 9pm. Sunday hours are noon or 12:30pm to 5 or 5:30pm. If you have questions regarding the Plaza or its retail outlets, stop by the **Plaza Association**, 4625 Wornall Rd. (tel. 753-0100), located just north of the 47th Street and Central intersection.

CROWN CENTER, 2450 Grand Ave., Kansas City, MO. Tel. 274-8444.

Located between downtown and the Plaza, Crown Center is a $500-million complex privately financed by Hallmark Cards, Inc. Virtually a city-within-a-city, the 85-acre development includes Hallmark Card's international headquarters, the Hallmark Visitors Center, two luxury hotels, apartments and condominiums, offices, theaters, cinemas, an outdoor ice-skating rink, and retail outlets.

Most interesting to shoppers, of course, is Crown Center's trilevel retail complex with more than 50 boutiques, shops, and stores. These include The Custom Shop Shirtmakers, with custom shirts and ready-to-wear shirts; Victoria's Secret, with fine lingerie; The Best of Kansas City, with souvenirs and edibles of Kansas City; Cat's Meow, packed with gifts for felines and their friends; Everyday's A Holiday, with decorations for Christmas and other holidays; Function Junction, Kansas City's most popular store for household items and kitchenware; Second Star to the Right, with Disney collectibles; and Hallmark Live!, a showcase of Hallmark greeting cards and related products. Halls Crown Center is a large department store with quality merchandise.

Crown Center offers a variety of customer services, including gift wrapping, mail wrapping, and UPS shipping. There's also a Ticketmaster outlet, and tickets for the Trolley are sold here. For information on Crown Center and a brochure listing all its shops and food outlets, stop by the Crown Center Information Booth, located on Level 2. As for parking, Crown Center allows three hours of free parking with validation from any Crown Center shop, no purchase necessary. An additional three hours of parking is awarded with the purchase of $25 in goods or food. On the weekend, parking is free, without validation.

Open: Mon–Wed and Sat 10am–6pm, Thurs and Fri 10am–9pm, Sun noon–5pm.

TOWN PAVILION, 1111 Main St. (Downtown), Kansas City, MO. Tel. 472-9600.
This is one of Kansas City's newest shopping centers, located right in the heart of downtown and built in sleek art deco style to match the city's surrounding architecture. Its anchor store is the Jones Store Company, and there are more than three dozen retail stores and food outlets. Shops include Paul Harris, with clothing for women; Woolf Brothers, with clothing for men and women; Hurst's Diamond Shop, which has been selling jewelry for more than 80 years; Demaree Stationery, opened since 1895 and selling fine writing instruments, leather briefcases, and office supplies; McClendon's Hats, Kansas City's oldest millinery; and St. Moritz Chocolatier.

A One Hour Photo shop will develop film in one hour; at the Pavilion Personal Services you can have your shoes repaired or your laundry done or altered, mail a letter or package by express delivery, or have a key duplicated. Parking is free the first three hours with validation Monday through Friday; on the weekend it's free. For more information, drop by the Information Desk located next to the north escalator on Level 1.
Open: Mon–Sat 10am–6pm.

BANNISTER MALL, 5600 Bannister Rd., Kansas City, MO. Tel. 763-6900.
Located in South Kansas City, just east of I-435 (take the 87th Street or Bannister Road exit), Bannister Mall is a huge mall with approximately 180 retail shops and outlets. Dillard's, Jones, J. C. Penney's, and Sears serve as anchor department stores, with many others selling clothing, shoes, accessories, formal and bridal wear, toys, home furnishings, jewelry, gifts, records, and more. An information booth is located in the center of the second floor, near Dillard's.
Open: Mon–Sat 10am–9pm, Sun noon–6pm.

OVERLAND PARK

OAK PARK MALL, 95th and Quivera Sts, Overland Park, KS. Tel. 888-4400.
Just off I-35 in Overland Park, two-level Oak Park Mall has 160 stores, shops, and food outlets. Major stores include J. C. Penney's, Montgomery Wards, and Dillard's. Its information booth is located in the center of the Lower Level, near Dillard's. Among its many food outlets and restaurants, particularly recommended is Paradise Diner, an upscale diner with a sleek white interior and a fun menu serving sandwiches and innovative dishes.
Open: Mon–Sat 10am–9pm, Sun noon–5:30pm.

2. ANTIQUES & ART

ANTIQUES
45TH AND STATE LINE, MIDTOWN

45th and State Line is the heart of antiques heaven in Kansas City, a three-block area with more than 20 independent dealers. Located in Midtown just six blocks west of Country Club Plaza, it is the best place in town to browse for high-quality antiques, much of them imported from Europe. Victorian birdcages, furniture, silver, glass, carousel figures, stained-glass windows, jewelry, decorative objects, light fixtures, Depression glass, miniatures, old books, and collectibles are for sale. The Georgian Village, 1708–1714 W. 45th St., is the largest shop, with 10 dealers under one roof.

Open: Tues–Sat 10am–5pm; a few are open Mon with the same hours.

WESTPORT FLEA MARKET, 817 Westport Rd. (Midtown), Kansas City, MO. Tel. 931-1986.

Just west of the nightlife action of Westport in Midtown, this is the city's oldest and largest indoor flea market. In operation for about 20 years, it houses dozens of dealers selling furniture, clothing, jewelry, and collectibles. A lot of the items are plain junk, but it's fun to walk through. Prices are low, and I've picked up some real bargains here. The hamburgers at the Bar and Grill in the center of the market, by the way, are the biggest I've ever seen.

Open: Sat and Sun 10am–5pm.

CHEEP ANTIQUES, 201 Main St. (Downtown), Kansas City, MO. Tel. 471-0092.

This huge, warehouselike store is one block north of City Market, near the Missouri River. I always enjoy coming here after visiting City Market on a Saturday. Cheep Antiques specializes in antique furniture, mostly wardrobes, kitchen tables, headboards, and buffets, spread on two floors of an old building. Lots to look at.

Open: Sat and Sun 9am–5pm.

ART

CENTRAL PARK GALLERY, 1644 Wyandotte (Downtown), Kansas City, MO. Tel. 471-7711.

This is a beautiful gallery, both in space and in content. Located in downtown Kansas City, it occupies what was formerly Wester School, built in 1885 and listed on the National Register of Historic Places. The gallery's grounds boast a garden, an aviary, and a fountain stocked with Japanese carp. The gallery itself is so large, with 15,000 square feet of gallery space, that it seems more like a museum than a retail gallery. Opened in 1989, it is the largest gallery in the Midwest, with two floors offering a mix of 1,500 paintings, sketches, watercolors, sculptures, and ceramics by approximately 50 regional and nationally acclaimed artists. Every item is marked with the price, and many are identified with biographies of the artists as well. Featured artists include Wong Shue, Watanabe, Eyvind Earle, Lu Hong, Yamin Young, Andreas Nottebohm, Marco Sassone, Michel-Henry, and Jim Buckels.

Open: Mon–Fri 9am–5pm, Sat 10am–4pm.

KANSAS CITY NIGHTS

Kansas City offers a wide variety of nightlife diversions, with something for everyone. You can sip a cocktail in a subdued and sophisticated lounge while watching the city lights twinkle in the distance, dance to the latest in aggressive rock, listen to some of the finest jazz in the country, eat at a dinner theater, or watch a musical being performed under the stars. And that's only the beginning.

Of course, Kansas City is most famous for its jazz, which it owes largely to such former local greats as Charlie Parker and Count Basie. The Kansas City Jazz Commission, the only group of its kind in the country, is dedicated to preserving and promoting the distinctive Kansas City style of jazz, which makes use of saxophones and background riffs. To find out what's going on in the weekly jazz scene in clubs across the city, call the Jazz Hotline, maintained by the Jazz Commission, at 931-2888.

To find out about upcoming productions in the theater, concerts, and other nightlife entertainment, pick up a copy of *The Fun Calendar,* a quarterly entertainment calendar published and distributed by the Convention and **Visitors Bureau of Greater Kansas City,** located downtown on the 25th floor of City Center Square, 1100 Main St. (tel. 221-5242). The Bureau also maintains a 24-hour **Visitor Information Phone** (tel. 474-9600), with recordings of this week's events.

In addition, *The Kansas City Star* features comprehensive listings of current and upcoming activities in its Friday and Sunday editions. Finally, available at various bars and restaurants throughout the city are free copies of *Pitch,* a weekly tabloid that covers Kansas City's nightlife scene in depth.

Capital Automated Ticket Services (CATS), is the largest ticket service in the metropolitan area, located at record shops and the Jones Stores. You can charge tickets for major events by calling Dial-a-Tick at 931-3330.

1. THE PERFORMING ARTS

THEATERS

AMERICAN HEARTLAND THEATRE, Crown Center, 2450 Grand Ave., Kansas City, MO. Tel. 842-9999.
This small 440-seat theater offers professional Broadway plays, musicals, mysteries, and dramas in an intimate setting. It's located on

---

MAJOR CONCERT AND PERFORMANCE HALLS

Folly Theater, 300 W. 12th St. (tel. 474-4444 or 842-5555)

Midland Center for the Performing Arts, 1228 Main St. (tel. 421-7500)

Music Hall, Municipal Auditorium, 13th and Central Sts. (tel. 421-8000)

Sandstone, 130th and State Ave., Bonner Springs, KS (tel. 913/721-3300)

Starlight Theatre, Swope Park, Meyer Blvd. and Swope Parkway (tel. 333-9481 or 363-STAR)

Level 3 of Crown Center, with a second stage, Stage Two, located in the Westin Crown Center Hotel.

Prices: $15–$21.

Open: Box office Mon–Sat 10am–6pm, Sun noon–2:30pm; performances Tues–Sat 8pm, matinee Sun at 2pm.

FOLLY THEATER, 300 W. 12th St. (Downtown), Kansas City, MO. Tel. 474-4444 or 842-5555.

This is Kansas City's only surviving turn-of-the-century playhouse, which served as a venue for burlesque, films, vaudeville, boxing, wrestling, and even strip tease before its renovation and reopening in 1981. On the National Register of Historic Places, the Folly now serves as a stage for a wide variety of events, including its own 12th Street Jazz Series, the Children's Series, World Travel Film Series, and dance.

Prices: Vary according to performance.

Open: Box office Mon–Fri 10am–5pm; telephone for performance times.

MIDLAND CENTER FOR THE PERFORMING ARTS, 1228 Main St. (Downtown), Kansas City, MO. Tel. 421-7500.

The Midland opened in 1927 as one of the region's most lavishly decorated movie palaces. It is still very ornate, with a three-story-high lobby, walnut wainscoting with gold overleaf, a 12-foot-wide marble staircase, chandeliers, and custom-cut Tiffany glass. Retaining many of its original furnishings and art objects, it seats 2,800 in its five-story-high auditorium, where Broadway hits, musicals, comedies, Las Vegas headliners, and other performances are held.

Prices: Vary according to the performance, with $15–$30 charged for most Broadway shows.

Open: Box office (located to the south of the main entrance) Mon–Fri 10am–5pm, Sat and Sun (on day of performance only) noon–5pm. Telephone for performance times.

MUSIC HALL, Municipal Auditorium, 13th and Central (Downtown), Kansas City, MO. Tel. 421-8000.

Located in Municipal Auditorium, this art deco theater was constructed in the early 1930s and is now a versatile facility, offering presentations ranging from dance and concerts to Broadway musicals. Both the State Ballet of Missouri and the Lyric Opera perform here.

Prices: Vary according to performance.

Open: Box office Mon–Fri 10am–4pm. Telephone for performance times.

SANDSTONE, 130th and State Ave., Bonner Springs, KS. Tel. 913/721-3300.

This natural amphitheater, off I-70 west of Kansas City in Bonner Springs, is where many visiting top artists perform. There are 3,000 permanent seats, but most people opt to bring blankets to spread out on the terraced lawns, where there is room for approximately 15,000 more people.

Prices: Vary according to performance. Tickets available through Dial-a-Tick (tel. 931-3330).

Open: Performances from late May–mid-Sept.

STARLIGHT THEATRE, Swope Park, Meyer Blvd. and Swope Parkway, Kansas City, MO. Tel. 333-9481 or 363-STAR.

You couldn't ask for a more delightful setting for musicals or outdoor concerts than this 7,862-seat amphitheater set in lush Swope Park. Since its opening in the early 1950s, the Starlight has served as a venue for Broadway musicals and top-name concerts, with 4 musicals and approximately 15 concerts performed each season. Musicals have ranged from *West Side Story* and *Oklahoma!* to *Grease* and *Annie,* while performers have included Bette Midler, Tina Turner, and Elton John.

Prices: $4–$25.

Open: Performances mid-May–Oct. Telephone for performance schedule.

MAJOR PERFORMING ARTS COMPANIES

MISSOURI REPERTORY THEATRE, Spencer Theatre, 4949 Cherry (Midtown), Kansas City, MO. Tel. 276-2700.

Celebrating more than a quarter of a century of live performances, this professional theater company presents approximately seven shows per year, with productions ranging from the great classics to premieres. *A Christmas Carol* is presented annually.

Prices: $17–$25.

Open: Box office Mon–Fri 10am–5:30pm, Sat and Sun noon–5:30pm; performances Sept–May, Tues–Sat 8pm, Sun 7pm, matinee Sat 4pm and Sun 2pm.

QUALITY HILL PLAYHOUSE, 303 W. 10th at Central (Downtown), Kansas City, MO. Tel. 421-1700 or 421-7500.

Located near Quality Hill and the Garment District downtown, this new theater presents contemporary plays, comedies, and musicals.

Prices: $8–$14.

Open: Box office (located at Midland Center, 1228 Main) Mon–Fri 10am–5pm, Sat and Sun (on day of performance only) noon–5pm; performances Sept–May. Call for exact times and schedule.

UNICORN THEATRE, 3820 Main (Midtown), Kansas City, MO. Tel. 531-7529.
This 200-seat theater offers off-Broadway–style productions, with an emphasis on contemporary and original scripts. It is one of only two companies in the country accessible for performers in wheelchairs.
Prices: $9–$14.
Open: Box office Mon–Fri 10–5, Sat noon–4pm; performances Oct–June Wed–Sun at 8pm, matinee Sun at 3pm.

OPERA

LYRIC OPERA OF KANSAS CITY, Box office at 1029 Central (Downtown); performances at the Music Hall, Municipal Auditorium, 13th and Central, Kansas City, MO. Tel. 471-7344.
Two operas are presented each spring, followed by three in the fall. Under the artistic direction of Russell Patterson, all productions are sung in English and performed in the Music Hall of Municipal Auditorium downtown.
Prices: $6–$35.
Open: Box office (1029 Central) Mon–Fri 10am–5pm, Sat (day of performance only) noon–5pm; performances Apr, Sept, and Oct Mon and Wed 7:30pm, Fri and Sat 8pm.

CLASSICAL AND ORCHESTRAL MUSIC

THE KANSAS CITY SYMPHONY, Box office at 1029 Central (Downtown); performances at Scottish Rite Temple, Linwood Blvd. and the Paseo, Kansas City, MO. Tel. 471-0400.
The Kansas City Symphony, under music director and conductor William McGlaughlin, presents a variety of programs. The Main Series features both classical and contemporary symphonies with guest soloists. The Sampler Series introduces audiences to classical music, while Nightlights teams the orchestra with major jazz and pop artists.
Prices: $11–$28.
Open: Box office (1029 Central) Mon–Fri 10am–5pm, Sat (day of performance only) noon–5pm. Performances for Main Series Fri and Sat 8pm, matinee Sun 2pm; Sampler Series Fri 7pm and Sun 2pm; Nightlights Wed 8pm.

DINNER THEATERS

TIFFANY'S ATTIC, 5028 Main (Midtown), Kansas City, MO. Tel. 561-PLAY.
    WALDORF ASTORIA, 7428 Washington (South Kansas City), Kansas City, MO. Tel. 561-PLAY.
Both these dinner theaters are under the umbrella of Dinner Playhouse, Inc., a professional equity company offering 16 performances per week at its two locations. Broadway comedies and musicals presented by famous TV and movie personalities are presented, along with a dinner buffet and pre-show entertainment.
Prices: $17–$24.
Open: Telephone reservations Mon 9am–6pm, Tues–Fri 9am–

8pm, Sat 9am–6pm, Sun 10am–6pm; performances daily 6pm, matinee Sun noon, some weekdays 11:45am.

2. THE CLUB & MUSIC SCENE

LIVE MUSIC HOUSES

Most of Kansas City's live music houses feature jazz or blues, although a few offer rock or alternative music as well.

DOWNTOWN

THE PHOENIX, 302 W. Central. Tel. 472-0001.
This jazz piano bar, located in the old Garment District, is popular with downtown businesspeople. Pianist Tim Whitmer performs everything from blues to be-bop, and he is often joined by local jazz artists. "Jazz Happy Hour" is Monday through Friday from 5 to 9pm.
    Prices: Drinks $2.50–$4. **Admission:** Free.
    Open: Mon–Sat 11am–1am.

VINE DISTRICT

In the 1930s, Kansas City jazz was centered in clubs at 12th and Vine. The action today has shifted a few blocks farther south to 18th and Vine, with these two locales featuring black musicians playing largely to black audiences, although all ages and races are welcome.

BIRDLAND, 19th and Vine. Tel. 842-8463.
This is an old-fashioned establishment, complete with 1950s furnishings and fixtures, including wrought-iron railings, red-vinyl chairs, Formica tabletops, and glowing red lamps. The clientele ranges from young couples to the middle-aged, and there's a small dance floor. This place is mellow and laid-back—a lot of fun. A band plays only on the weekend, from 8pm on Friday and from 9pm on Saturday.
    Prices: Drinks $3. **Admission:** Free.
    Open: Mon–Sat 4pm–1:30am.

MUTUAL MUSICIANS FOUNDATION, 1823 Highland St. Tel. 471-5212 or 421-9297.
The Mutual Musicians Foundation is a nonprofit social club for professional musicians and jazz buffs and was chartered in 1917 as an all-black Musicians Association. In the 1930s it produced some of the greatest musicians in jazz history—including Bennie Moten, Count Basie, Andy Kirk, Harlan Leonard, Lester Young, Jay McShann, and Charlie Parker. It has been at its same location off Vine since 1930, in a modest, two-story building; it now offers after-hour jam sessions Friday and Saturday night. This is where area musicians congregate after their regular gigs to jam all night long, with participants ranging from local celebrities to older men who once played with Count Basie and the bands. There's also a Saturday afternoon practice session.
    Prices: Drinks $2, beer $1.50. **Admission:** A donation of $3 or $5 is appreciated.
    Open: Jam sessions Fri and Sat after midnight; Sat practices 11:30am–1:30pm.

WESTPORT AND MIDTOWN

BLAYNEY'S, 415 Westport Rd. Tel. 561-3747.

This is an unrefined basement establishment, popular with a college crowd ever since its 1973 opening. The live music starts at 9pm and features blues, rhythm and blues, and old-style rock-'n'-roll from the late 1960s and early 1970s. There are a small dance floor and a pool table.

Prices: Beer from $1.85, mixed drinks $2.50–$4.50. **Admission:** Mon–Thurs $1, Fri and Sat $2.

Open: Mon–Sat 8pm–3am.

THE GRAND EMPORIUM, 3832 Main St. Tel. 531-1504.

This place is nothing fancy—in fact, it's kind of a dive—but it consistently brings in some of the best music to be heard in Kansas City. It's certainly the best place in town to listen to blues as well as alternative rock and reggae. The Grand Emporium is also a good place for barbecue, prepared by Grace, who is known for her sauce, ribs, ham, beef, and red beans and rice. The building itself dates from the 1920s and through the years has served as a plumbing shop, candy factory, grocery store, pool hall, speakeasy, brothel, and saloon. It's a small place, long and narrow, with a tiny stage, an even tinier dance floor, and walls plastered with promotional posters of various bands. If you're looking for Kansas City's most popular music house and dance hall, this is it.

Prices: Draft beer $1.25, mixed drinks $2.50. **Admission:** $4–$8 for most bands, sometimes higher for national acts.

Open: Mon–Sat 9am–3am.

THE HURRICANE, 4048 Broadway. Tel. 753-0884.

Located off Westport Road in the heart of the nightlife district, The Hurricane is a showcase for regional alternative acts, including bands that perform original material, whether it's blues, zydeco, or rock. There's a dance floor and an outdoor stage in the summer, making this the only place in Westport where you can listen to music outside. Live music starts at 10pm Monday through Thursday and at 5pm Friday and Saturday. Happy hour, with reduced prices for drinks, is from 3 to 9pm Monday through Thursday.

Prices: Beer from $1.25, mixed drinks $2.50. **Admission:** $1–$3.

Open: Mon–Sat 3pm–3am.

JIMMY'S JIGGER, 1823 W. 39th St. Tel. 753-2444.

This casual establishment opened the day after Prohibition ended. Its location near the University of Kansas Medical Center brings in an older crowd, including doctors, nurses, and students, who come not only for the drinks but also for the food. Jimmy's Jigger has gained a deserved reputation for good barbecue, prepared with its own sauce in its own smoker, including ribs and various sandwiches. There's live music every Friday and Saturday from 9pm and every Sunday from 5pm, featuring mostly jazz but also bluegrass, rock-'n'-roll, and zydeco.

Prices: Beer from $1.25, mixed drinks $2.50. **Admission:** $2–$3.

THE LEVEE, 16 W. 43rd St. Tel. 561-2821.

What a great place to while away a sunny afternoon, sitting on The Levee's outside patio or deck, sipping a beer. It's so pleasant that you'll be easily persuaded to stay through the evening to hear the band. Jazz and blues are the featured music, and "Never a cover" is The Levee's motto. Bands play in the main room on the ground floor, but you can still hear the music on the second floor and even outside. Live music begins at 8:30pm Monday through Thursday, 9pm on Friday, and 3pm on Saturday. With its exposed-brick walls, ceiling fans, and wooden floor, The Levee manages to be casual and stylish at the same time, attracting people of all ages. Salads and burgers are available. The Levee is located between Westport and the Plaza.

Prices: Beer from $1.50. **Admission:** Free.

Open: Mon–Sat 11am–1:30am.

MILTON'S, 815 W. 39th St. Tel. 753-9476.

Milton's is a classic jazz club, open since 1932 and certainly one of the longest-running jazz clubs in the United States. It's named after the original owner, Milton Morris—a flamboyant man who ran for governor several times; had gangsters for friends; and was an ardent fan of jazz and jazz musicians, including Count Basie and Charlie Parker, both of whom played at his club. Although the club has moved several times, it has managed to retain its simple, informal, and slightly seedy atmosphere, which is the way loyal customers like it. Live traditional jazz starts at 9pm, and admission is so low that it's almost embarrassing. As one of the present owners said, jazz is now much more appreciated in other countries, such as France and Japan—so much so that Milton's may soon open branches in Paris and Kyoto, where prices will be significantly higher.

Prices: Mixed drinks $2.50. **Admission:** Mon–Thurs free, Fri and Sat $2.

Open: Mon–Sat 2pm–1:30am.

THE POINT, 917 W. 44th St. Tel. 531-9800.

Ida McBeth, a local jazz and blues singer who has gained a faithful following of fans, packs them in every other week when she performs at The Point Thursday through Saturday. Other nights feature blues, jazz, and rock performers, with live music beginning at 9pm. There are two floors, each with its own bar, and the main floor can get so crowded that there's hardly room to move, much less dance on the small dance floor. Deli-type food, including soup and sandwiches, is available.

Prices: Draft beer from $1.25, mixed drinks from $2.25. **Admission:** Mon–Thurs free, Fri and Sat $4–$6.

Open: Mon–Sat 11am–1:30am.

SOUTH KANSAS CITY

CITY LIGHT, 7425 Broadway. Tel. 444-6969.

This jazz club is more sophisticated and subdued than those located in Westport and tends to draw in an older crowd, many of whom come here for dinner as well. The house band, the City Light Jazz Ensemble, ranks as one of the best bands in the city, playing mostly contemporary jazz but also accomplished at swing, be-bop, and rhythm and blues. Led by pianist Joe Cartwright, the ensemble plays most weekends beginning at 9pm, while the Joe Cartwright Trio entertains most weeknights starting at 8pm. There are also guest bands, and on Monday there's the Blue Monday Jam Session. The club is divided into three rooms, with windows that allow patrons to see into the main room. The view from the back room is limited, however, so if you come for dinner (which allows you to reserve a table and waives the admission price) be sure to request a table in one of the two front rooms. The menu includes seafood, steaks, and chicken, with most entrees ranging from $10 to $25.

Prices: Beer from $2.50, mixed drinks $2.75. **Admission:** Mon–Thurs free, Fri and Sat $4 (free with the purchase of dinner).

Open: Mon–Thurs 5–10:30pm, Fri and Sat 5pm–midnight.

COMEDY

COMEDYSPORTZ, 323 W. 8th St. (Downtown), Kansas City, MO. Tel. 842-ARGH.

Every Friday and Saturday night, a dozen or so local comedians come on stage for improvisational performances. Taking suggestions from the audience, they create skits that deal mainly with sports but include other topics as well. It's not stand-up comedy, nor is it a rehearsed play—but it is a lot of fun.

Prices: Beer from $2. **Admission:** $6 for ComedySportz only; $12 includes all the pizza you can eat.

Open: Performances Fri and Sat at 8pm and 10:30pm.

STANFORD'S COMEDY HOUSE, 543 Westport Rd. (Westport). Tel. 756-1450.

This is the best place in town for comedy, featuring nationally known comedians, some of whom have appeared on television with Johnny Carson or David Letterman. Roseanne Barr and Robin Williams both performed here, and each evening features an average of three comedians. There's a two-drink minimum, and snacks such as pizza and nachos are available. A great place to get those laughter muscles working. There's a branch at 9045 Metcalf Avenue in Overland Park (tel. 649-8288).

Prices: Drinks $2–$4. **Admission:** Mon–Thurs $5, Fri and Sat $7.

Open: Performances Mon–Thurs 9pm, Fri and Sat 8 and 10:30pm.

THE DANCING SCENE

In addition to the places listed here, a number of establishments described above offer both dancing and live music, including Birdland, The Grand Emporium, The Hurricane, and The Point.

WESTPORT AND MIDTOWN

GUITARS AND CADILLACS, 3954 Central Ave. Tel. 756-2221.

Claiming to have the largest dance floor in Kansas City, Guitars and Cadillacs is worlds apart from the other establishments in Kansas City—this is where you'll find cowboy boots, cowboy hats, and even some real cowboys. Co-owned by country-music star T. G. Sheppard, Guitars and Cadillacs is the place to go for country music. There's a live band on Monday, but otherwise there's a D. J., along with such promotionals as swimsuit contests (you won't find many feminists here), free dance lessons, and Friday happy hour that features reduced drink prices and a buffet. On Saturday, KFKF, the local country-music radio station, broadcasts live from here.

Prices: Draft beer from $2. **Admission:** Mon, Tues, and Thurs free; Wed $1; Fri and Sat $2.

Open: Mon–Fri 5pm–3am, Sat 7pm–3am.

LYNN DICKEY'S, 535 Westport Rd. Tel. 756-1010.
A popular sports café during the day, with 17 TV screens showing mainly sports, Lynn Dickey's transforms into a wild and crazy disco at night. The clientele, either college-age or college-educated, ranges from the preppie to the yuppie. There's a happy-hour buffet and special drink prices Monday through Friday from 4:30 to 7pm.
　　Prices: Draft beer from $2, mixed drinks from $2.75. **Admission:** $2; Thurs women admitted free.
　　Open: Daily 11am–2am.

OVERLAND PARK

STUDEBAKER'S, 10975 Metcalf Ave. Tel. 345-1951.
Studebaker's, located just south of I-435, is convenient if you're staying in Overland Park. Decorated in bright red and chrome, it features music of the 1950s, 1960s, and 1970s; the clientele tends to be an older professional crowd, many of whom work or live in Overland Park. You must be 23 or older to enter (isn't there a law against age discrimination?).
　　Prices: Draft beer from $1.75, mixed drinks $2.50. **Admission:** Tues–Thurs $2, Fri and Sat $3; Tues–Thurs women admitted free.
　　Open: Tues–Fri 5pm–2am, Sat 8pm–2am.

3. THE BAR SCENE

Many of the establishments listed in the preceding section are open throughout the day and are also good places for a drink.

DOWNTOWN

HITTER'S, Radisson Suite Hotel Kansas City, 12th at Baltimore. Tel. 221-7000.
This ultramodern bar broadcasts the latest in sports on its 11 TV screens, which can be found even in the bathroom to assure fans that they won't miss a minute of the action. One of the few bars in the downtown area, it offers a limited menu of sandwiches, salads, and burgers.
　　Prices: Beer from $2.50.
　　Open: Mon–Thurs 11am–midnight, Fri and Sat 11am–2am, Sun 11am–10pm.

MURPHY'S, 323 W. 8th St. Tel. 472-1516.
Located in the Garment District in a renovated brick building, Murphy's caters primarily to downtown office workers. A rustic establishment with exposed-brick walls and a wooden floor, it offers a wide assortment of salads and sandwiches and 18 beers on tap, including Kansas City's own Boulevard Beer.
　　Prices: Draft beer from $1.60, mixed drinks from $2.25.
　　Open: Mon–Thurs 11am–midnight, Fri and Sat 11am–1am.

CROWN CENTER

SKIES, Hyatt Regency Crown Center, 2345 McGee St. Tel. 421-1234.

Skies is Kansas City's only revolving restaurant, with a separate lounge where you can come simply for a drink. Located high above the city on the 42nd floor, it offers a fantastic panoramic view in a sophisticated, cocktail-lounge setting. The best time to come is during happy hour, from 4 to 7pm, when drinks and appetizers are half price.

Prices: Beer from $3, mixed drinks $4.

Open: Mon–Thurs 4pm–midnight, Fri and Sat 4pm–1am, Sun 4pm–11:30pm.

COUNTRY CLUB PLAZA

FRED P. OTTS, 4770 J. C. Nichols Parkway. Tel. 753-2878.

This simple bar has the advantages of a small outdoor patio and live entertainment on Tuesday night, for which there's no cover charge. In addition, happy hour on Monday through Friday from 4 to 7pm offers discounted prices for drinks and food. The menu lists typical bar food, including hamburgers, sandwiches, chili, and potato skins.

Prices: Draft beer from $1.60, mixed drinks from $2.25.

Open: Mon–Sat 11am–1am, Sun noon–9pm.

HOULIHAN'S OLD PLACE, 4743 Pennsylvania. Tel. 561-3141.

Just about everyone has a good time at Houlihan's, including families, the college crowd, and working professionals. This is the original Houlihan's, which opened two decades ago; the chain has since spread throughout the country. Happy-hour specials with discounts on food and drink are offered Monday through Friday from 4 to 8pm. The food menu is extensive, with a wide assortment of soups, salads, burgers, sandwiches, and entrees.

Prices: Beer from $2.25, wine from $3.75.

Open: Sun–Thurs 11am–11pm, Fri and Sat 11am–midnight.

LONGBRANCH SALOON, Seville Square, Pennsylvania and Nichols Rd. Tel. 931-2755.

Pay no attention to this establishment's claim that it has the city's "meanest waitresses" or that there's a 10-drink minimum. Instead, enjoy the convivial atmosphere over a beer or cocktail ("No Foo Foo Drinks," the menu says, "—This is a Saloon not a Drink Boutique") and take advantage of the daily food specials or regular menu items, such as hamburgers, steaks, and sandwiches.

Prices: Beer from $1.25, mixed drinks $1.85.

Open: Mon–Sat 11am–3am, Sun 11am–midnight.

PARKWAY 600 GRILL, 600 Ward Parkway. Tel. 931-6600.

This is *the* place in summer for an after-work drink on the Plaza, primarily because of the outdoor patio. In fact, so many people want to drink here that you'll probably have to wait for a table (be sure to get your name on the waiting list), unless you get here early. Because this is one of the few places on the Plaza serving alcohol in the morning, you can get here very early indeed.

Prices: Beer from $2.50, mixed drinks $2.85.

Open: Mon–Fri 7am–11pm, Sat 11am–11pm, Sun 9am–11pm.

WESTPORT AND MIDTOWN

FUZZY'S SPORTS BAR AND GRILL, 4113 Pennsylvania. Tel. 561-9191.

Yes, this is yet another sports bar, but this one claims to be the oldest one in Kansas City. Decorated with trophies, pennants, photographs, and other sports memorabilia, Fuzzy's features five TV screens and is at its rowdiest during big sports events. According to the management, everyone from businesspeople and young people to "sports nuts" make up its clientele. Happy hour is Monday through Friday from 4 to 7pm.

Prices: Draft beer from $1.25, mixed drinks from $3.
Open: Daily 11am–3am.

KELLY'S, Pennsylvania Ave. and Westport Rd. Tel. 753-9193.

Kelly's has the distinction of occupying the oldest building in Kansas City, built in 1837 when Westport served as an outfitting post for wagon trains heading for Santa Fe. In the 1850s a grandson of Daniel Boone set up shop here. Today Kelly's still has that unrefined, rustic atmosphere—a tavern in the true sense of the word. It is very popular with a young and enthusiastic drinking crowd. If you want beer for breakfast, this is the place to go.

Prices: Draft beer from 90¢, mixed drinks from $1.60.
Open: Mon–Sat 6am–1:30am.

4. MORE ENTERTAINMENT

MOVIES

GRANADA THEATRE, 1015 Minnesota Ave., Kansas City, KS. Tel. 621-2232.

Built in the 1920s in the style of a Spanish courtyard, this movie theater features silent movies, which are even accompanied by a theater pipe organ, just like they were in the olden days. There are approximately 75 films in the Granada's archives, with another 2,000 available from a private collection.

Ticket prices: $7 adults, $5 seniors, $4 students and children.
Open: Silent movies shown one Sat per month at 8pm, one Sun per month at 3pm. Call for exact dates.

TIVOLI, 425 Westport Rd. (Westport). Tel. 756-1030.

This movie theater, located in the heart of Westport, shows alternative and international films that never make it to the regular box offices.

Ticket prices: $5.
Open: Mon–Fri evening shows, matinee Sat and Sun. Telephone for exact schedule.

INDEX

GENERAL INFORMATION

KANSAS CITY

ST. LOUIS

SIGHTS & ATTRACTIONS

KANSAS CITY

KEY TO ABBREVIATIONS: * = Author's Favorite

ST. LOUIS

ACCOMMODATIONS

KANSAS CITY

KEY TO ABBREVIATIONS: *B* = Budget; *B&B* = Bed-and-breakfast; *CG* = Camping; *E* = Expensive; *I* = Inexpensive; *M* = Moderately Priced; *YH* = Youth Hostel; * = Author's Favorite; $ = Special Value

Raphael (*E**), 171–2
Ritz Carlton (*E**), 172
Riverview Inn, Kansas City, KS (*M*), 179–80

Trailside Camper's Inn, 182
Travelodge (*B*), 177
Westin Crown Center (*E**), 169–70

ST. LOUIS

Adam's Mark Hotel (*E**), 45–8
Archway Manor (*CG*), 65
Caverly Farm and Orchard (*B&B*), 64
Cheshire Inn and Lodge (*M*), 51, 59
Clarion Hotel (*E*), 48
Coachlight (*B&B*), 55
Coral Court Motel (*I**), 64–5
Corinne's Bed and Breakfast, Springfield, IL (*B&B*), 145
Daniele Hilton (*E*), 56–8
Days Inn (*M*), 51–2
Drury Inn Convention Center (*M**$), 52
Drury Inn Union Station (*M**$), 54
Embassy Suites (*E*), 48–9
Fifth Street Mansion, Hannibal (*M*), 139
Forest Park Hotel (*M**), 55
Garth Woodside Mansion, Hannibal (*M*), 139–40
Henry VIII Hotel (*M*), 51, 61–2
Holiday Inn Airport West (*M*), 51, 62
Holiday Inn Downtown/Riverfront (*M*), 52–3
Holiday Inn East, Springfield, IL (*M*), 144–5
Holiday Inn, Hannibal (*M*), 140

Hotel Majestic (*E**), 49–50
Huckleberry Finn Youth Hostel (YH), 61
Hyatt Regency St. Louis (*E**), 51, 53–4
Knights Inn (*I*), 65
KOA of St. Louis South, Barnhart (*CG*), 65–6
Lafayette House (*B&B*), 60–1
Marriott Pavilion Downtown (*E*), 50
Mayfair (*E*), 50–1
Motel 6 (*I*$), 63
Oakland Park Inn (*M**), 62–3
Old Convent Guesthouse (*B&B**), 61
Pinewoods Camp and Fishing Park, Wentzville (*CG*), 66
Radisson Hotel Clayton (*M*), 60
Ramada Renaissance Hotel, Springfield, IL (*E*), 144
Ritz-Carlton (*E**), 58
RV Parking (*CG*), 66
Seven Gables (*E**), 58–9
Sheraton Plaza Hotel (*E*), 63
Sheraton West Port Inn (*E*), 63–4
St. Louis RV Park (*CG*), 66
Super 8 Motel (*I*), 65
Thrifty Inn (*I*$), 53

RESTAURANTS

KANSAS CITY

Acapulco (*B*; Mexican), 189
American Restaurant (*E**; American), 191–2
Annie's Santa Festival (*B*; Mexican), 195
Arthur Bryant's (*B**$; barbecue), 189–90

Athena on Broadway (*I*; Greek), 197–8
Bangkok Pavilion (*I*$; Thai), 199–200
Barney's Café (*B*; burgers/snacks), 209

KEY TO ABBREVIATIONS: *B* = Budget; *E* = Expensive; *I* = Inexpensive; *M* = Moderately Priced; * = Author's Favorite; $ = Special Value

ST. LOUIS

NOW, SAVE MONEY ON ALL
YOUR TRAVELS!
Join Frommer's™ Dollarwise® Travel Club

Saving money while traveling is never a simple matter, which is why the **Dollarwise Travel Club** was formed 31 years ago. Developed in response to requests from Frommer's Travel Guide readers, the Club provides cost-cutting travel strategies, up-to-date travel information, and a sense of community for value-conscious travelers from all over the world.

In keeping with the money-saving concept, the annual membership fee is low—$20 for U.S. residents or $25 for residents of Canada, Mexico, and other countries—and is immediately exceeded by the value of your benefits, which include:

1. Any TWO books listed on the following pages.
2. Plus any ONE Frommer's City Guide.
3. A subscription to our quarterly newspaper, *The Dollarwise Traveler*.
4. A membership card that entitles you to purchase through the Club all Frommer's publications for 33% to 40% off their retail price.

The eight-page *Dollarwise Traveler* tells you about the latest developments in good-value travel worldwide and includes the following columns: **Hospitality Exchange** (for those offering and seeking hospitality in cities all over the world); **Share-a-Trip** (for those looking for travel companions to share costs); and **Readers Ask . . . Readers Reply** (for those with travel questions that other members can answer).

Aside from the Frommer's Guides and the Gault Millau Guides, you can also choose from our Special Editions. These include such titles as *California with Kids* (a compendium of the best of California's accommodations, restaurants, and sightseeing attractions appropriate for those traveling with toddlers through teens); *Candy Apple: New York with Kids* (a spirited guide to the Big Apple by a savvy New York grandmother that's perfect for both visitors and residents); *Caribbean Hideaways* (the 100 most romantic places to stay in the Islands, all rated on ambience, food, sports opportunities, and price); *Honeymoon Destinations* (a guide to planning and choosing just the right destination from hundreds of possibilities in the U.S., Mexico, and the Caribbean); *Marilyn Wood's Wonderful Weekends* (a selection of the best mini-vacations within a 200-mile radius of New York City, including descriptions of country inns and other accommodations, restaurants, picnic spots, sights, and activities); and *Paris Rendez-Vous* (a delightful guide to the best places to meet in Paris whether for power breakfasts or dancing till dawn).

To join this Club, simply send the appropriate membership fee with your name and address to: Frommer's Dollarwise Travel Club, 15 Columbus Circle, New York, NY 10023. Remember to specify which single city guide and which two other guides you wish to receive in your initial package of member's benefits. Or tear out the next page, check off your choices, and send the page to us with your membership fee.

FROMMER BOOKS　　　　　**Date**_____
PRENTICE HALL PRESS
15 COLUMBUS CIRCLE
NEW YORK, NY 10023
212/373-8125

Friends:

Please send me the books checked below.

FROMMER'S™ GUIDES

(Guides to sightseeing and tourist accommodations and facilities from budget to deluxe, with emphasis on the medium-priced.)

☐ Alaska. $14.95	☐ Germany $14.95
☐ Australia $14.95	☐ Italy $14.95
☐ Austria & Hungary $14.95	☐ Japan & Hong Kong. $14.95
☐ Belgium, Holland & Lux-	☐ Mid-Atlantic States $14.95
embourg $14.95	☐ New England $14.95
☐ Bermuda & The Bahamas $14.95	☐ New Mexico. $13.95
☐ Brazil $14.95	☐ New York State. $14.95
☐ Canada $14.95	☐ Northwest $16.95
☐ Caribbean $14.95	☐ Portugal, Madeira & the Azores. $14.95
☐ Cruises (incl. Alaska, Carib, Mex, Ha-	☐ Scandinavia $18.95
waii, Panama, Canada & US). .$14.95	☐ South Pacific $14.95
☐ California & Las Vegas. $14.95	☐ Southeast Asia $14.95
☐ Egypt $14.95	☐ Southern Atlantic States $14.95
☐ England & Scotland. $14.95	☐ Southwest. $14.95
☐ Florida $14.95	☐ Switzerland & Liechtenstein $14.95
☐ France. $14.95	☐ USA $16.95

FROMMER'S $-A-DAY® GUIDES

(In-depth guides to sightseeing and low-cost tourist accommodations and facilities.)

☐ Europe on $40 a Day $15.95	☐ Israel on $40 a Day $13.95
☐ Australia on $40 a Day $13.95	☐ Mexico on $35 a Day. $14.95
☐ Costa Rica; Guatemala & Belize	☐ New York on $60 a Day $13.95
on $35 a Day $15.95	☐ New Zealand on $45 a Day $14.95
☐ Eastern Europe on $25 a Day .$16.95	☐ Scotland & Wales on $40 a Day $13.95
☐ England on $50 a Day $13.95	☐ South America on $40 a Day. $15.95
☐ Greece on $35 a Day. $14.95	☐ Spain on $50 a Day $15.95
☐ Hawaii on $60 a Day $14.95	☐ Turkey on $30 a Day $13.95
☐ India on $25 a Day $12.95	☐ Washington, D.C. & Historic Va. on
☐ Ireland on $35 a Day $13.95	$40 a Day $13.95

FROMMER'S TOURING GUIDES

(Color illustrated guides that include walking tours, cultural and historic sites, and other vital travel information.)

☐ Amsterdam $10.95	☐ New York. $10.95
☐ Australia $10.95	☐ Paris $8.95
☐ Brazil $10.95	☐ Rome $10.95
☐ Egypt $8.95	☐ Scotland $9.95
☐ Florence $8.95	☐ Thailand $10.95
☐ Hong Kong $10.95	☐ Turkey. $10.95
☐ London. $10.95	☐ Venice. $8.95

(TURN PAGE FOR ADDITONAL BOOKS AND ORDER FORM)

FROMMER'S CITY GUIDES

(Pocket-size guides to sightseeing and tourist accommodations and facilities in all price ranges.)

☐ Amsterdam/Holland	$8.95	☐ Minneapolis/St. Paul	$8.95
☐ Athens	$8.95	☐ Montréal/Québec City	$8.95
☐ Atlanta	$8.95	☐ New Orleans	$8.95
☐ Atlantic City/Cape May	$8.95	☐ New York	$8.95
☐ Barcelona	$7.95	☐ Orlando	$8.95
☐ Belgium	$7.95	☐ Paris	$8.95
☐ Berlin	$8.95	☐ Philadelphia	$8.95
☐ Boston	$8.95	☐ Rio	$8.95
☐ Cancún/Cozumel/Yucatán	$8.95	☐ Rome	$8.95
☐ Chicago	$9.95	☐ Salt Lake City	$8.95
☐ Denver/Boulder/Colorado		☐ San Diego	$8.95
Springs	$7.95	☐ San Francisco	$8.95
☐ Dublin/Ireland	$8.95	☐ Santa Fe/Taos/Albuquerque	$10.95
☐ Hawaii	$8.95	☐ Seattle/Portland	$7.95
☐ Hong Kong	$7.95	☐ St. Louis/Kansas City	$9.95
☐ Las Vegas	$8.95	☐ Sydney	$8.95
☐ Lisbon/Madrid/Costa del Sol	$8.95	☐ Tampa/St. Petersburg	$8.95
☐ London	$8.95	☐ Tokyo	$8.95
☐ Los Angeles	$8.95	☐ Toronto	$8.95
☐ Mexico City/Acapulco	$8.95	☐ Vancouver/Victoria	$7.95
☐ Miami	$8.95	☐ Washington, D.C.	$8.95

SPECIAL EDITIONS

☐ Beat the High Cost of Travel	$6.95	☐ Motorist's Phrase Book (Fr/Ger/Sp)	$4.95
☐ Bed & Breakfast—N. America	$14.95	☐ Paris Rendez-Vous	$10.95
☐ California with Kids	$16.95	☐ Swap and Go (Home Exchanging)	$10.95
☐ Caribbean Hideaways	$14.95	☐ The Candy Apple (NY with Kids)	$12.95
☐ Manhattan's Outdoor		☐ Travel Diary and Record Book	$5.95
Sculpture	$15.95		

☐ Honeymoon Destinations (US, Mex & Carib) $14.95

☐ Where to Stay USA (From $3 to $30 a night) $13.95

☐ Marilyn Wood's Wonderful Weekends (CT, DE, MA, NH, NJ, NY, PA, RI, VT) $11.95

☐ The New World of Travel (Annual sourcebook by Arthur Frommer for savvy travelers) . . $16.95

GAULT MILLAU

(The only guides that distinguish the truly superlative from the merely overrated.)

☐ The Best of Chicago	$15.95	☐ The Best of Los Angeles	$16.95
☐ The Best of France	$16.95	☐ The Best of New England	$15.95
☐ The Best of Hawaii	$16.95	☐ The Best of New Orleans	$16.95
☐ The Best of Hong Kong	$16.95	☐ The Best of New York	$16.95
☐ The Best of Italy	$16.95	☐ The Best of Paris	$16.95
☐ The Best of London	$16.95	☐ The Best of San Francisco	$16.95

☐ The Best of Washington, D.C. $16.95

ORDER NOW!

In U.S. include $2 shipping UPS for 1st book; $1 ea. add'l book. Outside U.S. $3 and $1, respectively. Allow four to six weeks for delivery in U.S., longer outside U.S.

Enclosed is my check or money order for $_____

NAME_____

ADDRESS_____

CITY_____ STATE_____ ZIP____

0391